on track ...

Tori Amos

every album, every song

Lisa Torem

SONICBOND

sonicbondpublishing.com

Sonicbond Publishing Limited
www.sonicbondpublishing.co.uk
Email: info@sonicbondpublishing.co.uk

First Published in the United Kingdom 2021
First Published in the United States 2021

British Library Cataloguing in Publication Data:
A Catalogue record for this book is available from the British Library

ISBN 978-1-78952-142-9

Typeset in ITC Garamond & ITC Avant Garde
Printed and bound in England

Graphic design and typesetting: Full Moon Media

on track ...

Tori Amos

every album, every song

Lisa Torem

SONICBOND

sonicbondpublishing.com

Acknowledgments

With gratitude to interviewees: Joseph Chiccarelli, Noah Michelson, Gary Nobody and John Philip Shenale. A huge thanks to the talented team at *toriamosdiscography.info*. I am indebted to my diligent readers: John Clarkson and Christopher Torem. Thank you for the opportunity, Stephen Lambe. Finally, to Christopher, Allie, Emily, Madeline and Stella for unwavering support and to Tori Amos for her enduring discography. 'Ears with feet,' you rock!

on track ...

Tori Amos

Contents

Introduction: Can I Be You for a While?

Some aficionados believe that Tori Amos is ahead of her time. Others believe that she was born too late; but can't we agree on both? I believe that Tori Amos is one of the 21st century's most progressive artists, yet like Michelangelo, Tori could have been a Renaissance *cause celebre* with her triple-threat talents, or even further back: a cave-dwelling cantor.

Tori's creativity has rarely waned over an almost three-decade-long career. Her repertoire, seemingly unfazed by time, often rekindles memories of our own youthful fantasies and follies.

Still, even timeless artists must switch gears. In fact, Tori once said: 'Girls you've gotta know when it's time to turn the page.' So, I'm anxious to turn the page on her vast body of work, but first, let's talk.

Who becomes a Tori Amos fan and why? And once stricken, is this condition contagious? A quick look at fan forums reveals that some viewers commiserate online with like-minded others after nursing a broken heart – a tearful ballad brought them onboard. Others bond after parsing out a peculiar string of images – *was Tori talking to me?* Once the affliction takes hold, there's the question of longevity. Many yearn to bring a neophyte into the fold but don't know where to start. I mean, how do you rifle through hundreds of songs when asked to make a proper first choice?

You can't really fit a Tori Amos fan into a box (although she actually did just that on her debut album cover), and stereotypes still persist – but truthfully, Tori Amos fans come from all walks of life and every corner of the world. As such, her discography holds time and space for all.

Regarding Tori's legacy, there's rarely a hyphen after her moniker: she's not half of a team: a Lennon to a McCartney, a Goffin to a King or a Taupin to a John. Tori has consistently surrounded herself with talent, but as a songwriter/composer, she's pretty much a lone wolf, more in line with the likes of Alicia Keys, Stevie Wonder, Billy Joel, the late Laura Nyro or Joni Mitchell in terms of writing independently and taking charge of lead vocals and core instrumentals.

The likes of Nina Simone, Joni Mitchell, Bela Bartok, Robert Plant, Jimi Hendrix and The Beatles inspired Tori; her work too, has inspired a myriad of diverse acts, including, but not limited to: St. Vincent, Evanescence, Alanis Morissette, Fiona Apple and Regina Spektor.

She wears many hats, yet when an American talk show host asked how she'd like to be remembered, Tori emphatically replied: 'Composer.' Of course, female composers, historically, acquired little formal training, or if they exhibited talent, they likely hid behind a pseudonym, garnering little fanfare. But Tori's trajectory alters previous historical perceptions – she not only composed but produced the lion's share of her studio albums. That said, I aim to give fair shrift to her compositional and lyrical output. With fifteen studio albums alone, we'll have plenty of opportunities to chronicle her development.

Born with a strong visual acuity, Tori Amos has described 'seeing music as structures of light': a phenomenon that suggests a condition called chromesthesia. Perhaps that's led to her frequent alignment with visual artists. For each album project, her team has vividly carried out her concepts. For that reason, we'll leaf through album art, and profile three-dimensional tours.

We'll call out sexism: has a critic ever described Robert Plant as a male Tori Amos? Has a male act been reviewed solely on the basis of physical posturing, as opposed to the setlist?

In an interview with Nick Levine of *The Independent*, published on 8 December 2020, Tori reacted to a query regarding misrepresentation in the media: '...even if somebody doesn't really like what I do, they have to acknowledge that I've lasted. I mean, I turned pro at thirteen and I'm 57 now. You do the math.'

'The math' – she certainly put in her 10,000 hours. But what led to the achievement of that milestone? What made Tori Amos so musical? To what degree was young Myra Ellen Amos influenced by the tranquility, beauty, and perhaps, the birdsong of Newton, North Carolina, her birthplace, and where she spent many childhood summers? After all, images of natural settings abound in her work. In the novel, *Where the Crawdads Sing* (Delia Owens, 2018), the narrator observes, 'Birds sing mostly at dawn because the cool, moist air of morning carries their songs and their meanings much farther.' Did the 'cool, moist air of morning' inform Tori's creativity? Or did it evolve from the music and language at home, which flowed as freely as fresh water from a country stream? Was she influenced by her father's scriptures? Or the colorful stories told by her maternal grandfather, 'poppa,' who carried on the Cherokee oral tradition and mindfulness to the environment?

Tori's father, Dr. Addison Amos, was a respected Methodist minister. Her mother, Mary, a homemaker with a poetic soul. Tori's upbringing provided the schema for countless ballads. But did her lyrical depth stem from a desire to break away from the Judeo-Christian tradition and forge a unique spiritual path?

At two-and-a-half, she displayed a talent for memorizing piano melodies, although she needed telephone books to keep her slender frame from falling off the bench. Predictably, she sang in the church choir and eventually led her own: kids loved her, but parents were outraged over her red, leather trousers.

Back at home, her older siblings dropped the needle on a rich tapestry of sonic delights: joyful piano arrangements by Fats Waller and Nat King Cole made a lasting impression.

Picking melodies out by ear so effortlessly was a gift Tori's parents heeded. The prodigy received a Peabody Institute scholarship at Johns Hopkins University at the age of five. Being the youngest member ever admitted was an honor. Moreover, it was exciting to mingle with students in their upper teens, but the pressure to be perfect kept mounting: 'Then, all of a sudden, it stopped being fun,' she told journalist Paul Zollo. The rigor and exclusive menu of classical music study slowly wore her down; she yearned to improvise and compose, not merely interpret. It took forever to memorize a classical piece, and besides, many of her peers could more efficiently interpret a classical work.

She was also developing an appreciation for John Lennon, Jimi Hendrix and Jimmy Page; her open-mindedness created friction among the teachers. 'Unless it was Chopin and Mozart, they didn't wanna know,' she told Elf99. It wasn't that Tori didn't appreciate the works of the classicists – in fact, she'd explore the genre again seriously for *Night of Hunters* – but perhaps something she couldn't yet identify was burrowing within her: she longed to tap into it; allow the seeds to germinate on her own terms.

Ultimately, Tori and the Peabody Administration locked horns. She was expelled at eleven for 'musical insubordination' due to a preoccupation with all-things-rock, as well as a desire to create new works rather than interpret classics. To an emerging composer, this dire determination may have been the highest form of heresy, akin to jailing Galileo for holding the belief that the Earth revolves around the sun. Still, her parents were devastated after she lost her scholarship.

Tori's eventual success would come at a high, emotional cost: 'Getting kicked out of the conservatory was so traumatic for me; it was like a bad relationship ending,' she also revealed to Zollo.

Her songwriting talent became evident in autumn of 1980, when she and her brother Michael co-wrote the single 'Baltimore' in honor of the Baltimore Orioles' baseball team and garnered an impressive press clipping.

Tori's greatest fan, her father, stood fast in his determination to promote her professional career, which she first forged as a piano bar singer in Baltimore and in the Georgetown bars of Washington, DC. *Ellen* was still a minor, but the proprietor at Mr. Smith's agreed she could play if her father chaperoned. Dr. Amos knew his clerical collar alone would ward off potential predators. So, when Tori nabbed a steady gig at the popular gay bar amid a community with which she found unconditional support, worries about harassment were laid to rest. To that end, the LGBTQ community has continued to support Tori's career; she remains grateful.

'Being exposed to the gay community at thirteen would change my views forever and I have stayed close with that community ever since,' Tori exclaimed to Kalen Rogers in *All These Years.*

So, Tori earned her 10,000 hours, much like her heroes, The Beatles, did in Hamburg, Germany, churning out catchy standards from the Great American Songbook at night; attending junior high during the day, until a concerned friend mentioned that if she played the piano bar circuit too long, she'd hit a wall.

In 1984, Tori left for Los Angeles with conflicted feelings. There was the loneliness of being in a strange, new city, coupled with a self-identity crisis. But as luck would have it, she got back in touch with her muse after noodling around at a friend's piano. There would be rough times ahead (including a sexual assault which Tori has alluded to in interviews and which would thematically reappear in a number of her songs, such as 'Me and a Gun'), but then she'd be in a room where ideas would take over and her 'song girls' would instill a sense of calm.

Meanwhile, her father had been diligently sending out demos. Finally, producer Narada Michael Walden recognized Tori's talents, and Atlantic Records jumped onboard, ready to negotiate a contract. Her recording career officially began in 1987 with the self-titled album *Y Kant Tori Read.*

Personnel included rock drummer Matt Sorum: the future secret weapon of Guns and Roses; guitarists Steve Farris (Mr. Mister) and Steve Caton and vocalist Merry Clayton. Though not a commercial success, Tori's experience was life-altering: from then on, she only committed to creative projects that told 'her truth.' With that purpose in mind, she pushed on to write the songs for *Little Earthquakes*.

Atlantic urged Tori to relocate to London, where the cohesive club scene would be ripe for her sensitive lyrics and somewhat quirky personality. British audiences fell in love. In January 1992, *Little Earthquakes* was released in the UK, peaking at 14 in the charts and ultimately going gold. A month later, the album broke in the US.

Having established a reputation as a well-rounded pianist, versatile singer and songwriter, Tori also directed her energies to social causes. As a survivor of sexual violence, she became aware that survivors need unconditional support. In 1994, she co-founded RAINN (Rape, Abuse and Incest National Network). The organization's 24-hour hotline and 600 crisis centers have served thousands of survivors across the United States. Tori's resolve to address this trauma cannot be underestimated, Countless fans have reached out for her assistance and she has treated all of them with dignity and respect.

To this day, Tori remains committed to being fully focused onstage and off, well-evidenced by 'meet and greets' from which she incorporates requests and news bytes into her setlists.

To Bienne Huisman, at *timeslive.co.za*, she discussed staying hydrated, without wasting time chugging water: 'I chew cinnamon gum before shows. This keeps my vocal cords wet, helping me to reach notes with lots of space to breathe.'

That Tori developed a reputation as a hands-on musician who can manage technical issues is evident in the following story. Gary Nobody – a local, well-regarded studio engineer – attended the Atlantic Records pre-performance bash at Schubas' V.I.P. room in Chicago in April 1992. Chicago was a quick but essential stop on the 1992 *Little Earthquakes* World Tour (which began at London's Shaw Theater in January). He remembered Tori's flaming red hair, casual wardrobe and lack of makeup. He assumed she'd change into something flashy later, but she didn't. 'She was exactly who she claimed to be,' he exclaimed.

He was accustomed to seeing live acts accompanied by roadies or band techs, but as a pianist, Tori was on her own. That being the case, as she sat down to play, she frowned at the pedals. Something was out of whack. Nobody instinctively looked around; there was no one around to assist.

Briefly, Tori disappeared from the sightlines. When she reappeared, Nobody noticed that she was stretched out across the bare floor, like an auto mechanic. She whipped out a wrench to make a quick adjustment. Whatever minor surgery she performed did the trick. Tori popped back up to restart her song. Nobody exhaled – being from a working-class background, he was in awe of the songwriter's do-it-yourself mentality.

I, too, had been to Schubas' that night, having already developed an interest in Tori's music, but never got in; the concert had sold out. By the time she returned for her Park West appearance on 31 July, I'd become well-versed in her repertoire and in awe of her frank interview responses. After missing Schubas', I was dead-set on seeing Tori live. I actually found a babysitter. Now, I just needed a pair of tickets. I zipped over to Park West that hot, muggy afternoon with my young daughters. Breathless, I requested two tickets. This show, too, was completely sold out. I sat my daughters down with Ben and Jerry's bubblegum ice cream cones, waiting in the hot sun for a miracle. Suddenly, a pair of high tops with white laces tumbled out of a yellow cab. When I heard a voice, I squinted because the sun was in my eyes but did not look up. 'You look so sad,' the pretty voice whispered.

'I wanted to go to the concert tonight. I have a sitter and everything,' I babbled, like a sugared-up toddler.

'Come with me,' the voice replied. It all happened so fast. I had only seen a picture of Tori in a zine at the dentist's office. I didn't recognize the flaming red hair, the sparkly green eyes and certainly not the high-tops.

Finally, safe from the sun's glare and comfortable in the air-conditioning, I took in her full form. Tori doesn't walk, she bounces. When she bounces, her hair flies. When she speaks to you, she makes you feel like no one else in the world matters. As the iconic 'Cornflake Girl' lyric goes, I remember thinking, 'This is not a-really happening.'

Reaching the box office, Tori whispered to the attendant. The next thing I know, I'm on the guest list with a plus-one, with great seats directly behind the piano! Tori traipsed off to soundcheck before I could properly thank her; and while I was extremely grateful, my bigger takeaway was this: Now, I do believe in faeries.

At the concert, Tori didn't pick up the wrench, chug down fluids or crack gum. But what was clear, was that her fanbase was growing exponentially. She performed a you-could-hear-a-pin-drop set. Her acoustic-based music and compelling voice attracted a sophisticated, sensitive crowd. The tunes were contagious; the themes, relatable.

So yes, I'm a fan. And you are, too; that's what brought you here. Like many fans, I've pored over Tori's vast catalog with a discerning ear. Now, speaking of ears, you know that Tori affectionately refers to her many admirers as 'feet with ears!'

So, fellow 'feet with ears,' come along where 'the drifts get deeper' and compare notes. I'll likely cherish some cuts over others, point out themes that

Left: Gary Nobody, a well-known Chicago sound engineer, was impressed by Tori's practical, can-do attitude to playing live. *(Gary Nobody)*

Right: The author's daughters Allison (left) and Emily (right) – who met Tori Amos. (*Lisa Torem*)

immediately resonate with me (or leave me puzzled) and linger on those life-changers. So, let's lace-up our high-tops and get to work.

Lisa Torem
Chicago, Illinois 2021
lisatorem@gmail.com

What is included and what is not included:

For the veteran fan, I'll provide descriptive discography details so you can compare your own judgments of Tori Amos's work with mine.

If you are a neophyte, if your interest began surreptitiously, through a tip from a friend or otherwise, I've organized this discography chronologically and critiqued the work so that you can determine your own point of interest. In essence, my goal is to balance out my opinions (and that of other music critics) with documented facts. We'll browse *Y Kant Tori Read* and examine subsequent studio albums, devoting extra time to 1992s groundbreaking *Little Earthquakes*, and end with 2017's *Native Invader*: Tori's most recent studio album. Any contemporary non-album tracks, B-sides and known unreleased songs are also included. Single mixes and remixes are listed. Promo singles, international variants, bootleg recordings and unreleased demos of released songs are not included.

Finally, we can meet up at the concluding chapter, where I'll reveal my personal guilty pleasures. Hopefully, we'll gain a deeper understanding and appreciation of one of our most treasured (and inexplicably underrated) singer/songwriter/pianist/composers: Tori Amos.

Y Kant Tori Read (1988)

Personnel:
Tori Amos: lead vocalist, acoustic piano, except on 'Fayth'
Kim Bullard: co-producer, acoustic piano on 'Fayth,' programming, keyboards
Steve Caton: guitar
Paulinho Da Costa: percussion
Tim Landers: fretless bass, except on 'Fayth,' 'Floating City' and 'Pirates' – Fernando Saunders
Fernando Saunders: bass
Matt Sorum, Vinnie Colaiuta: drums
Additional Personnel:
Background vocals: Tori Amos, Ce Ce Bullard, Zobbin Rander, James House, Merry Clayton, Nancy Shanks, The Valentine Brothers and Rick Nelson ('Zobbin Rander' and 'Rick Nelson' are Robin Zander and Rick Nielson of Cheap Trick)
Richard Bernard: bouzouki
Gene Black: guitar
Devon Dickson: bagpipes
Steve Farris: guitar
Peter White: acoustic guitars
Eric Williams: mandolin
Producer: Joe Chiccarelli
Recorded by Joe Chiccarelli
Mixer: Ed Thacker
Co-producer: Kim Bullard
Executive producer: David Kershenbaum
Recorded in 1987 at Hollywood Sound, South Combe Studios, Ground Control Studios, Sound Castle Studios, Capitol Studios, The Grey Room
Label: Atlantic
Release date: UK: January 1988, US: July 1988, UK and Europe re-release: 2017
Highest chart rank: did not chart
Running time: 48:44

In hindsight, *Y Kant Tori Read* was propelled by the release of youthful, pent-up energy. But the recording of this synth-pop revelation revealed a complex backstory. Tori faced emotional obstacles from the outset. She was an L.A. transplant and sexual assault survivor, yet from the get-go, she spoke frankly to her fans, explaining in the promotional press release why her childhood was unique: 'I didn't play with dolls, I listened to my father's classical records, my mother's show tunes, my brother's rock 'n' roll records, and I played it all back by ear.'

In a tongue-in-cheek manner, she explained how she got her stage name: 'Tori came from 'notorious' for wearing red leather pants to my father's church on Sundays and directing the children's choir.' (She also revealed that an acquaintance suggested the name because she resembled a 'Torrey pine tree.')

She fronted *Y Kant Tori Read* with guitarist Steve Caton, drummer Matt Sorum and bassist Brad Cobb from 1984 to1989. Sadly, the original band disassembled before the album was recorded, although Sorum and Caton mutually agreed to stop in for random sessions. Over the coming years, Caton served as musical compadre on *Little Earthquakes*, *Under the Pink* and *To Venus and Back*. Sorum and Caton reunited in the late 1990s for the creation of Binge.

Nevertheless, Tori moved forward with a cadre of L.A. session musicians, including Mr. Mister's renowned guitarist Steve Farris; keyboardist and co-producer Kim Bullard; percussionist Paulinho Da Costa; Cheap Trick vocalists Robin Zander and Rick Nielsen; and Merry Clayton, famous for her duet with Mick Jagger and explosive solo on 'Gimme Shelter' (which she recorded after being awakened in the middle of the night). Clayton returned for *Under the Pink* to sing backing vocals for 'Cornflake Girl' and the phrase on the pumped-up bridge: 'and the man with the golden gun.'

Finally, Tori was paired with Pat Benatar and Frank Zappa producer Joe Chiccarelli (see comments below), who was eager to oversee the studio sessions. Always in demand, Chiccarelli went on to produce Brandi Carlisle, Jason Mraz, Alanis Morissette (a future Tori Amos touring mate) and The Strokes. And despite a still-circulating rumor, Chiccarelli did not discover Tori: Atlantic Records laid claim to that honor.

Functional illiteracy had little to do with the bohemian band moniker, which was actually in response to Tori's rebellious stance on sight-reading, and it underscored the obvious question: With such a perfect ear, why *did* Tori have to read?

Had she stayed at Peabody, sight-reading would have been compulsory, of course, as would a host of other skills. Classical training meant interpreting a piece precisely, and this required a strict routine: Hands gently lifted and lowered to indicate the end of a phrase; discrimination between dynamic markings: allegro, fortissimo and dolce and pedal usage on-demand. Inevitably, the restless prodigy rebelled; Who wouldn't crave an *entrée* into the world of high-decibel rock, after years of being a virtuosic shut-in?

In the pop world, Tori could stand out. With her enviable vocal range, beauty, solid piano chops, schooled technique and desire to write, she already had the goods. But in the late 1980s – as Tori has pointed out in multiple interviews – she was struggling to find her image, with little guidance and support. And if the album wasn't a godsend, so be it. But who would've guessed that she'd be sabotaged by an image? But she was when critics panned Aaron Rapoport's racy cover photo. When Tori appeared as a sword-swinging pirate in a bustier, all bets were off.

Maybe Tori tried a little too hard to impress. She didn't have to hiss like 'Rizzo' in *Grease* to dramatize her themes; her natural voice was fluid enough to make a point. So, chalk off these missteps to growing pains - Tori would discover her authentic self in a mere four years.

Still, there was a lot to be proud of on the album. Tori demonstrated great enthusiasm on each track and alerted the world to her multi-octave range. In addition, the album featured resilient melodies, and the personnel included the best from that era. Unfortunately, though, after its release, *Y Kant Tori Read* suffered from poor sales and promotion and thereby received little critical acclaim. Besides that, Tori found herself feeling somewhat abandoned. After all, the key musicians she'd worked with had quit, leaving the majority of the studio work to locals with whom Tori hadn't built up relationships, albeit she couldn't complain about lack of star power among the studio personnel.

In her 2005 book, *Tori Amos*: *Piece by Piece*, Tori reflects back to the *Y Kant Tori Read* era and concludes, 'I was playing a role then, and I learned from that. I decided, no, that doesn't fit me very well.'

Ultimately, an older, more successful Tori shrugged off the album's lack of success and thrust herself again into new projects, but that seemingly ill-fated album developed its own legacy. Once fans hopped on the Tori Amos bandwagon of 1992, keen to see what else she had accomplished, *Y Kant Tori Read* was infused with new life through a cadre of bootlegged copies and a subsequent skyrocketed value. In fact, in the spring of 2021, a sealed U.S. 1988 LP of *Y Kant Tori Read*, advertised as a *rarity*, could set the buyer back anywhere from $165 to almost $200. Finally, the album was shaken out of its one-night-stand status when Tori acknowledged the legacy and renegotiated the contract. *Y Kant Tori Read* then acquired honeymoon status.

Fans were, of course, excited about the album reissue in the fall of 2017, yet the timing seemed circumspect; a sleight-of-hand maneuver. Why weren't fans kept in the loop? Wasn't this release as newsworthy as *Native Invader*?

Certain critics were upended by the lack of promotion – David Michael Conner of m.huffpost.com (4 September 2017) cut to the quick: 'Who knew it would happen like this, just one week before her newest album release *Native Invader*?' Miffed about the reissue debacle, Connor expressed empathy for Tori: 'I wonder what she might have done with the same material without the constraints that were put upon her.' We'll never know, but Tori's decision to support said material, speaks volumes.

After coming full circle in her career, Tori was more consumed with the promotion of her fifteenth studio album, to which reviewers were consistently giving the thumbs-up. Ultimately, the dual release was a win-win. This was a perfect time to take stock of Tori's accomplishments and overall fruitful career. And so, with the Rhino Records negotiations over and the *Y Kant Tori Read* resurgence in full tilt, fans were in for a treat.

On Record Store Day of that same year, the remastered re-release of *Y Kant Tori Read* was streamed, and 4000 limited-edition vinyl copies were circulated. Was it just a coincidence that the gleaming transparent acetate version matched the singer-songwriter's campfire hair?

To get additional insight into the production of *Y Kant Tori Read*, I interviewed Joseph Chiccarelli. His analyses of specific songs are set forth below. The entire unabridged interview with Joseph Chiccarelli is included as Appendix A and contains additional insights into Tori and the music business.

Now, about those tracks.

Side 1

'The Big Picture' (Tori Amos, Kim Bullard)

No matter that this booming 1980's anthem is by default anachronistic, Tori's zeal is contagious. The storyline stays superficial, rarely moving beyond the theme of 'Gotta make more money,' but Tori's wild outro hints at her future vocal versatility.

'Cool on Your Island' (Tori Amos, Kim Bullard)

Bolstered by the beat of steel drums, Tori's fragile, yet incendiary vocals shore up the pretty melody of this calypso infusion. The simply-told story smacks of romantic urgency: 'I want you more than the stars and the sun,' she croons. The coda consists of an elongated instrumental. Eventually, she felt cozy enough with this calypso-infusion to include it in sets; much to the delight of future fans, the dreamy ballad has been included in 66-plus, far-flung performances.

As Chiccarelli remembers, 'As in every album, especially for a solo artist, the songs were all treated differently, just depending on the mood and the intensity of the song, and that's why different drummers were on different songs. Some of the tracks were very layered; some were very programmed. 'Cool on Your Island' might have been more synth/programmed-based.'

'Fayth' (Tori Amos, Brad Cobb)

Tori's vocals are especially vibrant before the sprawling electric guitar solo. The quasi-rap feels formulaic. Despite the title, there's little spirituality to be found in the sing-song pentameter, but the stomping beats and generous guitar work flesh out any soulless gaps.

'Fire on the Side' (Tori Amos)

The narrative continually circles back to a deep state of loneliness and romantic loss. 'Taste my tears... I am alone again,' Tori sings with an unhindered ache in her voice. Just a touch of exposition and we're there ('This girl was born just miles from here/Now she's coming home.') Take note of the crisp enunciation which would become a hallmark of Tori's enduring style.

Chiccarelli recalled: 'I remember 'Fire on the Side' in particular was a tough one for Tori because it was very, very personal, and it was something that she kind of didn't want to relive. The great thing about Tori, as an artist, is she really puts her entire being into a song, and for her to get up in front of a microphone and tell the story – which was really dark and intense and a sort of past part of her life that she didn't want to relive – was really difficult for her. I remember that particular song as being one where we took a few attempts at the lead vocal to get a performance that we really loved.'

Between October 1996 and November 2017, Tori heated up eleven stages – including grand European halls in Luxembourg, Germany and Finland; moving on to Australia. In the U. S., she hit Florida, Los Angeles, Georgia and Michigan (among others) – when performing this tender ballad about feeling painfully undervalued.

'Pirates' (Tori Amos, Kim Bullard)

As the title suggests, this aggressive arrangement holds no prisoners. There's little build, but then there's Matt Sorum firing like a madman on all possible cylinders.

Side 2

'Floating City' (Tori Amos)

The theme starts up on a personal note – 'You went away, why did you leave me?' – before a fantastical world opens up, anchored by shimmering chimes. This pre-*Little Earthquakes* ballad foreshadows the emotional transparency she would exhibit in the studio several years later.

'Heart Attack at 23' (Tori Amos)

This brand of guttural, tear-in-the-voice performance would also resurface several albums later. On the instrumental end, there's incessant squabbling between the electronic guitar and programmed bits, leaving very little breathing space.

'On the Boundary' (Tori Amos)

Tori's gritty contralto slowly grew on me. Peter White, with his Spanish guitar, made several dramatic excursions which were, each time, glossed over by other session musicians.

'You Go to My Head' (Tori Amos)

Tori's extraordinary range is the main ingredient. The overblown dynamics and unexpected sax solo don't quite hit the mark. I can't entirely make out the words of the backing vocalists, but their warmth comes through unequivocally.

'Etienne Trilogy' (Tori Amos)

This suite is comprised of two instrumentals and the ballad, 'Etienne.'

'The Highlands' (Tori Amos, Kim Bullard)

Because this 90-second track is sonorous and succinct, it balances out what follows. Yet, there's no actual distinctive thread between the three parts.

'Etienne' (Tori Amos)

Tori debuted 'Etienne' on the 1996 Dew Drop Inn Tour. After an affirmative response, the piece was added to subsequent setlists. Overall, this collection unfurls a romantic fantasy, rife with witches and knights and a breathless tribute to place: 'Running through the fields of Scotland by your side.'

The mid-point modulation is a welcoming lift. The piano interludes, while energizing, never interfere with the harmonies. When Tori utters, 'By the morning, maybe you'll remember who I am,' for the final time, her voice renders a beautiful sadness. As a songwriter, she'd dig much deeper in due time, but 'Etienne' stands as an infectious prototype. Chiccarelli recalled: ''Fire on the Side' and 'Etienne' were more personal and introspective storytelling songs, so they were treated much more simply.'

'Skyeboat Song' (Traditional)

I confess, I've a weak spot for bagpipes, particularly when played so expertly by Devon Dickson. Sure, this is not the typical end-game for a synth-pop album, but the trilogy demanded it.

Chiccarelli remembers: 'I believe it was Tori's idea to get bagpipes for the 'Skyeboat Song.' I mean, she really had visions for different colors; atmospheres. She really was quite dramatic and demonstrative about how she heard things, and I believe she mentioned bagpipes, and to be honest, I can't remember how I found Devon Dickson. It was, maybe, asking other producers that I knew that had ever worked with bagpipes. It doesn't happen that often. I've overdubbed bagpipes once since that record, and it was with The White Stripes. It's a tricky instrument to record and put in the track because it can only play in the key of C or F, so sometimes you can't fit in the song. Usually, you just get lucky. There are really only three or four notes that a guy can play that are within the song.'

Singles

'The Big Picture' (Tori Amos, Kim Bullard), 1988

'Cool on Your Island' (Tori Amos, Kim Bullard), 1988

Format: 12" vinyl, CD; US re-release: 12"-inch vinyl, CD and cassette

Album Art

Tori's hair is ratted sky high; lids are lavishly caked in pastel colors and there's no escaping the eye-level bustier. And yes, she's wielding a classic pirate's sword. Certainly, one's image can assume multiple iterations over the years, so why was Tori so harshly judged?

A cover featuring a male recording artist, decked out like an American greaser, metal head or punk, would have been considered cool; not out-of-bounds or a deal-breaker.

Leading Up To Little Earthquakes

Prior to her solo recording career, Tori was a session musician. The call she got from British singer-songwriter Al Stewart was not a routine shout-out. Stewart was in hot water: he was scheduled to play at London's Royal Festival Hall that night, but his pianist caught the flu. *Could Tori possibly help out?* She was hesitant to appear on a public stage due to visa issues, but Stewart told her not to worry, he'd work things out.

Tori bounced onstage, donning a floppy, brown beret, casual blouse and faded blue overalls. Upon seeing her, Stewart silenced his guitar, gestured to the young pianist and mumbled a hurried introduction which included a Russian-sounding name, Viliana Tchaikovskaya.

Seemingly unfazed, Tori played the rousing introduction to 'Year of the Cat', plus an elongated solo after Stewart sang and strummed a few verses. Finally, ending with a grand arpeggio, she skirted back to the green room, no worse for wear, visa intact (www.yessaid.com).

A unique friendship formed. When Stewart asked Tori to write him a song, she nearly handed over 'Silent All These Years', or at least the melody, but luckily, history had an alternate plan.

Tori sang backup on Stewart's 'Red Toupee' and the title song of *Last Days of the Century* (Enigma Records). They traveled in similar circles – Stewart's album was Chiccarelli-produced.

Little Earthquakes (January 1992)

Personnel:
Tori Amos: acoustic and electric pianos, lead vocals, background vocals, sampled strings
Steve Caton: Guitar, bass, background vocals
John Chamberlain: mandolin
Paulinho da Costa: percussion
Jake Freeze: rat pedal and saw
Stuart Gordon: violin
Ed Greene: drums
Will Gregory: oboe
Tina Gullickson: background vocals
Chris Hughes: drums
David Lord: string arrangement
Will McGregor: bass
Carlo Nuccio: drums
Philly: finger cymbal
David Rhodes: guitar
Eric Rosse: drum/keyboard programming, background vocals, Irish war drum
Jef Scott: bass
Matthew Seligman: bass
Nancy Shanks (Beene): background vocals
Phil Shenale: keyboard programming
Eric Williams: ukulele, dulcimer
Orchestra arranged and conducted by Nick De Caro
Produced by Tori Amos, Eric Rosse, Davitt Sigerson, Ian Stanley
Recorded at Eric Rosse's studio and Stag Studios
Label: Atlantic Records (US), East West (Europe)
Release date: UK: 6 January 1992, US: 13 January 1992
Highest chart rank: UK: 14, US: 54
Running Time: 57:11

To record her debut solo album, Tori just needed the right team. She'd put her fate in the hands of professional image makers for *Y Kant Tori Read*, but the album cover image had created a negative impression. The following review rubbed salt into the wounds. On 11 June 1988, *Billboard* magazine wrote, 'Classically-trained pianist pounds the ivories on her pop-rock debut, belting out self-written material with a forceful, appealing voice. Unfortunately, provocative packaging sends the (inaccurate) message that this is just so much more bimbo music.' *Billboard* didn't overtly pan Tori, but the word *bimbo* would be taken out of context thereafter. This time, Tori's image had to reflect the fact that she was an intelligent composer.

The sonic world was swirling with contemporary female (albeit guitar-driven) talent. In *Resistance, a songwriter's story of hope, change, and courage*, Tori recalls, 'At that time in music history, pop culture had not yet embraced the piano.' It's not that piano stars like Carole King and Laura Nyro, nor their progenitors, weren't appreciated anymore, but they were considered *classic* musicians.

Meanwhile, Melissa Etheridge, Suzanne Vega and Tracy Chapman had gained reputations for being surefire tastemakers in the early 1990s. Tori was distinctly aware of this shiny, new dynamic: 'The acoustic guitar was proving itself, with critics and sales. Synths were the keyboards of the day. The piano was seen as a snore and not fashionable.' Despite this perception, Tori worked hard to successfully integrate the 88-keyed outlier into her repertoire. She'd scrutinized her heroes' skill sets, paying rapt attention to Stevie Wonder's inventive left-hand maneuvers, as well as John Paul Jones' bass lines and Joni Mitchell's linear structures, not to mention George Gershwin's compelling inner-voicings.

On 21 May 2020, Matthew Barton, at thequietus.com (*Low Culture 6: Tori Amos and the Pretty Good Career'*), commented favorably on Tori's career: 'She used the piano with the intensity of a guitar, and in so doing, transformed its role in modern pop music. She bent it to her will, making it dirty or sweet or scary or fun, sometimes in the same song.' What sign couldn't Tori read this time? Could she have predicted this second folk wave, a phenomenon that was rapidly currying favor with industry honchos? What was the executive perspective? Wind Tori up, tune a guitar, repeat? Tori was not a guitarist. She'd earned her chops as a prodigy. She was an intensely creative pianist and one-off writer, yet she was being pigeonholed into a role that she could not, nor would not, agree to artistically fill.

Atlantic rejected the first version of *Little Earthquakes*: a ten-track demo recorded with Davitt Sigerson at Capitol Records, Los Angeles. This diverse offering included: 'Russia' (Later, 'Take to the Sky'), 'Mary,' 'Crucify,' 'Happy Phantom,' 'Leather,' 'Winter,' 'Sweet Dreams,' 'Song for Eric,' 'Learn to Fly' and 'Flying Dutchman.'

Tori has emphasized in interviews that she could have walked out of negotiations at any time, and returned to the piano bar circuit if it meant performing authentically. But after hashing out terms with executive Doug Morris, she agreed to work with then-partner Eric Rosse to produce a second *Little Earthquakes* demo. Despite a shoestring budget of approximately $6000, Tori and Eric forged ahead. Two studios were needed: Eric's home studio held a 24-track analog deck and a Yamaha CP-80. But to get Tori's signature sound, they scouted out Stagg Studios (now Stagg Street Studio), where she gained access to a gleaming Yamaha Grand.

They returned to Atlantic bearing sonic revisions. On this second listen, Doug Morris nodded his approval. This titan of a negotiating tool was comprised of 'Girl,' 'Precious Things,' 'Tear in Your Hand,' 'Mother,' and 'Little Earthquakes.' Fortunately, Tori's true believer had kept the faith: Morris' revised contract appeared on the table; Tori would add co-producer to her CV.

The label sent Tori off to London. First, she worked with former Tears for Fears member Ian Stanley, recording 'Me and a Gun' and 'China.' To create and sustain a buzz, she played pubs, clubs, and even put on concerts for moguls in her quaint London flat. Not every song wowed the higher-ups: 'Flying Dutchman,' for example, got canned.

The four-track *Me and a Gun* EP was released in October 1991 and achieved critical acclaim. In November, the renamed reissue included 'Silent All These Years,' which Tori would describe in an interview as 'A variation on a theme,' as far as its relationship to 'Me and a Gun'. The single charted just under the preferred 50 mark, but otherwise was well-promoted by BBC Radio where it was voted as Single of the Week. When the album was finally released in January 1992 in the UK, it shot up to number 14 in the album charts: a position it happily hovered around for 23 weeks. Fortunately, when the album came to America, it was also met with positive acclaim, although the *Billboard* 200 merely ranked it at 50.

Tori was finally getting the attention she deserved, although the stakes were still exceedingly high. She'd have to shake the trees with this debut, like label-mates Led Zeppelin, who went out on an artistic limb and had a hit with their self-titled maverick. The Who, Little Richard and Whitney Houston had hit the mark with their own debut efforts.

With *Little Earthquakes*, Tori would become a pop/rock influence on a legion of future female songwriters. But would the constant comparisons to late 1970s British soprano Kate Bush, cease? Could there be room at the top for another multi-ranged singer, pianist and composer?

Little Earthquakes was an unquestionable sea change. Rather than relying on bouzouki and bagpipes to bulk up her repertoire or pandering to the advice of *suits*, Tori explored a different path that involved cultivating her artistic integrity from within. To that end, Tori took a deep dive into the classics. She elaborated on this introspective journey to Robert Maril of rollingstone.com: 'From Rimbaud to Baudelaire, E. E. Cummings, Emily Dickinson and also the visual artists, I surrounded myself with the stories and the thinkers that formed me, not what those that had the power to push the button, wanted me to be formed with.'

The making of *Little Earthquakes* had a profound effect: In her second biography – *Resistance*, published in 2020 – Tori underscored the backlash she endured creating her debut; contending with 'the battle for the integrity of the songs' because powerful moguls wanted her to 'replace all the pianos with guitars.' Fortunately, after Tori 'found the piano again,' she recognized that *Little Earthquakes* was 'built around this rediscovery after my previous betrayal of the piano.'

Reviews were mixed: Jon Wilde of the popular *Melody Maker*, wrote that Amos 'possesses a rare ability to explore a multiplicity of emotions and a broad range of perspectives within the same song.'

However, Stephanie Zacharek of *Entertainment Weekly* disagreed, complaining that the lyrics 'are too self-consciously weird.' Roger Morton of

NME wrote, 'It isn't easy getting to grips with Tori.' (Morton, Roger, 11 January 1992). *Tori Amos: Little Earthquakes*, *NME,* London: IPC Media, pg. 28.)

On 2 April, Josef Woodard of *rollingstone.com* exclaimed, 'Newcomer Tori Amos's songs are smart, melodic and dramatic; the deeper you listen, the hotter they get.' Comparing her work to Kate Bush (does it ever end?) and Jane Siberry, Woodard concludes that, '...while they often deal in abstruse, poetic terms, Amos has a tendency to cut to the quick, to face facts....' Critics had a field day comparing Tori to other female alt-artists during this time: Jean Rosenbluth of the *Los Angeles Times* asserted that the album was 'a quixotic, compelling record that mixes the smart sensuality of Kate Bush with the provocative impenetrability of Mary Margaret O'Hara.'

Tori's discography has influenced a generation of recording artists. They have paid homage to her songwriting, vocal technique and performance style. But during the *Little Earthquakes* era, achieving 'street cred' entailed propelling her image beyond the prescribed circle of peers.

Fortunately, in the studio, Tori enjoyed her own support network. In 2018, singer Nancy Shanks (also known as 'Beenie') – Tori's best friend – was interviewed by podcast hosts Efrain Schunior and David Anderson of *Drive All Night*. Among other topics, she discussed singing backup during *Little Earthquakes* sessions and nicknames: 'Tori's nickname was Bee, and I was just B. There was a whole organic process which was wonderful when they were doing *Little Earthquakes*. We were doing a lot of growing then – both of us – it was reflected in the music.'

Shanks observed the metamorphosis that Tori underwent between the making of *Y Kant Tori Read* and *Little Earthquakes*: 'She just dug deeper into what she wanted to do. She went through that period where they wanted to change you. Don't change. There's always a maturing process when you do that.' (Sadly, 'Beenie' died in May 2019 of ALS.)

Ultimately, *Little Earthquakes* signifies an authentic period of self-discovery, untethered by trend. Critics in support wrote glowing reviews for all the right reasons. In 1998, *Q* magazine conducted a reader's poll in which *Little Earthquakes* reached the 66th ranking in their 'Greatest Albums of All Time by a Female Artist' category, according to *100 Women Who Rock the World* (*Q,* No. 186, London, 2 January).

In 2020, *Rolling Stone* awarded the album a ranking of 233 on its *500 Greatest Albums of All-Time* listing (*Rolling Stone*, 22 September 2020.)

'Crucify' (Tori Amos)

Released as the fifth single A-side, 12 May 1992 (US), 8 June (UK), 15 June 1992 (UK limited edition) b/w 'Here. In My Head', 'Mary,' 'Thank You,' 'Smells Like Teen Spirit,' 'Angie,' and 'Winter.'

Kicking into high gear immediately (kudos to percussionist Paulinho da Costa and mandolinist John Chamberlain for igniting the fireworks), 'Crucify' features a fistful of chords with a raised fifth, and that characteristic alone creates a palpable tension. Tori punches in the furious lower tones with the gusto of a five-star pastry chef, and her vocals are packed with personality.

Da Costa's bold signature sound emblazoned *Y Kant Tori Read*, so the team made a wise choice re-enlisting him on 'Crucify' and 'Happy Phantom.' By the age of five, the prodigy had already established a reputation as one of the best percussionists to emerge from Rio's Escola de Samba. In the following decade, he'd accompany (and this is just the shortlist) Diana Krall, Quincy Jones and Herbie Hancock. It's not just the infectious accompaniment or the support of backing singer Nancy Shanks – whose powerhouse vocals also reappear on the final track and title song; the whole gestalt makes 'Crucify' an epic.

Shanks told *Drive All Night*: 'I was doing that screaming on 'Crucify' and the producer nicknamed me the *antichrist* that day because I could do it over and over again.' Laughing, she revealed the ultimatum: 'Sit in the chair and be good now.'

The bullet-point lyrics come across as accusatory, bordering on paranoia: 'Every finger in the room is pointing at me.' Stark images of a 'bowling ball' stomach and 'desert mouth' are crucial components of this embittered landscape. Yet despite the cynicism, there's an element of mercy – in the pre-chorus: a promise of hope and escape. Finding 'a savior in these dirty streets' might be as elusive as finding *the goose that laid the golden egg* in a cul-de-sac, but the beauty of 'Crucify' lies in the quest, not in some fabricated fairy tale ending.

Moving forward, Tori whooshes back her anger and disenchantment with an introspective pronouncement: 'My heart is sick of being....' With resolve and fluidity, she extends the final word of that phrase, 'chains,' with an intriguing 16th-note melisma. Words, then, take a back seat to the wringing out of raw emotion in this self-sacrificial ballad.

Ultimately, she won't find her savior, but with fevered pitch, layered voices repeatedly chant, 'Why do we?' So, perhaps the moral is: while there's no precise formula for a happy ending, you've still got to hang in there and ask the good questions.

'Girl' (Tori Amos)

It was by a stroke of luck that 'Girl' came to life in the studio. In the *Little Earthquakes Songbook*, Tori recalls that co-producer Eric Rosse dug a cassette tape from a discarded stack, and urged her to react. Mercifully, Tori responded in kind. 'Girl,' one of four songs recorded in Rosse's home studio, landed Tori a deal and gave the team the opportunity to self-produce.

On the verses, Tori vamps on thirds, creating a catchy one-to-one correspondence to each steady beat. 'From in the shadow she calls,' is the elusive opening line. As the brush strokes of this tender portrait begin, we quickly get attached, as 'Girl' is deeply rooted in primal feelings. Tori's gut-punch honesty recalls John Lennon's plaintive rendering of 'Norwegian Wood'.

The setup is a sad one: 'She's been everybody else's girl.' 'Girl' goes beyond confessional, it's tearfully relatable, and the pathos – which extends beyond the struggle for young, female self-acceptance – bears a wider application. Tori cuts curiously back and forth between the first and third person in the verses. The 'response' lines – i.e. 'Rushin' rivers thread so thin.'– which are flush with poetic imagery, balance out the repetition.

Instrumentally, 'Girl' is a strong, radio-friendly ballad. The programmed drums contribute to the clean sound. The Kurzweil synth patterns add significant tonal color.

Little Earthquakes didn't lack coming-of-age epics, but 'Girl' brilliantly stands up on its own, thematically and harmonically. In *Resistance*, Tori recollects: 'The song 'Girl' had me putting up dreamcatchers around the house to salvage pieces of myself that I myself had gaslighted. She was encouraging me to be open to other sides I had not allowed myself to explore.'

'Silent All These Years' (Tori Amos)

Released as a single A-side with 'Me and a Gun,' 11 November 1991 (UK), April 1992 (US), 10 August 1992 (UK reissue), 17 August 1992 (UK limited edition), b/w 'Upside Down,' 'Thoughts,' 'Ode to the Banana King (Part One),' 'Song for Eric,' 'Smells Like Teen Spirit.'

Fortunately, the rest of the three-headed co-production team didn't mess with the sanctity. Tori remained in command of the maestro's baton. She would experiment liberally with zany vocalese effects in the future, but this sincere ballad remained pristine, with vocals upfront, and no intrusive wall-of-sound, give or take some sweetening. The shy, recurring piano motif immediately establishes a sense of calm and is as gentle on the ear as a quickly-opened jewelry box melody. Moreover, as harmonic textures heighten, Tori's vocal narrative remains steadfast.

Thematically, 'Silent All These Years' seems to be about achieving a sense of catharsis through artistic pursuits, submerging oneself in the creative process despite a fear of rejection or retribution. But feelings of loss and acts of repression also surface when this ballad is discussed on popular fan sites.

Certainly, politics came to bear. The 1991 hearing in which professor/attorney Anita Hill accused Supreme Court Justice Clarence Thomas of harassment, proved a perfect catalyst. Tori would continue to interject political and artistic views into future albums and memoirs, but perhaps this ballad was the prototype. Lyrically, a stream of consciousness soon gives way to authentic human observation, rendering one of Tori's most quoted lines: 'What's so amazing about really deep thoughts?' But there's a feminist flip side – she's young and in love but won't stand for being treated like a doormat: 'Boy, you best hope that I bleed real soon.'

In the bridge, she laments the passing of time: 'Years go by and I'm stripped of my beauty'; another standout phrase. With the passive voice, she leaves me wondering: who stripped the beauty away? Nature? DNA? The patriarch? The cosmetic industry, which benefits commercially when women perceive themselves as inadequate? (Later, Tori would address the double standard between older female artists and male counterparts.)

Instrumentally, the undulating introduction grabs our attention. But the arrangement didn't pop into a dream, like the iconic riff in Keith Richard's 'Satisfaction'; this song required painstaking attention to detail. She explained to journalist Paul Zollo that the ballad took six years to finish and grew out of 'that little bumblebee thing': essentially, recurring measures of 8th notes cycling around a minor second.

While 'that little bumblebee thing' forms the cinder block of this curious creation, its quiet dissonance allows for vocal *ad-lib*. With Tori's gentle execution, the figure floats as effortlessly as a buoy, under breathy vocals illustrating her penchant for onomatopoeia. After reading about that stepwise motif, every time I heard the melody, I envisioned an actual bee poking around a stack of wildflowers, landing on a stem with sweet pollen. This word-picture appeals to multiple senses.

Lyrically, the rapid switch from first to second person immerses the listener in a conversation: 'Well, I love the way you communicate/Your eyes focus on my funny lip shape.'

So, thematically, the ballad definitely holds a universal appeal. And, as mentioned earlier, fans have equated the backstory with not only the suppression of human rights but also a searing proclamation by a trauma survivor. Ironically, however, the iambic pentameter exudes playfulness and serenity that belies serious introspection.

Tori refers to her piano or songs in the third person, as if each were a close friend or child with whom she shares a divine pact. When regarding them as separate entities, it becomes clearer, album by album, song by song, how much Tori respects those boundaries. Creating a proper distance may be one key to her longevity. 'These songs demanded to be written. They are what they wanted to be,' she stressed to Zollo.

Producer Davitt Sigerson enriched the latter portion with Nick de Caro's orchestral arrangement, Tori's vocals blending seamlessly with the strings. But the arrangement also features less obvious touches. For the session, Sigerson asked 'Philly' to bring in his finger cymbal; although, unless you possess dog hearing, you may have missed the resilient ting.

'Precious Things' (Tori Amos)

Voila! The Bela Bartok influence! Bartok traversed the diverse regions of his native Hungary for simple folk music ideas, discovering beautiful melodies based on non-Western modalities. That Tori's a fan of his work, comes as no surprise.

In 'Precious Things,' the biting dissonance begins immediately, as mad packs of 16ths fence off against whole droning notes. That insistent phrase that your mind figures will harmonically resolve, does not, and therein lies the complex beauty. Everything about 'Precious Things' is intense: the painful relationships, the physical degradation, the wish to diminish the ills of puberty.

Harmonic tensions begin in the introduction, where a minor chord with a dramatic added 6th, 9th and major 7th, work in tandem. The riff is built around the melodic minor scale, where the 6th note is raised. Those distinctive harmonies continue into the verse, with a brief suspension and resolution at the end of the cadence.

In the chorus, Tori uses a single syllable of text while moving from pitch to pitch. For instance, she stretches out the syllables in the hook: 'These precious things.' 'Precious' ticks off two syllables, with two pitches in succession, but 'These' breaks up into four. Such melismatic singing, when used in Gregorian chant, often creates a hypnotic reaction. Another novel device is the penetrating use of breath percussion.

Returning to the verse, she matches words to beats until the phrase ends, subtly contrasting the sections. Remember the idea of Tori Amos being an enlightened Renaissance woman? Well, Leonardo da Vinci made use of chiaroscuro in his oil portraits. Similarly, Tori creates her own brand of light-dark, but with contrasting lengths and pitches.

Then there's the physicality of the narrative: 'So I ran faster,' Tori murmurs, exposing a quiver of fatigue in her chest voice. The piano figures move rapidly as she exaggerates her performance. To convey her altered state, she sighs and pants, reminding us that mere words could not reveal or conceal her anguish. During this sequence, she is the crowned princess of onomatopoeia.

Janis Ian used the phrase 'ugly girls like me' in 1975's 'At Seventeen.' The ballad was a bittersweet revelation after much on-the-air saccharin. Years later, that descriptor still stings. In 'Precious Things,' we hear 'ugly girl' spewed out by 'Billy.' In retaliation, the subject rants about 'pretty girls' and 'little fascist panties. 'Schoolboys' are depicted as entitled gnats. And amid this rubble of childhood cruelty, there's a lingering sadness, a sense of inconceivable loss.

I once watched a Buddhist monk build a perfect sand mandala and blow it all away to illustrate impermanence, and I think about that image when Tori sings, 'Let them bleed, let them wash away.'

The male voices in the chorus perfectly complement Tori's triple-tracked vocals and also contrast the higher-pitched female harmonies that ring out near the end.

'Precious Things' is one intense song. Tori's anguished wails – especially during the final measures – are supported by Steve Caton's thrashing blues-soaked guitar. He'd also have her back, recording 'The Waitress' on *Under the Pink* and 'Caught a Lite Sneeze' on *Boys for Pele.* On that album, Tori would hold back, being more constrained in her vocal antics. But I like that she doesn't hold back here vocally; plus, the instrumentals circle back with equal intensity.

Producers Tori and Eric Rosse utilized a conventional but superbly experienced ensemble: guitarist Steve Caton; bassist William McGregor; and drummer Carlo Nuccio. Rosse added rhythms through strategic keyboard programming. With all these dizzying effects, I dare you to fish out the 'rat pedal' bit by Jake Freeze.

'Winter' (Tori Amos)

Released as a single A-side, 9 March 1992 (UK), 16 March 1992 (UK limited edition), 24 November 1992 (US), b/w 'The Pool,' 'Take to the Sky,' 'Sweet Dreams,' 'Angie,' 'Thank You,' 'Upside Down,' 'Smells Like Teen Spirit.'

'Winter' is a striking example of the role Tori's classical background has played in her instrumental scoring. The piano starts out gently, but the dynamics and voicings go through several iterations. Chording in the verses is stately and reminiscent of classic Beethoven. Tori liberally flavors the melodic line with parallel 4ths and 5ths in the right hand, giving the song a gorgeous hollow texture. She allows a wide berth for the left-hand voicings, where she favors octaves and torpedoing 5ths.

Touring drummer Matt Chamberlain (not around during the *Little Earthquakes* era) later became accustomed to Tori's early repertoire during concerts. In interviews, he has suggested that Tori has a heavy left hand, which he has learned to work around. It's always a challenge for a bassist to play alongside a self-contained pianist, especially one who is capable of creating sweeping arrangements on her own. But with 'Winter', Tori illustrates her efficiency as an all-around arranger: with just a few well-placed accented notes, she creates powerful phrasal statements.

In the first four measures, there is almost a singsong feel to the vocal. But when Tori moves on to the following measure, she quickens the pace, using 16th notes for contrast: 'I get a little warm in my heart….'

Tori awakens multiple emotions; Rosse renders a blowtorch effect with the *war* drum, which also soldiers us through the season.

'Winter' has become an anthem for fathers and daughters, or perhaps any parental figure and child. That story is heartbreaking but wistful. 'Snow can wait/I forgot my mittens.' What follows is a chronology of subjective moments: The little girl puts her hands in 'my father's glove'. Like most youth, she's impulsive, 'I run off where the drifts get deeper,' the central character rails against fast, furious chording and strings. By this point, Tori has created such a vulnerable protagonist that one would plow through the polar vortex to salvage her shivering body.

Years later, 'hair is grey/the fires are burning.' Her father is aging as his little girl looks on helplessly. Is it time for father and daughter to switch roles? Time travel is plausible within this magical world. We needn't be slapped in the face with floating calendar pages to understand the inter-generational irony of this beautiful, albeit painful, dynamic.

Tori's 'song girls' have changed over the years. 'Winter' originally depicted Tori as a young girl, but she's just as likely to witness an assortment of images when performing live. 'It's always shifting. When I sing 'Winter' now, I don't necessarily get the same pictures I did on the last tour or the tour before or the tour before or the tour before. Sometimes now, I see a girl walking over that hill with a mommy. Yet the pictures can still be of my Poppa and my father. It's not always an even/or when I'm singing a song live,' she explained in her 2005 bio *Piece by Piece*.

As a fan, I retain the same image. To this day, I tear up when I hear 'Winter,' as I also had a close relationship with my father. I longed to wear his faded, corduroy jacket, even though my little fingers would only reach the elbow patches. And when the father tells the daughter, 'Things are gonna change so fast,' and 'I won't always have you near,' I wonder how Dr. Amos felt about his younger daughter growing more independent, whether he grew despondent thinking about their ultimate separation.

Throughout popular music history, many songs have been written about parents and children, i.e., Harry Chapin's 'Cats in the Cradle' and John Mayer's 'Daughters.' In Suzanne Vega's 'Luka,' a physically abused child is the protagonist, but 'Winter' is unique. To me, it's about watching your parent age, and feeling utterly helpless in the process. It's about facing mortality. 'Winter' reveals a subtle but sobering dialogue between the generations. As such, remorse and gratitude are likely to inhabit both sides.

Tori's vocal tone changes abruptly in the chorus, morphing into a low growl, and at that point, one can imagine the little girl becoming an irritable tween, rolling her eyes at the cautious parental figure. These are the word pictures that run through my mind, and that's why I consider 'Winter' one of Tori's most cinematic arrangements.

As a fan, 'Winter' makes me feel protective of Tori's work and even selfish. That selfish part of me wanted to keep her in check and keep fans, like me, in her back pocket. I wanted her to continue to write songs that were relevant to me. It felt prophetic when she sang 'Things are gonna change so fast' because I knew that that change was going to happen, and, knowing that she would ultimately expand her thematic range, I despaired at being left in the tundra.

After a number of exploratory albums, Tori would come full circle and write songs that harkened back to 'Winter' and 'Silent All These Years.' And while that was a welcome return, the years when she explored alternative songwriting avenues were just as critical. Remember when Bob Dylan got booed off the Newport Jazz Festival stage for going electric? Many will agree that he grew exponentially after that self-defining moment. Tori's fanbase has proven that they could accommodate and grow too.

Davitt Sigerson – who also produced 'Silent All These Years' – made a similarly intelligent choice. The orchestral parts – arranged and conducted by Nick de Caro – are lush, yet never overbearing. With such teamwork, the piano texture is enhanced rather than steamrollered.

Tori told the *Los Angeles Times* on 21 September 2003: 'Someone said, 'Bury the strings in 'Winter' because it won't be commercial.' And now I'm trying to preserve what was on tape, not necessarily what got released because of a decision that was made in twenty seconds of time.'

'Happy Phantom' (Tori Amos)

As much as we loved getting uncomfortably intimate, maybe Tori suspected that we needed a breather. As such, 'Happy Phantom' is a saloon-style pleaser, clocking in at about the same length as 'Leather' and just as hummable. The introductory bars are clanky and definitive, comprised of jolting octaves and striking Debussy fifths.

The progression marches merrily along like a John Philip Sousa anthem, yet the story begins with: 'And if I die today....' Now, how ironic is that?

Further afield, freewheeling fantasies are in full bloom with 'And I will never need umbrellas in the rain' and 'I'll wake up in strawberry fields every day.' But soon enough, words are cast aside: Tori has a ball singing 'Oo-hoo' while stomping out syncopated chords that would titillate the iconic Thelonius Monk (One of a few pianists that, just by virtue of instrumental ingenuity, can make us laugh; Chico Marx and Victor Borge are two more).

I see visions of The Rockettes at Radio City Music Hall, arm across arm, shoulder to shoulder, kicking legs in unison to the infectious beat. This is a visually rich song. When Tori ruminates about the afterlife, she envisions a Dorothy-in-the poppies surrealism, where Judy Garland, Buddha and Confucius comically intersect. Yet, there is an undercurrent of irony. Under the sunny exposition, clouds loom. I mean, it is about the grim reaper, right? So, after the catchy refrain, the eternal damnation begins. The songwriting pivots to post-mortem retribution, envisioning her real-time lover moving on. Thus, the recurring line, 'And if I die today,' takes on a darker meaning, even as those Rockettes swivel their shapely hips.

Eric Williams – who performed on *Y Kant Tori Read* – plunks out heady riffs on his dulcimer, and I can't imagine this piano-driven arrangement without this novel touch. And the other pre-debut player, Paulinho da Costa, also returns. As I mentioned earlier, da Costa began his career as one of Rio's most renowned percussionists. To date, he has performed on almost 2000 recordings. He knew how to flesh out the song while leaving enough space for Tori to pound out her own rhythmic persuasions.

'China' (Tori Amos)

Released as a single A-side, 20 January 1992, b/w 'Sugar,' 'Flying Dutchman,' 'Humpty Dumpty.'

The first song Tori wrote for *Little Earthquakes* back in 1987 was released as the third single and had originally been titled 'Distance,' as the line, 'I can feel the distance,' is the pillar on which the narrative leans. According to Eric Rosse, this was the only track on which the piano and vocals were recorded in tandem; others were subject to technological limitations.

On the surface, the theme appears to be loneliness and getting too close and backing away and how challenging that can be. Tori expresses a great deal of vulnerability in general, but specifically where she sings, 'In your eyes.' At this point, she lingers on that last word for dear life, finally concluding, 'I see a future together,' but her hesitance speaks volumes. Because the physical and emotional distance is so great, this love affair seems destined to go south. A long-distance affair with an emotionally disengaged lover can equal nothing but heartbreak. Then again, with this one-sided conversation, are we sure which lover is creating that distance?

On the other hand, why get stuck in that gauzy set-in-stone space? Tori invariably shows resilience in her 'song girls.' Regarding that line, 'I can feel the distance getting close…', Tori explains in *Piece by Piece*: 'That situation can be with a girlfriend, or with a different man than the one I wrote it about.'

I guess Tori's asking us not to pigeonhole her, nor claim that we comprehend the intricate backstories that lurk outside of her vivid imagination. I often relate to the colorful characters that hover between the stanzas, but only she can validate their motivations. As a writer, she gives and gives, but there's probably a part of her that wants to keep a few stories to herself; in fact, this seems to be a common thread in past interviews.

Each producer had a particular bent, and Ian Stanley definitely had his own vision: one which truly brought out the melody's elegance. As such, Stanley procured some fine instrumentalists: violinist Stuart Gordon; oboe player Will Gregory; guitarist David Rhodes; bassist Matthew Seligman, and drummer Chris Hughes. As the consummate arranger, David Lord gilded the final knot.

'China' is a song with an uncompromising structure. Setting the stage in the introduction by pummeling out 5ths in the left hand before the vocals, Tori employs pulsating fifths and penetrating octaves though out the verses. At the bridge, she reiterates her vocal lines instrumentally, and when returning to the final verse, she expands the bass part substantially, acting as her own independent orchestra.

Here, geography acts as a metaphor for romantic detachment. Tori explores metaphor further down the line; 'China' is but one compelling example.

'Leather' (Tori Amos)

Like 'Happy Phantom,' 'Leather' provides comic relief, but it's also a metaphor for playful sensuality. Played live, it's an extraordinary tour de force: one of Tori's most crowd-hungry requests. Fortunately, that sensuality comes through on the recording as well. Similar to 'Happy Phantom,' 'Leather' has a delightful burlesque overtone.

But Tori has explained in interviews that the story is not about having a wild time; nevertheless, fans on Tori Amos forums have put forth their own creative spins.

This is another one of co-producer Davitt Sigerson's gems. He's created a unique wall of sound using just a few variables. That's Tori on sampled strings and acoustic piano, with bass player, Jef Scott, buttressing the low end.

'Mother' (Tori Amos)

Tori premiered this ballad on the Little Earthquakes Tour in 1992 and has performed it on every subsequent tour. The heartbeat here manifests in another gripping piano motif. The solo acoustic piano intro is well-crafted and spacious. Written in cut time with a swath of suspended chords, 'Mother' evokes a dream state, through sustained end-of-phrase notes and jagged tempos. Tori's vocal performance is cutting and ethereal: often within the space of a solitary thought.

The shifting images in this intense ride bear witness to 'a dancing girl', 'brides in veils,' and 'breadcrumbs lost under the snow.' I initially assumed the phrase 'Mother the car is here' alluded to mental illness, especially given the distorted background effects, but Tori explained to yessaid.com that the line was actually about 'arriving on a place like earth, where that energy is very dark and attractive and sensual.'

She also explained to *rollingstone.com* that 'Mother' 'represented not just the father, but the grandfather – Poppa, my mother's father.' Imagery in subsequent work is also closely influenced by family members.

The repetitive commands haunt. 'Go, go, go now,' Tori coos. On the surface, a mother bird orders the clueless chick out of the nest. It's a cruel and confusing directive but loving and obligatory at the same time. Who can't relate to the dichotomy? The lyric imbues a perplexing push-me-pull-you: an ambiguous tension that muddles many familial relationships. 'First my left foot, then my right behind the other….' This sojourn of self-awareness is even more convincing when the narrative is filtered through the first-person perspective. Multi-instrumentalist Steve Caton crafts a schizoid blast of chord progressions and effects: simultaneously scary and stunningly beautiful.

At a running time of 6:59, Sigerson had plenty of time and space in which to oversee a number of nuances, but it's really Tori who steals the show, with soul-throbbing chord changes and immaculate articulation.

Ironically though, 'Mother' might never have seen the light of day sans Eric Rosse. By identifying Tori's germinal ideas and encouraging her to expand on them, her co-producer became a proactive sounding board. So, what happened? According to yessaid.com, Tori got up early one morning to noodle around on the piano. Pretty soon, a melody emerged. Of course, if you're Tori Amos, you might come up with 50 random melodies a day, but Rosse detected this one's distinctive beauty and challenged Tori to elaborate.

In Disc A of the box set, *A Piano: The Collection*, an alternative version was included. In addition, the ballad was remastered for inclusion in the *Little Earthquakes* 2015 reissue.

'Tear in Your Hand' (Tori Amos)

'All the world is dangling…' Tori sings. The most inviting part of this breakup song is not just Tori's breathy delivery and the whirling-dervish riff, but the sense conveyed of going back in time. Although it appears to be a ballad about lost love, there are reams of intelligent reflections here, as opposed to the bitterness found in the just-got-dumped-and-I'm-out-for-blood radio standards.

'Me and a Gun' (Tori Amos)

Released as a single A-side with 'Silent All These Years,' 21 October 1991, b/w 'Upside Down,' 'Thoughts.'

Keep in mind that Tori recorded this decades before the #MeToo movement. She became the first spokesperson for RAINN (Rape, Abuse & Incest National Network) and thereafter reached out to thousands of survivors, offering emotional support.

This acapella anthem was inspired by Tori's own frightening sexual assault, but not, as some critics and fans thought, an actual account. After seeing a related scene in the American film *Thelma & Louise*, Tori chose to become transparent about her own experience. On the track, as she references hymns she was forced to sing, her voice remains low and hesitant; the melody is simple but immensely moving.

Recording this track was a brave move on Tori's part, and there were risks: Socially, maybe the personal nature of the content would cause fans to feel invasive as if they were voyeurs that didn't have the right to participate.

The world in the early 1990s was still a harsh place; survivors were more often ridiculed than validated. Fortunately, Tori's stark and earnest presentation created a forum through which fans could discuss post-traumatic effects. Moreover, bonding with her audience was a blessing. Unfailingly, though, certain interviewers and fans crossed the line of decency by probing for details. In such cases, Tori remained remarkably grounded.

In this era, when Nirvana released *Nevermind*, the band awakened insular minds to other still-taboo themes, when referencing a drug prescribed for bipolar disorder in the truculent track, 'Lithium.'

Five years after the release of 'Me and a Gun,' Fiona Apple released 'Sullen Girl' about her own sexual assault. Tori swung open the door that encouraged artists to come forward with their traumas, giving future survivors an opportunity to openly dialogue.

Singer Judy Collins has frequently dealt with suicide – another historically taboo subject – in her music and memoirs. Joni Mitchell wrote about domestic abuse in 'Not To Blame,' and Janis Ian in 'These Hands.' Trauma is most dangerous when it's kept secret; when survivors can't benefit from the support of their peers or heroes. These female artists should be hailed for their transparency, for not shying away from tough subjects, and for providing opportunities for healing via their craftsmanship and willingness to share.

Ian Stanley is credited for the recording. Perhaps his contribution was underrated, with seemingly little room for production, as 'Me and a Gun' consists entirely of Tori's achingly beautiful voice. But Stanley executed an acoustically perfect track that magnifies the senses and captivates the heart.

'Little Earthquakes' (Tori Amos)

There's exceptional chemistry between Steve Caton's wailing electric guitar and Tori's shimmering synth. Eric Rosse exceeded expectations with his over-the-top programming ideas, and bassist Will McGregor simply tore up the bottom. This phenomenally complex closer is structured like a classical suite with several formidable parts. The penultimate section consists of a headbanging cacophony. It's only after Tori rants about being ripped to pieces that we can unapologetically exhale.

Nancy Shanks – the aforementioned Beenie – sang backup along with Steve Caton, Tori and Eric Rosse. This rich spectrum of voices added a lasting sparkle to the grand finale. Shanks sorted out the soaring harmonies on this jittery title song, which at six-plus minutes, holds the honor of being the lengthiest album track. Essentially, it is a queasy roller coaster ride. And lyrically, whatever vampires Tori alluded to at the beginning, lay in state by the second half.

Perhaps this self-produced tizzy was *Little Earthquake*'s most intrepid effort, with the inclusion of devilish tricks, such as Jake Freeze on musical saw. Freeze would guest again on *To Venus and Back* (1999) and *Tales of a Librarian: A Tori Amos Collection (2003).*

Interestingly, live versions varied in length. That *Venus* version expanded to 7:37 from the original 6:51.

Alas, without adequate space, not all recorded songs made it onto *Little Earthquakes*. 'Take Me With You' was one of the casualties until 2006, when Tori re-recorded the vocals for *A Piano: The Collection*.

Album Art

On Cindy Palmano's cover, a bright-eyed, barefoot Tori in rolled-up jeans and sleeveless shirt crouches inside a wooden box, with one hand touching the outer edge and a look of anticipation on her face: a sign that she's ready to spring? Palmano completely captured Tori's innate sense of curiosity and playfulness. A matching blue toy piano rests on the right side; her name in attention-grabbing gold, but turn the cover and – Where's Tori? The box is empty!

Inside the accompanying booklet, lyrics are printed in tiny letters. There are also some grainy illustrations. I wish, I could read the lyrics, but in terms of the cover shot, it's perfect for *Little Earthquakes* because it's whimsical, attractive, and even a bit suspenseful.

Related Tracks:

The 'Me and a Gun' single from the EP of the same name dropped on 21 October 1991. The release of the subsequent tracks was staggered: 'Silent All These Years', 18 November 1991; 'China,' 20 January 1992; 'Winter,' 9 March 1992; 'Crucify,' 12 May 1992.

'Crucify' (U.S. EP)

Crucify (U.S. EP)
'Crucify' is the fifth single from Little Earthquakes.
Personnel: See Little Earthquakes

Produced by Ian Stanley and Davitt Sigerson
Label: Atlantic, East West
Release date: US: 12 May 1992, UK: 8 June 1992, UK (Limited edition): 15 June 1992, AUS: 20 July 1992
Running time: 21:35

'Winter' (Tori Amos)
Always an epic; perhaps the song which most completely defines Tori's early career by way of expressive, linear lyrics. (See *Little Earthquakes*).

'Angie' (Mick Jagger, Keith Richards)
Tori set precedence, as female artists hadn't always covered songs written by men about women. She replaced Richard's acoustic guitar with titillating, gospel-spiked piano. Her vocal performance is sultry and magnetic. Produced by Ian Stanley.

'Smells Like Teen Spirit' (Kurt Cobain, Krist Novoselic, Dave Grohl)
Live, Tori articulates with keen technical expertise. Each note rings out with the utmost clarity as she chants 'Hello' repeatedly. She takes liberties by altering a lyric and leaving out a verse, but stays present.

After churning out sterling measures of solo piano, she delivers a restrained first verse: 'With the lights out, it's less dangerous,' using her chest and head voice interchangeably. She'd have had big shoes to fill had she elected to approximate the heavily-produced Nirvana version but wisely toned the song down, making it entirely her own.

Kurt Cobain once mentioned in an interview that he and his then-girlfriend, Courtney Love, used to wake up to Tori's version to do interpretive dance.

Fans and critics applauded her crisp, clear enunciation, as opposed to the somewhat undecipherable vocals of the original. Instrumentally, Tori's acoustic piano version is especially demonstrative. She illustrates that even without thrashing electronics, the song embodies truth and veracity. True to form, Tori uses her head voice to escalate tension, thus making this unplugged gem one of her best. Produced by Ian Stanley.

'Thank You' (Jimmy Page, Robert Plant)
Tori retains the raw, vocal humility that lead singer Robert Plant conveyed in the Led Zeppelin classic. Clearly intent on making the lyrics evocative, Tori creates an intricate arrangement that echoes and shades her vocals. Produced by Ian Stanley.

'Crucify' (Remix)
Other than highlighting the rich backing vocals, there's not much difference between this remix and the original version. Produced by Davitt Sigerson.

Me and a Gun (UK EP)

Personnel:
Tori Amos: Piano and vocals
Arranger: Nick De Caro
Produced by: Davitt Sigerson
Label: East West Records (UK), Atlantic (North America)
Released: 21 October 1991
A-side: 'Silent All These Years,' 'Upside Down.' B-side: 'Me and a Gun,' 'Thoughts'

Silent All These Years (UK EP)

Personnel: see Little Earthquakes
Produced by: See Little Earthquakes
Label: East West Records, Atlantic
Release date: UK: 11 November 1991; AUS: 3 February 1992; US: April 1992; UK (Reissue): 10 August 1992; UK (Limited edition): 17 August 1992
A-side: 'Me and a Gun.' B-side: 'Upside Down'/ 'Thoughts'/ 'Ode to the Banana King (Part One)'/ 'Song for Eric'/ 'Smells Like Teen Spirit.'
Note: Because the track 'Silent all These Years' received more radio attention than 'Me and a Gun,' the label reissued the EP with this new title. Alas, the EP only reached 51 in the UK, but Tori's lucky break came when BBC Radio 1 crowned the song 'Record of the Week.'

Crucify (U.K. CD single)

Label: East West
'Crucify' (remix)/ 'Here. In My Head'/ 'Mary'/ 'Crucify (Alternate Mix)'

Limited U.K. Live EP

Label: East West
'Little Earthquakes'/ 'Crucify'/ 'Precious Things'/ 'Mother' (Live)
(See *Little Earthquakes* personnel)
Excellent live renditions of four songs from Little Earthquakes.

Reissues:

Little Earthquakes Deluxe Edition: Bonus Disc 2:

'Upside Down'/ 'Thoughts'/ 'Ode to the Banana King'/ 'Song for Eric'/ 'The Pool'/ 'Take to the Sky'/ 'Sweet Dreams'/ 'Mary'/ 'Sugar'/ 'Flying Dutchman'/ 'Humpty Dumpty'/ 'Smells Like Teen Spirit'
Plus, five tracks recorded live at Cambridge on 5 April 1992:
'Little Earthquakes'/ 'Crucify'/ 'Precious Things'/ 'Mother'/ 'Happy Phantom,' plus the B-side, 'Here. In My Head.'

When the *Deluxe Edition* bonus disc of the remastered *Little Earthquakes* was reissued in 2015, the following bonus tracks that were added:

'Humpty Dumpty' (Tori Amos)

With fat, bluesy riffs, excitement builds, along with a zigzag of emotions. It is based on an American nursery rhyme.

'Upside Down' (Tori Amos)

See *Under the Pink*

This first appeared with 'Me and a Gun,' 'Silent All These Years' and 'Winter' singles in 1991, and then on *More Pink* in 1994, *A Piano* in 2006, and in the *Little Earthquakes Deluxe Remaster* in 2015.

With raw emotion, and against a meandering, melodic accompaniment, Tori recycles the thought, 'Any kind of touch is better than upside down.' This melodic ballad includes sharp touches: church bells, courtesy of Davitt Sigerson, and John Philip Shenale's woozy Mellotron. Bassist Jef Scott provided bold outlines. While Tori deeply regrets that the song was omitted from *Little Earthquakes*, fans shared in her excitement when she rattled off the rhythmic lyrics on *Live at Montreux*.

Upside Down 2 (Tori Amos)

This pretty, slow-moving ballad sounds like it needs a musical to go along with it. Tori, are you listening? When the theme is first established, the narrator keeps the listener at a distance – 'Watch the boats go by in someone else's life' – but the story quickly becomes inclusive: 'No, that is not our life, not today.' Ultimately, it morphs into a cheerful song: 'We got to turn that frown upside down,' although the background chords tell an alternative tale.

'Thoughts' (Tori Amos)

'Me and a Gun' and 'Silent All These Years' singles; *Little Earthquakes Deluxe Remaster*.

A shuttle through fierce times where 'burning witches' and 'burning books' were the norm.

'Ode to the Banana King (Pt. One)' (Tori Amos)

'Silent All These Years' single; *Little Earthquakes Deluxe Remaster*.

Over a heavy-handed bassline, Tori breathlessly stretches out a Middle Eastern melody.

'Song for Eric' (Tori Amos)

This plaintive ballad (which only clocks in at 1:32) with a circuitous melody, is about pining for and dreaming about one's true love. It's about Eric Rosse, with whom Tori shared a seven-year relationship and co-produced *Little Earthquakes*.

'The Pool' (Tori Amos)

'Winter' single; *A Piano, Little Earthquakes Deluxe Remaster*.

Be prepared for a sonic paradox, as the instrumental portion employs both a meditative and unsettling vibe. But to be clear, Tori's vocals are enchanting.

'Take to the Sky' aka **'Take to the Sky/Russia'** (Tori Amos)

'Winter' single, *More Pink*, *A Piano*, *Little Earthquakes Deluxe Remaster*.
Tori punches her right fist against the baseboard; her left tears off an ostinato. Lyrics suggest early career woes: 'This house is like Russia, with eyes cold and gray.'

'Sweet Dreams' (Tori Amos)

Remixed in the *Little Earthquakes Deluxe Edition*, incandescent vocals float over cantankerous beats and swooning harmonies. There's lots of personality in each verse. 'Your house is on fire – come along now,' she incants, echoed by a riveting chorus and bright piano.

'Mary' (Tori Amos)

'Crucify' single, *Tales of a Librarian, A Piano, Little Earthquakes Deluxe Remaster.*
Bridging the gap between folk-rock and Americana, this guitar-driven song takes no prisoners.

'Sugar' (Tori Amos)

See *Hey Jupiter* EP.
Against an extraordinary sea of effects, Tori's voice exudes warmth. The lyrics of the verse of this quietly-stated love anthem suggest an entirely different story, but the chorus can't not pull you in, as Tori sings: 'The robins bring me many things, but Sugar, he brings me sugar.' Verse to verse, her voice grows incrementally sweeter.

Maybe a flip of the coin would determine whether the live version on *To Venus and Back* or *Live from Sunny Florida* is the champ. Maybe there's no contest: both versions retain the intended amount of sweetness.

Tori has performed many iterations of this beloved ballad, which was inspired by the memory of a childhood suitor. Hoping to win her affection, the shy lad asked how many sugars she likes in her tea. Although the earnest suitor lost his dream girl, he's got fun stories to share.

'Sugar' was a surefire hit during the 1998 tour.

Live, Tori's voice has remained low and empathetic. Lingering over a pocketful of chords, she's been known to amp it up along with the band before ad-libbing with fervor.

'Flying Dutchman' (Tori Amos)

'China' single, *A Piano*, *Gold Dust*, *Little Earthquakes Deluxe Remaster*.
See *Under the Pink.* The title spawned *Comic Book Tattoo*: a graphic novel collection inspired by Tori's discography. 'They say your brain is a comic book

tattoo,' but in Tori's world vision, even nerds become heroes. Tori mentioned in interviews that 'it was the hardest one to lose.'

'Straight suits, they don't understand,' she sings to calm the misunderstood boy at the center.

The arrangement conflates other-worldly effects, a futuristic theme and deep dives into the universal search for human potential.

There is a lot of vitality in the orchestral version; the counterpunching flute is a nice surprise, but the dynamics are overblown during the extended outro. At a snappier tempo, it still shines.

Early fans got access to this song with the 'China' single and it's become a classic.

'Here. In My Head' (Tori Amos)

'Crucify' single, *More Pink*, *A Piano*, *Little Earthquakes Deluxe Edition*.
See *Under the Pink*

Under the Pink (1994)

Personnel:
Tori Amos: piano, vocals, Vox on 'Past the Mission'
Steve Caton: guitar
Paulinho da Costa: percussion
Ross Cullum: mixing
Shaun DeFeo: assistant engineer
Melissa 'Missy' Hasin: cello
John Beverly Jones: engineer
Kevin Killen: mixing
Ezra Killinger: violin
Dane Little: cello
Bob Ludwig: mastering
Paul McKenna: producer, engineer
Cynthia Morrow: viola
Carlo Nuccio: drums
Cindy Palmano: art direction, photography
George Porter Jr.: bass
Chris Reutinger: violin
Trent Reznor: backing vocals
Jimbo Ross: viola
Eric Rosse: producer, engineer
Nancy Roth: violin
John Philip Shenale: strings, Hammond organ
Nancy Stein-Ross: cello
Francine Walsh: violin
John Wittenberg: violin
Produced by Tori Amos and Eric Rosse
Recorded at The Fishhouse, New Mexico, and Westlake Studios, Los Angeles in February-October 1993
Label: Atlantic (US), East West (Europe)
Release date: UK and US: 31 January 1994
Highest chart rank: UK: 1, US: 12
Running time: 56:40

In May 1994, Adrian Deevoy at *Q* magazine published the cutting-edge article, 'Hips Lips Tits Power,' where Tori, Bjork and PJ Harvey were profiled, although their skills and musical approaches were incomparable. While no one would question that each woman had great talent, what made the press insist on lumping three dissimilar female artists together when in male-oriented articles, editors ordinarily grouped shredders with shredders? And can you imagine a title broadcasting the private body parts of men? (Okay, let's not go there...).

Despite the bias, Tori's work was enjoying acclaim, but after the incontestable success of *Little Earthquakes*, she faced the pressure of releasing a sharp, relevant follow-up.

In August 1994, she spoke to John Everson of the *Illinois Entertainer* about dealing with that challenging transition: 'There is the sense that the sophomore record can really trip you up. There are a lot of people whose second record doesn't get heard, and I was aware of that. I don't have to worry about the sophomore jinx anymore. I've passed that, so I've got a career!'

Under the Pink was a game-changer, an investigation of stark rhythms and unorthodox instrumentation, sweeping character arcs and historical re-imaginings. Tori explained to the *Baltimore Sun*, '*Little Earthquakes* was more of a diary, and *Under the Pink* is more to me of an impressionist painting.'

Early on, the team rinsed off the palette knife and prepped the canvas, but those days were far behind. Tori had learned so much more about musical collaboration, business negotiations and transparency during and after her studio experiences with *Y Kant Tori Read* and *Little Earthquakes*. She acquired all the right tools, but statistically speaking, the follow-up could have flopped, leaving Tori to become a one-hit-wonder.

But… that's not what happened. *Under the Pink* holds the record of being Tori's highest-charting album in the UK and internationally, with more than 2,000,000 copies sold. So, she clearly avoided the sophomore jinx. According to the RIAA, *Under the Pink* achieved double platinum status in October 1999 in the US, after achieving those 2,000,000 sales. *Rolling Stone* includes it in their greatest albums of the 1990s list.

The singles were promoted worldwide. The first, 'Cornflake Girl,' reached Europe in January of 1994, followed by the Australian release in February. In May, it became the second single in the US, reaching its zenith at number four in the UK.

'God,' the second single released in Australia in May 1994, was the fourth in Europe in October. 'Pretty Good Year' was the second single released in Europe that same month, but the fourth in Australia, in November. The promotional campaign was like an invigorating game of musical chairs, fetching new fans at a frantic rate.

The third single, 'Past the Mission' – featuring Tori's sonorous Vox organ – rose to number four on the UK singles chart, while the album itself racked up an impressive number one slot. Although it did get released in the UK by East West Records on 16 May 1994, it was solely in the form of a limited edition and on 23 May in a double-CD format. Similar promotional activity followed on 4 July 1994 in Australia and on 27 September in the U.S., through Atlantic Records.

Perhaps the eight-month production setting brought the team good fortune. After all, recording conditions were exceptionally serene. They communed under cumulus skies, surrounded by the all-around spirituality of New Mexico, in a 150-year-old hacienda. As the locale was on Native land, the local community adopted Tori.

There were repeat performers: guitarist Caton and percussionist da Costa. Eric Rosse and Tori immediately set about exchanging creative ideas, with Rosse moonlighting as a technician.

As for the material, time proves that Tori easily generates new ideas. While she's been known to tirelessly explore archetypes and mythology, she could complete several volumes of work just based on her fascinating family history. Tori's forebears include her fearless great-grandmother, Margaret Little. Her grandfather explained that Little escaped the Trail of Tears in the Smoky Mountains, 'with a tomahawk hidden under her apron', but at-the-ready.

On the paternal side, Tori could draw upon stories from her Scottish roots; her ancestors ultimately settled in the mountains of Virginia. Tapping into the richness of her southern childhood, native lineage and spoon-fed Christianity guaranteed an abundance of storylines.

Even if such cultural cornerstones didn't find their way into a specific track, the residual emotions often would. Still, selecting final album tracks can always be harrowing, especially for a prolific composer who considered her songs 'friends.' 'Friends' need to be loyal, right? Tori still harbors regrets about abandoning the orphan tracks: 'Sister Janet,' 'Peeping Tomi,' 'Daisy Dead Petals' and 'Honey' would've made a copacetic quartet.

On the romantic front, there'd be another major change: Eric Rosse and Tori – together for seven years – would split up after production. But for the duration of *Under the Pink*, they'd work intensively: like first-responders tending to a five-alarm fire.

Guitarist Steve Caton – from the *Y Kant Tori Read* camp – would not return to the studio with Tori until *To Venus and Back*, although they would tour together from 1996 to 1999.

But a new creative partnership was brewing: 'Yes, Anastasia,' 'Bells for Her', 'Pretty Good Year,' and 'Cloud on My Tongue' would be enhanced by John Philip Shenale, who had previously arranged keyboard parts for *Little Earthquakes*. The L.A.-based arranger describes the augmentation of his role:

> Tori called and said, 'Phil, you've got to come down to Ocean Way. We're going to drink and we're going to tell you about stuff.' I knew they were recording strings. They basically told me that Tori came in and started listening to what arranger Clare Fischer was doing. Tori couldn't recognize any of her songs. It was so far out. And by the way, I have the DAT, which had just the orchestrations, which I never listened to until after. It's the most beautiful music that never fit that I've ever heard in my life.
>
> We didn't even have a click at the time. This was '92. To generate the click, because Tori was playing in rubato, she was playing in freestyle. We didn't have those tools, so I actually had to synch two computers up and run the audio track from one computer into the other one in order to get the tempo mapped and the click, so the players could play to her easily because she moves around a little less now – it's a little easier and I love it.

Tori's insecurities surfaced during the making of *Y Kant Tori Read*, and she fought to be heard during *Little Earthquakes* pre-production, but positive factors were now impacting her success. Her enviable fanbase and record of sold-out performances proved that she was sonically versatile and endlessly creative.

Working at her craft since the age of five had made Tori a quick study. Whatever the setbacks, she'd come around. After experimenting with synth-pop and finding the genre vacuous, she'd moved on. With great enthusiasm, she opened herself up to alternative means of expression.

The making of *Little Earthquakes* allowed Tori to convey her truths, mostly within the context of a confessional ballad. But post-debut, Tori was ready to move on, expand her thematic range, and purge unapologetically into her hyper-aware writer's heart.

In an *AllMusic* review, Ned Raggett suggests that *Under the Pink* 'has been unfairly neglected, when in fact it has as good a claim as any to be one of the strongest – and maybe even the strongest – record she has put out.'

Was it neglected? In hindsight, maybe so. I do concur that it's one of Tori's strongest studio albums. There's a relaxed vibe that runs through many of her vocal and instrumental performances, and at this point, she demonstrated a confidence that could only come from bleary-eyed studio sacrifice and egoless editing – she'd shown her true colors as a certifiable team player. Furthermore, she'd won over the naysayers. How else could she have gotten away with 'Yes, Anastasia': a nine-and-a-half-minute ode to a dead Russian princess? It was an epic undertaking, but certainly not radio-friendly.

In 1968, Jimmy Webb, with actor and occasional singer Richard Harris, released an unprecedented seven-plus-minute ballad and certainly had to fight for his share of the pie, um, I mean cake! Had 'Yes, Anastasia' been Tori's 'MacArthur Park' moment?

Native American folk singer, Bill Miller, warmed up the house. As Tori walked onstage, the *Rawhide* theme echoed across the house. With the Bosendorfer and prepared piano at the ready, the wrench used at Schubas could be designated a relic.

'Pretty Good Year' (Tori Amos)

Released as an A-side, 7 March 1994 (UK), 7 November 1994 (AUS), b/w 'Home on the Range (Cherokee Edition),' 'Daisy Dead Petals,' 'Honey,' 'Black Swan.'

Tori has built a reputation for taking her fan letters to heart, but one letter affected her so personally that she dedicated the opening song to the contents. This fan, Greg, lamented that his girlfriend Lucy left him. It was clear that he was in a depressed state, generally wallowing in self-pity. Tori namechecked Lucy but made Greg the centerpiece: 'Tears on the sleeve of a man/Don't want to be a boy today.' One of Tori's objectives for writing the *Under the Pink* songs was to work through any feelings she had about being a victim. And here was Greg. It struck a chord.

In the book, ***In Their Own Words: Songwriters Talk About the Creative Process*** (Bill DeMain), Tori says, 'I was just telling Greg's story, and it affected the singer so much that it brought my own stuff into it, and that was kind of a near surprise.'

The strings – arranged by John Phillip Shenale – give a real touch of class to this organically conceived, upbeat opener, which is universally accessible. Shenale offers: 'There's a bit of a rock and roll event. More of an Elton John and Paul Buckmaster kind of thing in a way.'

'God' (Tori Amos)

Released as a single A-side, 1994, b/w 'Home on the Range (Cherokee Edition),' 'Piano Suite: All the Girls Hate Her,' 'Over It' (US).

'God sometimes you just don't come through/You need a woman to take care of you.' There's Tori, putting the quintessential feminist spin on theology.

There's so much eclectic electricity here: the zany effects that bleed forth from Caton's sunburst Strat and the imperious Rat Pedal, billowy chorus, echoing bassline and exclamatory lyric, with intoxicating rhythms from a barrage of electronic drums.

Drummer and future touring companion, Matt Chamberlain, wasn't around at this point, but once he came aboard, he became well aware of how a studio arrangement could change during the excitement of a concert: 'Live, it can become way funkier, an almost improvisational thing. And she'll work off that.'

This controversial song inspired director Melodie McDaniel's video, which placed Tori's character in a darkened temple, undergoing a ritual which includes handfuls of roaming rats, burning candles and spiritual leaders – not for the weak of heart if you detest crawly things, but the bold imagery makes for a definitive think-piece.

American audiences had a cassette single version at their disposal, b/w 'Sister Janet,' but their European counterparts had a wider format choice: CD, 12-inch, 7-inch vinyl single, as well as the cassette version. Fascinating ambient and remix versions include: Detroit techno artist Carl Craig's 'God (The Thinking Mix 2)' and 'The Rainforest Resort Mix' (East West 1994), 'God,' the 2015 CJ Bolland remix, and 'God (The Dharma Kaya Mix)' by The Joy.

'Bells for Her' (Tori Amos)

The introduction to this delicate waltz consists primarily of broken minor chords. In the first four measures, the tonic note is held over, serving as a seductive drone – although the piano plays a starring role, Caton also infuses alchemy.

The theme pertains to a quarrel Tori had with a friend over an act of domestic violence. Hinging on an implied-moral judgment, the storytelling is both evocative and mysterious; the melody line is refreshingly plaintive: 'Blanket girl, there's nothing we cannot ever fix,' 'You have your face and her eyes, but you are not her.' Critics pounce on Tori for using elusive imagery, but here – even with the narrative shifting from first-person plural to second and third – the fragmented phrases' disregard for time and ethereal ambience form a stunning symbiosis.

The prepared piano technique harkened back to the avant-garde tradition used by composer John Cage in the 1940 piece, 'Bacchanale,' which similarly intrigued Brian Eno and The Velvet Underground. Shenale elaborates:

> Eric Rosse and Tori wanted to experiment with the timbres of the piano. They would experiment with electric piano later, but for that period of time, it was strictly acoustic piano. One of the best ways of extending the sound is to use prepared piano, which is standard in progressive classical music.
>
> Tori said, 'Just prepare a bunch of things and then I'll use them or not.' We started with one of her grands. We used rubber mutes and various things at the time. It was a technique that sounded a lot like an electric, distorted guitar on the piano, which was pretty wild. We went to Walmart and picked up bolts and a few large steel balls and just let them roll down the strings that we were using and recorded it. We used a sampler to record some of the weirder-prepared piano stuff.
>
> Then we finally got to the grand, and I said, 'Let's detune it by two octaves and make it basically a monochord.' Normally, there's three strings on most of the keys, and then on the lower keys, there are only two and then one. We basically cut out two of the strings on each note, and basically, what you're hearing on 'Bells for Her' is a tuned piano, down two octaves and with only one string. It's a very efficient sound. The harmonics begin to be stretched, and they become further apart and they're not actually musically in tune with each other. They get spread out, so it begins to sound more like a tubular bell or bell tones like that. That was the main technique she ended up using for *Under the Pink*.

'Past the Mission' (Tori Amos)

Released as an A-side, 16 May 1994 (UK limited edition), 23 May 1994 (UK CD2), 4 July 1994 (AUS), 27 September 1994 (US), b/w 'Black Swan.'

'Past the Mission' is a radio-friendly tune with a deeper meaning. Tori told *St. Louis Dispatch*, 15 July 1994, that the song 'refers to a personal experience with sexual violence, which I had a song about on *Little Earthquakes* also.' She also exclaimed: 'Though I can't change what happened, I can choose how to react.' To avoid 'being bitter,' she deliberately added this line: 'Past the Mission, I smell the roses.'

The tempestuous Vox adds a muted texture, approximating Ray Manzarek's zeal on The Doors' 'Light My Fire.' With a winning ostinato and abrupt end, the track zips by in a flash.

The juxtaposition of short and long phrases keeps the pace moving, although the lyrics have a decidedly dark theme: 'Past the Mission/Behind the prison tower.' Tori radically changes mood by alternating her vocal tone: on the verses, which are in a major key, she sounds optimistic – her head voice is bright and fearless.

On the chorus, she engages her chest voice; the mood turns melancholy. Sounding appropriately world-weary, she blends exceedingly well with baritone Trent Reznor.

So, how did Reznor turn up on a Tori Amos album? Musically, they came from disparate worlds, but after a friend turned Reznor on to *Little Earthquakes*, he grew infatuated with Tori's progressive songwriting skills and contacted her.

She'd been an admirer of his battle-cry vocals yet detected a softness and vulnerability beneath the anguished screams. When they finally got together at the home that Reznor was renting (where actress Sharon Tate had been murdered by members of the Charles Manson Family), Tori attempted to bake the Nine Inch Nails vocalist her family's tried-and-true chicken recipe. Unfortunately, she ruined the meal by burying the hot poultry in too much flour. In tears, Tori had to call her mother for advice. Despite the calamitous meeting, Tori and Trent became quick friends and perhaps would've become more.

But in February 1996, Reznor updated *Spin* regarding his personal relationship to Tori: 'We're not that close now. Some malicious meddling on the part of Courtney Love.'

'Baker Baker' (Tori Amos)

In a highly transformative performance, Tori again struggles with the aftermath of sexual assault. Yearning to be made 'whole again,' she lays out a series of persuasive, gentle chords. 'I ran from him in all kinds of ways,' she sings, suggesting a terrible fear of intimacy. Although it serves as an aftermath to the a cappella 'Me and a Gun' from *Little Earthquakes*, 'Baker Baker' is more structurally complex, yet the subtlety behind the metaphor is easily gleaned. Shenale's restrained strings illuminate the raw, spare beauty.

'The Wrong Band' (Tori Amos)

The piano is mesmerizing; Tori's steampunk vamps are as palpable as a carnival barker's pitch. She lights up the ivories with a playful fugue. When played live, she whips fans into a frenzy as she swivels and switches from acoustic to electric, all while keeping the audience in full sight.

But like many of Tori's themes, this one takes a dark turn, so don't let the cavalier bass line fool you. 'The Wrong Band' is essentially about a sex worker whose client is a powerful politician; because she knows too much about him, she's forced to leave the country. But the political references and *Sturm und Drang* are only half the experience; the overrides include that rousing accompaniment and hummable melody.

'The Waitress' (Tori Amos)

'I want to torture the people who don't understand the world of faeries,' Tori told *Rolling Stone*'s Steven Daly (*rollingstone.com*, 26 June 1998). There may be a hidden message in this passive-aggressive rant, but if there is, I haven't quite found it. Still, 'The Waitress' is fundamentally a harrowing ride. Framed by Jerry Garcia-esque electric guitar courtesy of Caton, and Carlo Nuccio's swaggering drums and other-worldly effects, Tori combusts her inner-punk and whatever else her imaginative brain boots up.

Performed live, what's really cool is her quasi-scat singing, or then again, is she speaking in tongues? The point being that this anti-paean allows for lots of levity.

Matt Chamberlain wasn't there for this original recording but would perform live with Tori in the future. He told Jake Brown, the author of *Tori Amos in the Studio*: 'The versions of the songs we did live, were different than on the record, which made them unique. 'Waitress,' for example, is a nine-minute space jam that's totally different from the version on the record.'

The contrasts give off heat. In the verses, Tori meanders along in cut time. At the chorus, she's hell on wheels; the receptive bass line is also off-the-charts.

Engineer, Paul McKenna, felt the album was unfinished until Tori returned a few days later after an altercation with an aggressive server. She told *Blender* in the February/March 2002 edition: 'She was a meanie. She became the embodiment of a few women in my life that I was having it out with, and 'The Waitress' got written. And Paul said, 'The record's complete.'

'Cornflake Girl' (Tori Amos)

Released as an A-side 'edit', 1994 (US), b/w 'Sister Janet,' 'Dead Daisy Petals,' 'Honey.' Released as a limited-edition, 1994 (UK), b/w 'Sister Janet,' 'Piano Suite: All the Girls Hate Her,' 'Over It'; Disc 2: 'A Case of You,' 'If 6 Was 9', 'Strange Fruit.'

I assumed Tori borrowed the title from Lennon-McCartney's 'I Am the Walrus': you know the line, where Lennon belts out, 'Sitting on a cornflake,' but Tori proved me dead wrong.

The spry piano chops that form the framework, belie the cruel back story which influenced this immortalization. In *Possessing the Secret of Joy*, by Alice Walker, there's discussion of the female genital mutilation practiced in Africa, whereby female family members coerce other females to engage in the procedure. When Tori discussed the book with stylist Karen Binns, the topic turned to acts of betrayal of women by women. Tori referred to a female betrayer as a 'cornflake girl,' as opposed to a 'raisin girl,' a designation with which she identifies strongly.

If you hadn't heard that back story, you could innocently bop along to this pop gem because, musically, there's a lot to love. Like the sexy smoke rings good-looking actors blew into the cosmos in the classic films, or a shot of honey-colored brandy after an amazing meal, 'Cornflake Girl' is the ultimate *aperitif*.

Nancy Shanks (Beenie) backs up Tori's overdubs. You'd sway along with your best friend too if she were a 'raisin girl....' And what's not to love, when 'And the man with the golden gun' acquires street cred due to Clayton's burnished contralto?

The playful, 'Rabbit, where'd you put the keys, girl?' has insidious roots. Tori told the *Baltimore Sun* in January 1994 that in certain Indian traditions, 'rabbit' represents fear.

But about that resounding piano riff. Do you recall chewing gum commercials that you couldn't get out of your mind because they were catchy but dumb? I can't get this devilish riff out of mine either, but that's because it's catchy and brilliant.

The instrumentalists rock hard, beginning with Caton's maniacal mandolin strums and Tori's assertive piano voicings, which grow more syncopated on each consecutive verse. George Porter Jr. introduced a loop based on Tori's original reggae-inspired riff, to which Paulinho Da Costa added a sleigh bell. If that wasn't over-stimulating enough, Tori was headstrong about sampling a whistle: hence that eerie high pitch in the introductory bars. No, that wasn't your tinnitus acting up. And that effect especially excited fans from down under. Yessaid.com noted: 'In 2000, alt-rock station, Triple J, included 'Cornflake Girl' in a list of the 'Greatest Whistling Songs of all time.'

'Cornflake Girl' led to a role playing piano in a commercial for a Kellogg's cereal. Tori triumphed over seasoned American actress Sarah Jessica Parker. The label promoted Tori's work with a series of corn flake boxes on which her image appeared. If you've got one in the cupboard, don't recycle! You've won the lottery – it's a collector's item.

The UK video is better than the US version, hands-down. Tori wanted two: in the UK version, *Dorothy* goes to hell rather than Oz. In following the oeuvre of the album, this decision makes complete sense; a young innocent thrown cavalierly under a bus.

'Icicle' (Tori Amos)

With 'Baker Baker', Tori longed to be made 'whole again' by some outside entity, but for this sensitively performed waltz, the narrator seeks solitude for a spell. Drawn from Tori's strict upbringing, the backstory hints that religion and sensuality are often at odds in the real world: 'I think the good book is missing some pages,' the subtle songwriter observes.

Initially, as Tori concentrates on the upper keys, the repetitious motif sounds luminous and echoey, but as the song moves forward, the pleasing harmonies grow incrementally dissonant. As such, the real beauty resides in the subtle changes. A fan who noted the multi-sensorial effect, wrote on YouTube: 'It's like looking at the Sistine Chapel with your ears.'

Thankfully, no overly-produced orchestral fills muck up the simple elegance. Live or on video, it's thrilling to watch Tori's left-hand cross over the right: it's as if her fingers are sprouting invisible wings that are gently gearing up for flight.

'Cloud on My Tongue' (Tori Amos)

Tori uses her highest vocal register sparingly, but when she does (and because it's so random), she elicits goosebumps. Even if she hammered the rhythms out on a jaw harp or discarded oil drum, we'd still experience this ballad's warmth, which is generated by an undulating motif and plaintive vocals; Shenale's lush accouterments make it sparkle.

'Space Dog' (Tori Amos)

At first, the descending bass line and erratic percussion perpetuate Tori's pleas. But in an instant, the instrumental structure drastically changes. 'Space Dog' is an unpredictable assemblage of feelings and quirky phrases. Tori namechecks her dear friend, Neil Gaiman, as well as the incomparable 'Colonel Dirtyfishydishcloth.'

Sometimes it's droll: 'Deck the halls, it's you again, it's me again,' but overall, 'Space Dog' is loopy and poetically disarming. With its sing-song rhythm, it could be a prequel to a Dr. Seuss book; but on the other hand, the brash instrumentality brings to mind the theme song to the film, *Goldfinger.*

Tori told *Upside Down* fanzine, issue #5: 'This song is about giving your power to someone else – passing the torch.' She compares the theme to that of 'Past the Mission,' although, musically, the songs are oceans apart.

On the surface, 'Space Dog' is an innocent indulgence. But beyond the tongue twisters and anachronistic bass line, there's a dance of disillusionment: 'Space Dog' points to Tori's loss of faith in religious leaders, as well as in rock contemporaries who strayed too far from the cause.

'Yes, Anastasia' (Tori Amos)

This aforementioned intricately structured closer foreshadows Tori's rich compositional future, where she'd reclaim her classical roots for *Night of Hunters*. Pianistically, Tori wires several distinctive parts into an air-tight structure. The piano arrangement sprints before accelerating to a proper gallop – each subsequent section moving the simply-told story forward.

Inspired by the life of the young princess, Anastasia Romanov, Tori brings us loosely into that pre-Soviet world, with repetitive lines, such as: 'Show me the ways to get back to the garden' and 'We'll see how brave you are.' But the real pizzazz comes from the vocal gymnastics and exemplary shifts from head to chest voice. Orchestral effects come into play and are most effective when synching up rhythmically with pervasive vocals.

Although Anastasia was killed with her family in 1918, some claimed that she was still alive. Even Tori claimed to have felt Anastasia's presence during a Richmond, Virginia soundcheck. She told *B-Side* in April/May of 1994: 'She comes, and goes, 'You've got to write my tune.''

Little Earthquakes was telling and beautiful, but like many debuts, it's insular; a sonic memoir, as subjective as Joni Mitchell's 'Song to a Seagull.' Tori's ode to the Russian princess proved to fans that she could accept the challenge of writing about historical figures and show their humanity without sounding pedantic. So, did her then-label, Atlantic, flinch when they heard about the length? Songwriter Jimmy Webb often explains how Los Angeles-based radio station, KHJ, requested a shortened version of his 7:20 'MacArthur Park,' but when Webb wouldn't budge, KHJ played the entire song, paving the way for The Beatles' 'Hey Jude' at 7:11.

In this commercial tug-of-war, Tori won the final round, for 'Yes, Anastasia' was allocated more than enough space to create a proper narrative. With the piano, she built and released harmonic tensions for the beginning stanzas. Shenale broadened the theme by contrasting lithe and dramatic orchestral touches. Vocally, Tori sounded swept away by the imperious setting. But the epic outcome didn't come easily. This composition could not be hurried.

Shenale recalls:

> At that time, we had long discussions since *Little Earthquakes* about the Russians and the early 20th century and the grand works; that was one of our lunchtime musings. I think she was very influenced by Stravinsky, late 19th century composers, Rimsky-Korsakov: I think that's where she was going with that. It came out as an epic work because she intended it. It was interesting because my first thought when I heard it was, 'Let's start at the beginning,' and she said, 'No, let's start in the middle, because that's where the new scene happens.'

Their collaborative process yielded a balanced portrait, which conveys vibrant emotion. And live, 'Yes, Anastasia' never fails to bring down the dacha.

Album Art

Cindy Palmano returns to design the striking album cover on which Tori wears a long, sleeveless white dress, arms affixed firmly by her side. Flimsy articles of cellophane shimmer off the ground. On the back, a mini-Tori poses on a huge, white fluffy ball. Lyrics are included in small print. The photographs are of a high quality, especially the colorful headshot.

Related Tracks

On 15 April 2015, Rhino Records reissued both *Little Earthquakes* and *Under the Pink* with revised liner notes and in remastered formats. The project was titled: *Little Earthquakes & Under the Pink Deluxe Editions*. Wasn't this the perfect opportunity to celebrate a boatload of B-sides, sadly left adrift?

The live versions of 'Past the Mission,' 'Icicle,' 'Flying Dutchman,' 'Winter' and 'The Waitress' captured the excitement of the moment as expected, and probably pleased the cross-section of fans from Chicago, Boston and Manchester that were fortunate enough to enjoy this spontaneous performance.

Overall, this collection of live and studio tracks was exciting and well-balanced, but I was befuddled by the inclusion of dance track: 'The CJ Bolland Remix.' I'm not dismissing 'God' as a suitable candidate for a dance tune, but frankly, this version felt out of place, given its proximity to the neighboring tracks.

'Sugar' and 'Take to the Sky' are underrated songs that Tori re-sculpted in the concert halls and arenas. Here, they're grand too, but in comparison to the live versions, they merely whet the appetite.

Selects on the second discs were remastered and mostly culled from B-sides: 'Sister Janet,' 'Honey,' 'Daisy Dead Petals,' 'Over It,' 'Black Swan,' 'Here. In My Head' and 'Upside Down.'

'Sister Janet' (Tori Amos), **'Daisy Dead Petals'** (Tori Amos), **'Honey'** (Tori Amos), **'A Case of You'** (Joni Mitchell)

'If 6 Was 9' (Jimi Hendrix) (Originally by the Jimi Hendrix Experience)

This *Under the Pink* B-side is a tribute to one of classic rock's most influential guitarists, Jimi Hendrix, and appeared on the Jimi Hendrix Experience 1967 album, *Axis: Bold as Love*. Tori didn't feel she measured up musically but felt a calling simply out of respect for the iconic shredder. She needed no disclaimers; there's heaps of soul in Tori's rendition. She reimagines this much-covered classic with an impressive ostinato. Enough said.

'Strange Fruit' (Lewis Allan) (Recorded initially by Billie Holiday and her Orchestra in 1939)

The pacing is unique: false starts and stops add a strong degree of tension. The piano accompaniment and singing sound eerily out-of-synch, creating a further layer of agitation.

To capture a sense of vocal ferocity in the studio, Tori awakened with the songbirds, knowing that her voice would retain a grainy quality that would help express the solemnity of the heartbreaking theme: the lynching of black people in the American South during Jim Crow.

She related to the theme because she and her Cherokee grandfather felt racial hatred during her own early years growing up in the south.

Knowing that the iconic Billie Holiday made this ballad famous back in 1939 and that Nina Simone followed suit in 1965 would be enough to intimidate the most progressive songstress, but Tori identified with the racially explosive theme, nixed Holiday's orchestral approach, and came up with this haunting, piano-vocal construct. Produced by Eric Rosse and Tori Amos.

'All the Girls Hate Her' (Tori Amos)

Originally on the 'Cornflake Girl' single.

The thrashing bass notes, which occur in the introduction, foreshadow the drama to come. Why do I say this? For a few measures, the chordal harmonies sound cheerful – like something out of a classic American animated film – but then an over-arching dissonance creeps into the cracks. This song brings to mind the beauty and irony of Stephen Sondheim's *Into the Woods*.

'Over It' (Piano Suite) (Tori Amos)

This song was on the 'Cornflake Girl' single, the 'God' single in 1994 and the *Under the Pink Deluxe Remaster* in 2015.

Instrumentals on solo piano were rarely recorded during this time period. On this somber piece, Tori bears witness to strident melodies in both hands, as she toys with articulation and tempo.

'Black Swan' (Tori Amos)

'Home on the Range' (Cherokee Edition) (Tori Amos)

This song first appeared with the 'God' single in 1994, *A Piano* in 2006, and the *Under the Pink Deluxe Remaster* in 2015.

Tori puts a unique spin on the age-old folk tune, with historical finger-pointing: 'But Jackson made deals/A thief down to his heels.'

'Hello, Trail of Tears' (Tori Amos)

With references to Andrew Jackson's forced evacuation of about 60,000 native Americans between the years 1830 and 1850 by the U.S. government, Tori's impassioned vocals and instrumental interludes examine her frustrations about this historical atrocity.

'God' (The CJ Bolland Remix) (Tori Amos)

This was from the 'God' 12" record.

This outrageously cool and creative track stands out here and would be better-served alongside other dance tracks.

Two CD singles titled 'Past the Mission' contained mostly live B-side versions of the following songs, which were released in the UK by East West Records on 16 May (UK limited edition) and 23 May (UK CD2) 1994. The peak position was 31. The promotion was followed up with a 4 July release in Australia, and a 27 September launch in 1994 by Atlantic Records:

U.K. CD single:

'Upside Down' (Live)/ 'Past the Mission'(Live)/ 'Icicle' (Live)/ 'Flying Dutchman' (Live)

U.K. Single 2:

'Past the Mission' (LP)/ 'Winter' (Live)/ 'The Waitress' (Live)/ 'Here. In My Head' (Live)

'Upside Down' (Tori Amos)

See Little Earthquakes Deluxe Remaster in 2015.

'Past the Mission' (Tori Amos)
It's best-known for the intense harpsichord backing, and Trent Reznor's baritone on the dramatic, minor-tinged chorus, but this song is so well-structured that it stands alone.

'Icicle' (Tori Amos)
Tori expands the instrumental section, suspending time with the image-filled narrative.

'Flying Dutchman' (Tori Amos), **'Here. In My Head'** (Tori Amos)

Under the Pink Deluxe Edition: Bonus Disc 2

'Sister Janet'/ 'Honey'/ 'Daisy Dead Petals'/ 'Over It'/ 'Black Swan'/ 'Home on the Range (Cherokee Addition)'/ 'All the Girls Hate Her'/ 'God' (The CJ Bollard Remix)
Plus, seven live tracks:
'Here. In My Head' (Colston Hall, Bristol, 7 March 1994)/ 'Upside Down' (The Sanders Theater, Boston, 31 March 1994)/ 'Past the Mission' (The Vic Theater, Chicago, 24 March 1994)/ 'Icicle' (Wadsworth Theater, L.A., 22 March 1994)/ 'Flying Dutchman' (The Vic Theater, Chicago, 24 March 1994)/ 'Winter' (Free Trade Hall, Manchester, 1 March 1994)/ 'The Waitress' (The Sanders Theater, Boston, 31 March 1994)

Cornflake Girl (Limited-edition U.K. 2-disc EP)

Produced by Eric Rosse and Tori Amos
Label: East West
Released: 17 January 1994
Disc 1: 'Cornflake Girl'/ 'Sister Janet'/ 'Piano Suite: All the Girls Hate Her/Over It'
Disc 2: 'Cornflake Girl'/'A Case of You' (Joni Mitchell)/'If 6 Was 9' (Jimi Hendrix)/'Strange Fruit' (Lewis Allan)

Hey Jupiter (EP)

Personnel:
Tori Amos: acoustic piano, vocals
Steve Caton: guitars
Justin Meldal Johnson: bass
Andy Ling: programming
Produced by: Ian Stanley and Tori Amos
Label: East West (UK), Atlantic (US)
Release date: US: 20 August 1996
Running Time: 25:14

'Hey Jupiter' (The Dakota Version) (Tori Amos)

In complete contrast to the melodic and soft-pedaled version on *Boys for Pele*, Tori ruminates against thunderbolt rhythms and elasticized synth tones. A brand-new bridge appears, along with an extended outro, but the original third verse has gone missing.

This version was played widely on the 1996 American Doll Posse international tour and makes another shiny appearance on *A Piano*. This is essentially an apples or oranges debate, but while this modern experiment might satiate the forward-thinking, I don't feel it holds a candle to the original. Produced by Ian Stanley.

'Sugar' (Live) (Tori Amos)

Maybe a casual flip of the coin would help determine whether the live version on *To Venus and Back* or *Live from Sunny Florida*, is the champ. Maybe there's no contest: both versions retain the intended amount of sweetness.

Tori has performed many iterations of this beloved ballad, which was inspired by the memory of a childhood suitor. Hoping to win her affections, the lad asked how many sugars she likes in her tea. While the earnest suitor may have lost his dream girl, he certainly has fun stories to share. 'Sugar' was a surefire hit during the 1998 tour. Produced by Tori Amos.

'Honey' (Live) (Tori Amos)

The repetitive, instrumental drone effect pumps the conversational narrative with zest. 'It got kicked off at the last minute because I'm such a ding-a-ling,' Tori laments onstage about the track's omission from *Under the Pink*. Produced by Tori Amos.

Past the Mission (Limited edition CD single)

Personnel: See Under the Pink
Produced by Davitt Sigerson
Label: East West (U.K.)
Released: U.K. (Limited edition) 16 May 1994; U.K. (CD 2): 23 May 1994; AUS: 4 July 1994; U.S: 27 September 1994
Running time: (U.K. limited edition version) Disc 1: 23:59; Disc 2: 19:76
Note: The U.S. version was solely available in a cassette format, with tracks: 'Past the Mission' b/w 'Black Swan.'

Disc 1 (Limited edition live CD single)
'Upside Down' (The Sanders Theater, Boston, 31 March 1994)/'Past the Mission' (Vic Theater, Chicago, 24 March 1994)/'Icicle' (Wadsworth Theatre, L.A., 22 March 1994)/'Flying Dutchman' (Vic Theater, Chicago, 24 March 1994)

Disc 2 (UK CD single 2/German CD/Australian CD)
'Past the Mission' (LP version)/'Winter' (Live in Free Trade Hall, Manchester, 1 March 1994)

'The Waitress' (The Sanders Theater, Boston, 31 March 1994)

It's a more unplugged version than we're all accustomed to, but the passive-aggressive spirit is in full force.

'Here. In My Head' (Colston Hall, Bristol, 7 March 1994)

Featuring an extended piano introduction.

More Pink: The B-Sides (1994)

Personnel:
Tori Amos: piano, vocals, producer, Vox organ on 'Past the Mission'
Steve Caton: guitar
Paulinho da Costa: percussion
Carlo Nuccio: drums
George Porter Jr: bass
Chris Reutinger: violin
Trent Reznor: backing vocals
John Philip Shenale: strings, Hammond organ
Violin: Michael Allen Harrison, Ezra Killing, Nancy Roth, Francine Walsh
Viola: Cynthia Morrow, Jimbo Ross
Melissa 'Missy' Hasin: cello
Cello: Dane Little, Nancy Stein-Ross
Paul McKenna: producer, engineer
Eric Rosse: producer, engineer
John Beverly Jones: engineer
Shaun DeFeo: assistant engineer
Russ Cullum: mixing
Kevin Killen: mixing
Bob Ludwig: mastering
Julie Larson: production co-ordination
Cindy Palmano: art direction, photography
Alan Reini: design
Recorded: 14 November 1994
Label: Atlantic, East West
Release date: U.K. and U.S. 14 November 1994
Highest chart rank: U.K: 1, U.S: 12, AUS: 5, AT: 6
Running time: 48:49

A double-disc of *Under the Pink* was released by East West on 14 November 1994 in conjunction with the Australia and New Zealand tour. Ironically, the chosen tracks were drawn from a hodgepodge of singles, and a holiday song was thrown in for good measure. Perhaps the project should have been called *Less Pink*?

More Pink: The B-Sides was not released as a separate entity, and as such, is considered a rarity. Fans would not see another collection of B-sides until the release of 2006's *A Piano: The Collection.*

'A Case of You' (Joni Mitchell)

Tori imbues this ballad, from the 1971 charmer *Blue,* with unbridled emotion. Peals of piano follow the vocal line faithfully. In contrast to Mitchell's original version, where the singer fancies falsetto, Tori imbues passion with a burning contralto. Moreover, an appreciation for the romantic lyricism comes across with each carefully-paced measure.

Tori exclaimed to the *Chicago Tribune* on 8 October 1992, 'If you're going to do a cover, it has to be a complete challenge.' Tori may have done hundreds, but she's darn selective.

Being an age-old Mitchell fan probably helped Tori bring out the seduction of the original, and with stunningly executed phrasing, she accomplished the task. Since the debut on the 1994 *Under the Pink* tour, she's done hundreds of repeat performances.

'As constant as a morning star' describes not just one of the poetic phrases, but Tori's presentation of this classic. Like Mitchell, 'I could drink a case….'

'Honey' (Tori Amos)

'Honey' first appeared with the 'Cornflake Girl' single, *More Pink* in 1994, *A Piano* in 2006 and the *Under the Pink Deluxe Remaster* in 2015.

This was originally supposed to be on the album, but 'Past the Mission' got the golden ticket. The light harmonies, dissonant strings and chilling effects combine to create a mysterious beauty. Tori's voice cycles through lively iterations.

'Daisy Dead Petals' (Tori Amos)

This song was also on the 'Cornflake Girl' single, *More Pink* in 1994, *A Piano* in 2006, and the *Under the Pink Deluxe Remaster* in 2015.

This brightly-orchestrated track, a poetic portrait of an outsider, is underscored by the subject's quickly shifting moods: 'Dancing on a dime, hearing mother cry….' Tori's vocals move as effortlessly as a Ferris wheel.

'Sister Janet' (Tori Amos)

B-side on the 'Cornflake Girl' single which circulated in Australia, Germany, France and the UK in January 1994, and as a B-side to 'God' and 'Cornflake Girl' in the US in February and May 1994..

Too bad this B-side didn't make the cut. Tori's rhymes are delightful: 'Nobody is slippin' the blade in the marmalade.' The instrumental portion is equally breathtaking.

The lyrics suggest symbolic spirituality with: 'the master shaman,' the reference to 'a demon and an Englishman' plus the pedestrian imagery of 'angels' and 'wizards.'

Browsing through the discography, it's clear that Tori frequently cites dualities and groups together supernatural entities; in fact, it's almost par for the course given her religious upbringing and desire to understand its repercussions. But what grounds the lyric here – other than the lovely harmonic structure – is the reference to the late 'sweet' Marianne, Tori's dear friend, whose presumed overdose at fifteen would forever haunt her close friends, and for whom Tori would dedicate a touching ballad on *Boys for Pele*. The instrumental portion is also awe-inspiring. Tori's playing is subtle and nuanced.

The premiere occurred on the *Under the Pink* Tour in 1994, and the song has been a setlist favorite ever since. *A Piano: The Collection* also includes a remastered version.

These tracks were recorded live. Venues and dates are listed below:

'Past the Mission'; (Live at the Vic Theater, 24 March 1994, Chicago); 'Icicle' (Live from Wadsworth Theater, LA, 22 March 1994); 'Flying Dutchman' (Live from Vic Theater, Chicago, 24 March 1994); 'Winter' (Live from Free Trade Hall, Manchester, 1 March 1994); 'The Waitress' (Live from The Sanders Theater, Boston, 31 March 1994)

'Sugar' (Tori Amos)

Against an extraordinary sea of effects, Tori's voice throbs with pleasure. While the lyrics in the verse of this quietly-stated anthem suggest an entirely different story, the chorus can't not pull you in: the robins, 'bring me many things, but Sugar, he brings me sugar.' As Tori ruminates, each verse grows incrementally sweeter.

'Take to the Sky' (Tori Amos)

A complete one-off, Tori curries favor with a raucous left-hand ostinato, while her right fist punches out rhythms against the baseboard.

'Upside Down' (Tori Amos)

This melodic ballad includes sharp touches: church bells courtesy of Davitt Sigerson and John Philip Shenale's woozy Mellotron. While Tori deeply regrets that the song was omitted from *Little Earthquakes*, fans shared in her excitement when she rattled off the rhythmic lyrics on *Live at Montreux*.

'Flying Dutchman' (Tori Amos)

This inspirational song first appeared on the 'China' single in 1992, *A Piano* in 2006, *Gold Dust* in 2012 and the *Little Earthquakes Deluxe Remaster*.

'They say your brain is a comic book tattoo,' but in Tori's magical world, even nerds become heroes. 'Straight suits, they don't understand,' she tells the shy boy. She's drawn up a fascinating character. Her vocals know no limits.

'Here. In My Head' (Tori Amos)

The track first appeared on the 'Crucify' single, then *More Pink: The B-Sides* in 1994, *A Piano* in 2006 and the *Little Earthquakes Deluxe Remaster* in 2015.

Tori's phrases are divinely poetic, with this line being my favorite: 'I'll show you the roses and brush off the snow.' Slowly and methodically, she sketches out a genteel blueprint sure to make romantics swoon. Don't ignore the innuendo: 'Thomas Jefferson wasn't born in your back yard.'

The ballad premiered during the 1992 *Little Earthquakes* Tour, and was published as a short story in the 2008 anthology, *Comic Book Tattoo*. Tori calls it 'one of my special heart songs.'

'Black Swan' (Tori Amos)

This song was first up on 'Pretty Good Year' in 1994, on *A Piano* in 2006, and finally on the *Under the Pink Deluxe Remaster* in 2015.

The piano part has a life all its own on this cinematic track. The lyrics may be spare, but what is said is revealing: 'Gum drops and Saturdays/Did Eric call by the way.' Dynamics are measured and images are bite-sized, but Tori offers clues about her state of mind post-breakup.

'Little Drummer Boy' (Traditional)

Tori sang this at the KROQ Acoustic Christmas event. First, she plays it through conventionally, then adds a personal touch.

Boys for Pele (January 1996)

Personnel:
Tori Amos: vocals, harpsichord, Bosendorfer piano, harmonium organ, clavichord, harpsichord
Steve Caton: guitar, electric guitar, mandolin
Alan Friedman: drum programming (Including the 'cry of a bull' effect)
Manu Katche: drums
Darryl Lewis: percussion
George Porter Jr: bass
James Watson: trumpet, brass conductor
The Black Dyke Mills Band
The Sinfonia of London Strings
Produced by Tori Amos
Mark Hawley: recording engineer
Recorded in Ireland and Louisiana in June-October 1995
Label: Atlantic (US), East West (Europe)
Release date: UK: 22 January 1996, US: 23 January 1996, AUS: 29 January 1996
Highest chart rank: UK: 2, US: 2
Running time: 70:09

'There's an opportunity when there are troubles. There's an opportunity to write, and you put it out there and it might move somebody that day to make a different choice that isn't destructive. And I think that's the reason to wake up in the morning,' Tori told *Slant* in November 2020.

Tori used creativity as a tool to communicate in a more visceral manner than she'd ever attempted previously. *Little Earthquakes* had served as a sonic memoir; *Under the Pink* contained excellent pop and rock tracks, and had appeased the commercial suits. But with *Boys for Pele* – her third studio album – she took a significant cultural turn. The buzz started three weeks before the release. As a teaser, 'Caught a Lite Sneeze' was distributed.

It was during the *Under the Pink* Tour that the concept for a new album began to percolate. Fragments of ideas even came to Tori onstage. A couple of years before *Boys from Pele* was released, she spilled the conceptual beans to journalist John Everson: 'On *Little Earthquakes*, I dealt with the son, and on *Under the Pink*, I dealt with the father, so… I've handled the men – I'm gonna go deal with the women.' (Tori would dig more deeply into the female psyche with *American Doll Posse*).

So, on *Boys for Pele*, Tori constructed the gender groundwork. But it was not until a trip to Hawaii – the lusty land of volcanoes – that she found the inspiration to coin the title. In Hawaiian mythology, Pele is known as the fire goddess: a powerful creator and myopic destroyer. Rumor has it that this lava-infested diva also delights in eating male flesh. Why wouldn't Tori be captivated by this physical manifestation of female empowerment?

'First, I wanted to sacrifice all these guys to the volcano goddess, and roast them like marshmallows, then I decided they gave me a really wonderful gift,' she proclaimed. As such, *Boys for Pele* became a catharsis; a definitive way to evaluate and contend with trauma, anger and failed relationships. And like the independent goddess Pele, Tori would be completely in charge this time, not only as a passionate storyteller, singer and composer, but sole producer.

There was a ton of material ready to unearth. Tori had broken up with Eric Rosse. She had wrestled with religious ambiguities in *Little Earthquakes* but felt compelled to focus on how women were treated within the parameters of the patriarchy. To that end, Tori examined the material through an uncompromising feminist lens. She explained this concept to journalist Howard Cohen: 'God (is) a patriarchal force, a very masculine energy, with the feminine having been subservient, either being the mother, the lover, the virgin, but never the equal, never to have the whole.'

This ambitious album boasted eighteen tracks, but not all were fleshed out. Perhaps Tori was reflecting back on The Beatles' iconic *White Album* when composing several songs that were intriguing thematically, but that clocked in at under 90 seconds: 'Mr. Zebra', 'Agent Orange' and 'Way Down.' Was it the right decision? The theme of 'Agent Orange' – the chemical known for killing Vietnam vets – certainly deserved more time.

The songs, though, which speak to failed relationships are so well-crafted they balance out any missteps: 'Blood Roses,' 'Caught a Lite Sneeze,' 'Hey Jupiter,' 'Doughnut Song' and 'Putting the Damage On' are clear examples.

Production setting has always played a part in Tori's trajectory. This time around, much of the project was recorded in a church in County Wicklow, Ireland, and the rest in New Orleans. Regarding the church setting, Tori was interested in 'claiming fragments that I had suppressed for a long time.' It made sense to return to a house of worship.

But recording in a church required major acoustic adjustments. Tori wound up recording with her instruments enclosed in a box with a Leslie cabinet, where physical adjustments had to be made. For example, when she stood up to go back and forth between the harpsichord and piano, there were time gaps that impacted the recording.

There was the grating sound of the Leslie speaker being switched on and off, but maybe these factors added to the ambience; after all, Tori was making and producing her first quasi-experimental album. She even left a few moments of silence before the first track (perhaps to channel her inner John Cage).

But putting aside the technological components, Tori experimented with more than production techniques on *Boys from Pele*; she questioned the concept of feminine beauty and the judgments therein. Author Amy Gentry, for the *33 1/3* series, observes: 'Women and girls have a particularly complicated relationship with disgust. We learn at an early age to be grossed out by our bodies.'

For *Boys for Pele*, Tori stripped away the notion of the contemporary superwoman model. The aesthetic – both thematically and visually – is anything but airbrushed. It's as if, to contend with her demons, Tori had to make herself as unapproachable and untouchable as they are. The cover and graphics eradicated any preconceived visions of shallow beauty. It was Tori's time to explore all sides of womanhood; not just the commercially acceptable kind.

So, ironically, in the space of four studio albums (here I'm including *Y Kant Tori Read*), Tori goes from hair sprayed vixen; to a young woman safely ensconced in a box, yet ready to spring; to an angelic soul in bridal white; and finally, to a dirty-footed female on a rough-hewn, wooden porch, baring her darkest soul, holding nothing back, possibly on the edge, yet presumably, more powerful than ever before. She exposed the phlegm of the patriarchy, and dished on mythology and spirituality through an enlightened woman's prism.

Stereogum writer, Michael Tedder, said, '*Boys for Pele* is an album only a rock star would make. It's way too long, often wildly self-indulgent, and designed to dazzle you with its virtuosity. This, of course, is also what makes it great.' Tedder adds: 'I truly believe that becoming a fan of Tori made it easier for me to see women as not *the other*, but as people. She helped free me from a trap many people fall into and made me a better man.'

Tori's influences were making the rounds. She would continue exploring gender on *American Doll Posse* and *Strange Little Girls*. But at this juncture, she had plenty on her steaming lava plate, simply by virtue of becoming a producer.

'Beauty Queen/Horses' (Tori Amos)

In this quickly-escalating medley, Tori sings wistfully over a singular, penetrating note. 'I've got me some horses to ride on.' The lilting piano matches Tori's vocal dynamic until she goes off into a more beat-stealthier trot. Although the skips in the verse are pleasing, I can't wait until she gets back to the refrain. That's where the action is; that's where you can envision wild mares racing against a menacing wind.

'Blood Roses' (Tori Amos)

This song holds special memories. I'd ride around in the summer with the windows down, singing fecklessly along to the verse. My toddlers in the back seat followed my lead, shouting the choral lyrics so loudly that I was afraid a cop would cite me for using inappropriate language in front of minors. Little voices screaming 'blood roses, blood roses,' I suppose, would be a legitimate cause for concern for the authorities.

There are more than a few heart-wrenching images. For example, 'Chickens get a taste of your meat,' circles back to the sobering topic of female mutilation. The theme brings to mind feelings of desperation, humiliation and disrespect. 'At least when you cry now, he can't even hear you,' Tori murmurs with a gruffer-than-usual inflection.

The harpsichord is bitingly goth and embracing, but because the instrument notes have little sustain, there's an intense clamping-down effect after key

Left: Chicagoan Kara Marselle caught Tori in Dublin and Cork on the 2017 *Native Invader* tour; in Madison, Wisc., they reminisce. (*Courtesy of Kara Marselle*)

Right: In the Emerald Isle, Tori graciously autographs tickets for Kara and best friend Diane Marselle. (*Courtesy of Kara Marselle*)

Left: When *Y Kant Tori Read* morphed into a limited-edition format, super fans flocked to record stores. (*toriamosdiscography.info*)

Right: 'Ellen' Amos and brother Michael paid homage to The Baltimore Orioles' team on their co-written 1980 acetate version of 'Baltimore.' (*toriamosdiscography.info*)

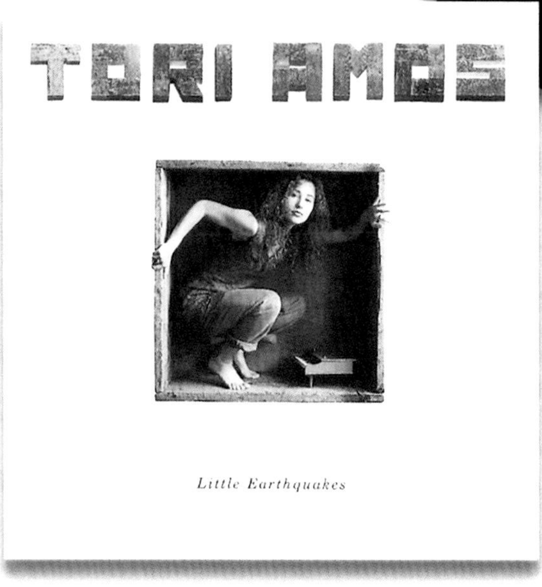

Left: With 1992's *Little Earthquakes*, Tori Amos evaporated the fourth wall between fan and artist. (*Atlantic, East West*)

Right: *Under the Pink* soared to the top of the UK Albums Chart upon its 1994 release. (*Atlantic, East West*)

Left: *Boys for Pele*. In 1996, on her first self-produced studio project, Tori Amos experimented electronically while examining all sides of femininity. (*Atlantic, East West*)

Right: Chamberlain's killer beats launch Tori's biting lyrics, breathy vocals and driving harpsichord on the 'Professional Widow' single. (*Atlantic, East West*)

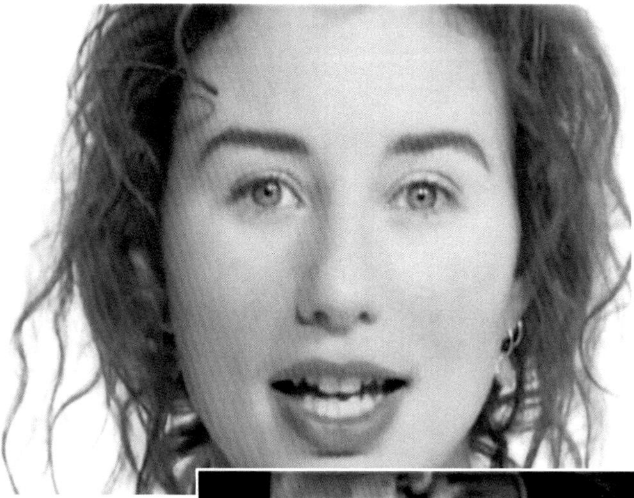

Left: The epic 'Winter' rekindles touching childhood memories.

Right: The compelling story behind 'Corn Flake Girl' is brought to life by its reggae-inspired beats.

Left: In 'God,' Tori explores spirituality in a unique way, but not without reprisals!

Right: 'Caught a Lite Sneeze' points at the troubles lovers face when they've been too long at the fair.

Left: In 'A Sorta Fairytale,' the fictional Scarlet searches for love and identity. (*Epic Records*)

Right: 'Raspberry Swirl' resulted in Tori's first Grammy nomination for a single.

Left: *From The Choirgirl Hotel* features fiery performances from drummer Matt Chamberlin, bassist Jon Evans and guitarist Steve Caton. (*Atlantic, East West*)

Right: When Tori's imagination exploded, *To Venus and Back* accommodated and became a two-disc album. (*Atlantic, East West*)

Right: For the 2001 concept album *Strange Little Girls*, Tori fields bold narratives through a masculine lens. (*Atlantic, East West*)

Left: Through 2002's *Scarlet's Walk*, Tori explores her proud Native heritage. (*Atlantic, East West*)

Left: Arranger John Philip Shenale has spread his magic on nearly every studio album. (*Courtesy of John Philip Shenale*)

Right: *Huff Post* journalist Noah Michelson knows what to ask when interviewing Tori or drumming up hot topics for his podcast. (*Courtesy of Noah Michelson*)

Above: Drummer Matt Chamberlain, a five-time touring member, got involved initially with the *From the Choirgirl Hotel* project. (*Matt Chamberlain website*)

Below: Multiple Grammy-winning L.A. producer Joe Chiccarelli (Morrissey, Elton John, The Strokes) reflects back on *Y Kant Tori Read*. (Courtesy of *JoeChiccarellimusic*)

Left: A Hammond B-3, African drums and working-class bees define the tone of *The Beekeeper*. (*Epic Records*)

Right: *American Doll Posse*. Tori channels five fictional women to clarify her perspectives on American life. (*Epic Records*)

Right: Of *Abnormally Attracted to Sin*, Tori said, 'It is not a concept album. It is a red-headed woman singing songs.' (*Universal Republic*)

Left: With vocals by Natashya Hawley, percussion by Chamberlain and strings by Shenale, *Midwinter Graces* ushered in the New Year. (*Universal Republic*)

Left: To further promote *The Beekeeper*, Tori chills with brilliantly colored butterflies while striking a seasonal pose. (*toriamos-discography.info*)

Right: When Tori supported *Boys for Pele* with the Dew Drop Inn Tour of 1996-97, she reached into the vault. (*toriamos-discography.info*)

Above: *Under The Pink* features the prepared piano and mysterious imagery of 'Bells for Her.' (*toriamosdiscography.info*)

Right: 'Corn Flake Girl.' Ears on feet, if you saved this box, you've won the lottery. (*Atlantic, Kellogg, toriamosdiscography.info*)

Left: Compositions 'Shattering Sea' and 'Snowblind' trigger a myriad of emotions on the classically inspired concept album, *Night of Hunters*. (*Deutsche-Grammophon*)

Right: Songs from Tori's 13th studio album, *Gold Dust*, were recorded with the Metropole Orchestra. (*Deutsche Grammophone*)

Right: Having completed *The Light Princess*, Tori returned home to pop and alternative genres with *Unrepentant Geraldines* in 2014. (*Mercury Classics*)

Left: Tori dishes on the 'climate blind,' 'shooting stars' and the 'Great Mother' on 2017's *Native Invader*. (*Decca*)

Left: *Under the Pink*, Access All Areas. Judging by sales of more than two million, Tori was definitely not in 'The Wrong Band.' (*toriamosdiscography.info*)

Right: *Strange Little Girls*, September 19, 2001 Virgin Records, Union Square. Tori reimagines work by Eminem, 10cc, Neil Young, Slayer, Tom Waits, the Velvet Underground, the Stranglers and the Beatles. (*toriamosdiscography.info)*

Left: VIP pass, *Unrepentant Geraldines* Tour, 2014. For *Unrepentant Geraldines*, Tori channels Cezanne, Rosetti and more to create palpable, visual pieces. (*toriamosdiscography.info)*

phrases, which, I believe, adds to the solemnity. Traditionally, baroque composers like J. S. Bach and Domenico Scarlatti favored the upper range of this age-old instrument. Maverick that she is, Tori defiantly concentrated on the lower rungs. Unlike her myopic predecessors, she noodled around the entire keyboard.

Harmonically, 'Blood Roses' is the quintessential showstopper. The first chord – the relative minor of the key signature – is simultaneously dark and fantastically beautiful. The distortion occurs because Tori played the song through a Marshall amp. Like Scarlatti and Bach, she dotes on contrapuntal lines, flavoring her work with precise ornamentation.

The song starts out in 6/8 time but then halves to a waltz rhythm. Many elements combine to make 'Blood Roses' a masterpiece, and they come together magically here. But keep in mind that, despite the harpsichord's unarguable beauty, the instrument and song weren't necessarily joined at the hip outside the studio walls, back in the real world. Tori only played the harpsichord live on her 1996 Dew Drop Inn Tour, but fans claim she still nailed it at the 1999 Las Vegas concert. She continued performing 'Blood Roses' for years afterwards as well. On a 2010 Australian and European tour, she graced the stage with a Bosendorfer grand and multiple synths; you'll witness the instrument's resurrection on *To Venus and Back*.

'Father Lucifer' (Tori Amos)

'Father Lucifer' has enjoyed many incarnations. But what made the *Boys for Pele* recording a classic in the song's first life? Piano interludes are sharp, sprightly and dance-like, with the precise harmonic structure immaculately set down in verse one. (This unique pattern brings to mind the tightly-structured 'Mother' from *Little Earthquakes*, where Tori also inserted a mesmerizing motif.)

In verse two, James Watson's grieving trumpet erupts (he also performed on 'Putting the Damage On'); then on the bridge, Steve Caton's stabbing guitar, George Porter Jr.'s spot-on framing and Watson's brooding ad-libs collide. To top it off, a joyful choir pops out of the blue.

There's that constantly moving bass line, the chords in the verses march on every beat, and genteel grace note add cosmetic flair. These embellishments appear in the first measure, skip the second, but reappear in the third and fourth. Tori enhances the mood by faithfully repeating this pattern throughout.

And those seismic shifts – From the pro-active line in the bridge: 'Nothing's going to stop me from floating,' and the celebratory, 'Every day's my wedding day,' to the colloquial, 'How's your Jesus Christ been hanging?' – there's much lyrical variety.

The laid-back bridge lies in stark contrast to the aerobic verses. After that rigorous piano workout, you can imagine Tori's fingers loosening their grip and settling into a more conventional groove. Her vocals sound more relaxed here too.

On 7 May 2020, Tori spoke to journalist Noah Michelson for a YouTube Crowd Cast Talk. When asked which part of a song she likes writing the most – verse, chorus, bridge – Tori replied: 'I love writing bridges. I don't just see it as a middle eight. I see it as another world – anything can happen.'

'Father Lucifer' makes use of multiple skills. 'I'm pretty ruthless with lyrics. I don't let anything slide. The music is more stream of consciousness and it's always done first, with a line here and there,' she told Bill DeMain.

But like many 'song girls,' solemnity hung in the balance: 'Father Lucifer' is as light as it is dark. Although the song was stamped with Tori's airy tones, detractors spoke out about her thematic intent. Was the devil in the details? Here's one 'really deep thought' she shared with *The Baltimore* for the Sunday, 21 January 1996 edition, ''Father Lucifer' is about needing to go to the space of shadow, to go where we hide. Not Satanism. A whole different plane.' Tori's defense continued into the spring when she told *Spin* in March 1996, 'Shadow defines light. The shadow is where I hang out a lot because I like chasing and diving with those forces... '

Tori's London girlfriends expressed disbelief at her choice of subject. By examining the devil, Tori stirred up considerable controversy. And despite the fact that the theme had no bearing on her relationship with her dad, he sat in judgment at Thanksgiving, confiding that he'd been hurt by the insinuation. Tori simply explained that she was taking ayahuasca (a supposedly life-altering elixir) with a South American shaman when the songwriting muse hit. 'I really did visit the Devil, and I had a journey,' she formally admitted to *VH1 Storytellers* in 1998.

From Mitch Ryder and The Detroit Wheels' 'Devil With a Blue Dress On' (1966) to The Rolling Stones' 'Sympathy for the Devil' (1968), pop culture has generated many a hellfire tune. Mitch Ryder got a free pass, but the latter was initially banned: Jagger and Richards were accused of being 'devil worshippers' by certain religious groups who misinterpreted the songwriters' intentions. The writers were chronicling – not celebrating – the violence Jagger sang about: such as the blitzkrieg, the Kennedy assassinations, and how 'Anastasia screamed in vain.'

In contrast, Tori's narrative seemed pretty tame. Humanizing the Devil, making Lucifer less-than-scary is evident here: 'You always preferred the drizzle to the rain,' where the subject comes off as an amiable chap; and unlike Jagger and Richards' song, Tori wrote 'Father Lucifer' in the second person, which should've removed some of the sting.

Still, as the daughter of a minister, Tori had always been held to the highest standards. Despite the fury of her detractors, she maintained her sense of humor: 'I finally realized that Lucifer was a woman, wears white and drives an ice cream truck,' she joked to host Roseanne Barr on *The Roseanne Show* in 1998.

I feel like an insider because of the lyrical namechecking. First off, there's that line about her best friend: 'And Beenie lost in the sunset'; and secondly, faithful Norma Jean fans may get misty here: 'Does Joe bring flowers to Marilyn's grave?' Despite their divorce, Monroe's second husband, Joe DiMaggio, fought on the starlet's behalf after she was sent to a sanitarium.

Tori first played 'Father Lucifer' live on 25 February 1996 at the Manchester Apollo on the Dew Drop Inn Tour, along with guitarist Steve Caton. It was smartly sequenced as a spirited break after the somber 'Silent All These Years' and before the meditative, 'Bells for Her'.

At the Palace Theatre on 29 November 1998, Tori performed the 'Lucy Improv' version, over Matt Chamberlain's exuberant percussion, plus string effects and bass. She tiptoed vocally with the title phrase before immersing herself in the groove. In 2002/2003, she partnered with her 'Wurly' (Wurlitzer electric piano) to create an even wilder texture.

On *The Late Show with David Letterman* on 4 October 1996, Tori performed 'Father Lucifer' with Steve Caton. After the bridge, she peppered the arrangement with several measures from Mike Oldfield's hypnotic *Tubular Bells*, leading a journalist from Oneweekoneband.tumblr.com to exclaim: 'The look in her eyes as she begins to play 'Tubular Bells'… it's otherworldly.'

The recording was artfully remastered for the 2006 boxset, *A Piano: The Collection.* Even though the sound quality was excellent, some fans felt that the track's organic feel was compromised. Wasn't *Boys for Pele* a warts and all undertaking?

Two years on, 'Father Lucifer' acquired a cult fascination when a nine-page story was printed in the graphic novel, *Comic Book Tattoo*; Composer Ross Burton's vibrant acoustic piano version is accented by distorted bleeps; and Philadelphia DJ King Britt's steroidal 'Sylkscreen' remix was released as a B-side to the vinyl version of the 'Jackie's Strength' single in 1998. So, if you need a wider berth, other versions abide.

'Professional Widow' (Tori Amos)

Released as an A-side CD single, 2 July 1996 (US), b/w 'Armand's Star Trunk Funkin' Mix,' 'MK Mix,' 'Just Da Funk Dub,' 'MK Vampire Dub' (All four are also on 12"), 'Armand's Instrumental,' 'Bonus Beats.'

Released as A-side, 30 December 1996 (UK), b/w 'Armand's Star Trunk Funkin' Mix' (Radio Edit), 'Mr. Roy's 7" Edit', 'Armand's Star Trunk Funkin' Mix,' 'Mr. Roy's Cosmic Cottage Mix', 'Just Da Funk Dub' (All but the first are on 12" single).

Johnny 'D' DeMairo at Atlantic Records suspected that the song's Internal beats could cross-bleed into the dance genre. This was no hunch. After handing an acapella version to Arman van Helden, the Boston DJ/producer created a hallucinatory hybrid of jungle and house, helmed by Tori's woozy vocals. Remember, remixes represented new territory in the 1990s, but once green-lighted, Van Helden's remixes ushered in a savvy new crowd.

'It's one thing when somebody adds something; it's another thing when your work is being cut up and reduced to *moon and June*. I don't think van Helden did that. I think he retained an attitude and made it about a vibe,' Tori said on a promotional video. Amen.

But who *was* the subject? Some claimed that the 'widow' in question was singer Courtney Love, the former wife of the late Kurt Cobain. Trent Reznor suggested in interviews that Courtney Love created conflict between him and Tori (Reznor and Love had also been involved). When Reznor borrowed the term, 'starf*cker' from Tori's song, and used it on his own blasphemous 'Starf*ckers, Inc.', was he intentionally adding fuel to the fire?

Armand van Helden and MK released a remix of 'Professional Widow' in July 1996. The 'Star Trunk Funkin' Mix' enhances the vitality and brings out the essence of the lyric, but other than that, why compare this exhilarating dance mix to the original, where an alpha-state-inducing harpsichord is the bedrock?

Besides the 'Star Trunk Mix,' there were a series of other mixes that the single inspired, including a 4:31 LP mix; 'Just Da Funk Dub' which clocked in at only 3:44; the 'MK Vampire Dub' at 6:56; and 'Armand's Instrumental' at 5:35.

Mr. Zebra' (Tori Amos)

Tori lightens up this probing album with loopy lyrics and accents of brass courtesy of The Black Dyke Mills Band: conducted by the aforementioned James Watson. The namesake, 'Mr. Zebra' – a charismatic being in his own right – is no lone wolf. Tori has a lark introducing the fictional 'Ratatouille Strychnine' (beware) and 'Mrs. Crocodile,' whom the striped African wild horse befriends. Did Tori use pseudonyms to hide the identity of a character in the narrative? She knows fans love to unravel her mysteries. Isn't that why, as she ramps up the bass notes, she boldly utters, 'Figure it out?'

'Marianne' (Tori Amos)

Tori would revisit the theme of possible suicide on *The Beekeeper*. 'And they said Marianne killed herself/And I said, 'Not a chance,' she posits in this touching tribute to a childhood friend.

'Marianne' has a deeply moving melody. Yet it feels like two songs. In her inimitable way, Tori uses curious imagery to lure us into her unique world. 'Tuna, rubber, a little blubber in my igloo.' Huh? But it's okay, she gets to say this. Besides, Tori got this one nailed in only one take. Like I said, she gets to say this.

'Caught a Lite Sneeze' (Tori Amos)

Released as an A-side, 1 January 1996 (UK), 2 January 1996 (US), 29 January 1996 (AUS), b/w 'This Old Man,' 'Hungarian Wedding Song,' 'London Girls,' 'That's What I Like Mick (The Sandwich Song),' 'Samurai,' 'Graveyard,' 'Toodles Mr. Jim.'

This was the first single available for download on the internet. Before you shrug, consider that hearing an audio track before the album release was then a state-of-the-art phenomenon that built a promotional buzz. But that's not the only newsflash: some fans believe Tori left coded messages to singer Trent Reznor in this harpsichord-savvy ballad. She sang, 'Made my own pretty hate machine': *Pretty Hate Machine* being the title of the 1989 Nine Inch Nails debut.

Regarding secret codes, wasn't Taylor Swift also guilty as charged? Carly Simon eventually leaked the truth about the narcissist of 'You're So Vain,' and who knows what Billie Joe MacAllister threw off the Tallahatchie Bridge in the 1967 epic, 'Ode to Billie Joe.' So, Tori is in good company. But shouldn't it be called, 'Caught a Lite Tease?'

Apart from the sleuth-y connotations, there's delightful alliteration: 'Caught in a lightweight lightning seed.' Tori revealed in promotional materials, 'It's really about a relationship. And she's kind of given herself away, so she's trying to get pieces back in any way she can.'

A sneeze can be a metaphor for a passing thought or a superficial relationship. 'Boys on my left side, boys on my right side': in other words, boys in every conceivable nook and cranny – but the one who should matter? 'You're not here.'

The lead vocals are captivating, but keep an ear out for the extraordinary backing vocals, where Tori sings 'Inanna' in her mind-blowing upper range. Lest you forgot, Inanna – the ancient Mesopotamian goddess – is equal to the Greek Aphrodite and the Roman Venus.

For the American TV show *Saturday Night Live*, Tori invited The Harlem Boys Choir to back her up. It was a sensation. This song is that little black dress one can wear anywhere and still look great. It merely needed Tori's catchy melody and keyboard chops, but with an electronic flourish, a sensual behemoth alights.

'Muhammad My Friend' (Tori Amos)

Clarence J. Johnson III's soprano sax lends an enduring touch, as confident George Porter Jr. infiltrates the bottom end. Tori premiered the song as a duet with the sultry tones of Tool's Maynard James Keenan on the 1996 Dew Drop Inn Tour.

In one of her most religious-centered songs yet, Tori name-drops Muhammad, Moses and the Pope. She questions the authority of biblical icons with a clear-eyed cynicism. 'And I've never seen light, but I sure have seen gold.' Ultimately, she crafts a fresh, feminist twist: 'We both know it was a girl back in Bethlehem.'

'Hey Jupiter' (Tori Amos)

Released as an A-side, 'Hey Jupiter' (The Dakota Version), 1996, (AUS and UK) b/w 'Professional Widow (Armand's Star Trunk Funkin' Mix) (Radio Edit)', 'Sugar' (Live), 'Honey' (Live).

'No one's picking up the phone, guess it's me and me.' Loneliness is currency in this haunting ballad. Breaking up with Eric Rosse was reason enough to pour out her heart, but then – against better judgment, alone in a strange hotel room, knowing full well that the relationship had run its course – Tori grabbed the phone.

Tori's head voice and the searing instrumental arrangement are inseparable. 'Hey Jupiter' has one of the prettiest melodies on the album and one of the saddest themes. Tori takes her time bringing us into the story. It's as though she's asking us to respect her post-breakup state of mind. The piano part feels grievous and spare, almost like a funereal dirge, but in a touching, efficient way. Virtuosic piano would feel out of place here – see 'Father Lucifer' for that.

'Way Down' (Tori Amos)

Tori goes for a gospel sensibility here. The warm, male voices in the chorus are a definite plus. We'll hear similar textures in *The Beekeeper*. Unfortunately, this is one of her shorties, but fasten your seat belts: we'll hear an extended version down the line.

'Little Amsterdam' (Tori Amos)

'Little Amsterdam shut down today /They buried her with a butter bean bouquet' – a doomed inter-racial relationship set in the American south finds the white female subject placating the white sheriff in an effort to protect her man. When a murder takes place, the female subject panics and appears to be emotionally divorced from the politics at hand. The dramatic theme is balanced by soulful slide guitar and blues-drenched piano.

Author Amy Gentry, in her *Boys for Pele* publication (33 1/3), pointed out that 'Little Amsterdam' 'was the first explicit story about race to appear on one of her albums and the first specifically to tease out Amos' own racial identifications with both the oppressor and oppressed.'

Interestingly, back in 1965, singer Janis Ian – then age sixteen – explored interracial tensions in the then-controversial 'Society's Child,' where the Caucasian female subject also ghosts the relationship, something which the older Ian later insisted she would have changed.

'Talula' (Tori Amos)

Released as an A-side, 11 March 1996 (UK), 21 May 1996 (US), 22 April 1996 (AUS), b/w 'Amazing Grace/Til' the Chicken,' 'Frog on My Toe,' 'Sister Named Desire,' 'Alamo,' 'Samurai,' 'London Girls.'

It's like lounging in a lanai over a Mai Tai after the first couple of bars. They say that a good storyteller brings the audience right smack into the middle of the situation; that surely happens here. Musically, Tori delves freely into the blues, marking time with a hypnotic motif.

'Not the Red Baron' (Tori Amos)

Baron von Richthofen – the World War I flying ace who got shot down in a dogfight, and who was popularized in a *Peanuts* cartoon – may have been the muse, but Tori actually wrote the song to commemorate men who have died of Aids – liberally using the phrase, 'Another pilot down,' as a reliable metaphor. She also juxtaposes wartime against 'heroes in beautiful capes, taking them to the flames.'

The engineers were chatting in Dutch as the tape rolled. By keeping their indistinct musings on the track, one might think that a radio message is being intercepted. This smart move sits well with the empathetic outcome.

Piano is truculent and vocals are electrifyingly sincere. While easy to disregard, with the inclusion of similarly strong tracks, 'Not the Red Baron' deserves a sacred space.

'Agent Orange' (Tori Amos)

Along the same spectrum as 'Talula,' this ditty is short, sweet and ever-so-bluesy. It references the toxic chemicals used by the U.S. army during the Vietnam war; but on the 2016 *Pele Deluxe Edition* liner notes, Tori stated: 'It's a homage to somebody who, in the early days of tanning, was a beautiful shade of orange.'

'Doughnut Song' (Tori Amos)

The 'holes' in this toxic relationship are only growing larger. 'There's the idea that you can't have two whole beings together, and I couldn't live like that,' Tori told *B-Side* in May/June of 1996. 'You'll never gain weight from a doughnut hole,' sums up this flailing relationship, devoid of sustenance.

The harmonic changes that lead from verse to chorus to bridge are subtle but effective. This breakup song is not written from a victim's point of view – it's as if Tori is looking back and resolving what happened pragmatically. Case in point: 'You've been wasting my time this time.'

'In the Springtime of His Voodoo' (Tori Amos)

Released as an A-side (LP Mix), 24 September 1996, (US) b/w 'Hasbrouck Heights Single Mix, Club Mix, Quiet Mix, Sugar Dub.' (Also promoted as 12" single.)

Tori opens up with: 'Kind of standing on a corner in Winslow, Arizona…' What's with Winslow, Arizona? Isn't that where The Eagles crooned 'Take It Easy'?

Geography aside, Tori adds class to her normative bag of tricks by honoring the heyday of big band singers, such as Peggy Lee, Anita O' Day and Queen Ella, who scatted with temerity. Joni Mitchell's beatnik-like cover of 'Twisted' and the cool flirty bass on 'Fever' also come to mind.

In 1996, Tori commented to *Fanzine* about the making of this album: 'I would like to be able to fly off cliffs.' That said, if she could fathom ziplining while scatting to 'In the Springtime of His Voodoo,' she wouldn't need a pulley. The strength of her imagination would be the guiding force. The song was expertly remastered in 2016.

'Putting the Damage On' (Tori Amos)

After The Black Dyke Band's brawny introduction and a few off-topic lines, the intensity of this breakup epic sincerely unfolds: 'You said you packed my things and divided what was mine.'

The tear-stained melody is set against a simple progression. Tori's trembling vocals tug earnestly at the heartstrings. The four-bar interlude prior to the B section allows time for catching a breath; this affair won't end well.

At the short C section, Tori sings, 'I'm trying not to move, it's just your ghost passing through,' and then repeats the key line hesitantly, revealing deep sadness and an understandable regret. Horns blare in the outro, furthering the intensity.

'Twinkle' (Tori Amos)

After cooing over a battery of dissonant single acoustic piano notes, Tori moves from verse to verse, barely indicating a change of mood. I'm not certain that contemporary listeners pay attention to sequence, but while this simple song is beautiful, I anticipated a stronger finale for this eighteen-track smorgasbord. 'It just wasn't finished until that song,' Tori told *B-Side*, May/June 1996.

'Twinkle' felt more like a resting place to me, rather than a stopping point. 'Putting the Damage On' would have been my preferred finale.

Album Art

Cindy Palmano snapped the cover photo in New Orleans; this shot is far from pretty. Tori purses her lips and stretches a rifle across her lap. One leg swings over the edge of a cheap, wooden porch chair. Bare legs are caked with mud. A serpent hides on the ground; a rooster lurches from the roof. With her name set to the side, there's little or no visual star power to be found.

Tori's image brings to mind a hungover binge-drinker, but the disturbing cover is tame compared to the most talked-about illustration, where she's nursing a suckling pig! But in keeping with the theme, this disquieting image makes sense. *Boys for Pele* is about telling and discovering the truth, warts and all; filthy feet and suckling pigs, notwithstanding.

Not that the trashy image influenced sales: *Boys for Pele* skyrocketed to number two in the US and UK. Tori scaled the transatlantic heights, and all 'without a safety net.'

B-sides / additional tracks on remastered editions

'This Old Man' (Traditional)

Tori gives this repetitive and banal nursery rhyme a legitimate purpose when the piano takes on a distinctive persona.

'Hungarian Wedding Song'

After a groaning piano motif, Tori matches each vocal utterance with the piano, and the result is crisp and spellbinding.

'London Girls' (Chas Hodges, Dave Peacock)

It's hard to argue with easy-on-the-ears pop, that's light, innocent and justifiably self-indulgent.

'That's What I Like Mick (The Sandwich Song)' (Chas Hodges, Dave Peacock)
This pint-slugging novelty song appeared on the Chas and Dave 1982 album *Job Lot*. It's fun to hear Tori tick off the tongue-twisting gastronome.

'Samurai' (Tori Amos/George Porter Jr.)
Tori's melodic line skirts back and forth while the bass line sits pretty.

'Graveyard' (Tori Amos)
'I'm coming in the graveyard to sing you to sleep now,' the narrator gently informs. Knowing Tori's reverence for her own ancestry and elders in general, I suspect she's honoring a special family member rather than a made-up character. The gentle piano-playing put me in a relaxed state until the song ended with a thunderbolt.

'Toodles Mr. Jim' (Tori Amos)
The undulating intro. measures lead to a steady stream of marching chords. Tori's playful words: 'picker' and 'sticker' quickly give way to more graphic language.

'Amazing Grace/Til' the Chicken' (Tori Amos)
On 'Amazing Grace,' Tori's chords are basic, as is George Porter Jr.'s purposeful bass, allowing for a soulful, stellar and church-like vocal. 'Til the Chicken' is set afire by finger snaps and humorous mimicry: 'I'm gonna wrangle his wings,' Tori asserts with a giggle.

'Frog on My Toe' (Tori Amos)
The discourse between a child and the 'Poppa' sounds perfunctory at first, but emotions heat up in the subsequent verses. Tori's voice is angelic; the uniform chording puts us in the pews.

'Sister Named Desire' (Tori Amos)
Fans still wonder why this *Boys for Pele* B-side didn't get on the album, as it is certainly in keeping with the album's tone. With skyward pitches and staggered breathing, Tori pulls off an impassioned performance. Although the rubato piano part almost suggests a separate piece, the two instruments miraculously find the center.

The androgynous 'Desire' circles back to Neil Gaiman's *Sandman* comic book series. Amos and Gaiman are known for mutual namechecking, both lyrically and visually.

'Alamo' (Tori Amos)
A regal piano introduction sets the stage for the soaring melody and got-to-dance-along lyrics.

From the Choirgirl Hotel (1998)

Personnel:
Tori Amos: keyboards, vocals
Steve Caton: acoustic and electric guitar; mandolin on 'Black-Dove (January)'
George Porter Jr: bass
Justin Meldal-Johnsen: bass
Matt Chamberlain: drums, marimba on 'Cruel'
Andy Gray: programming
Stewart Boyle: guitar, 'Northern Lad'
Willy Porter: guitar on 'Playboy Mommy'`
Al Perkins: steel guitar on 'Playboy Mommy'
Sinfonia of London: 'Jackie's Strength'
David Firman: conductor
John Philip Shenale: string arranger
Produced by Tori Amos
Recorded at Martian Engineering, Tori's home studio, Cornwall, England, Sept 1997 to Feb 1998
Label: Atlantic
Release date: UK: 4 May 1998, US: 5 May 1998
Highest chart rank: UK: 6, US: 5, AUS: 8, NOR: 9
Running time: 57:00

From the Choirgirl Hotel is Tori's fourth studio album. There was much to celebrate, as she had married engineer Mark Hawley, in February 1998. Additionally, serendipity was in the cards for this album, when in the fall of 1997, Tori met Matt Chamberlain: an in-demand drummer who'd worked with Fiona Apple, Chris Isaak and Sam Phillips. Chamberlain and Tori hit it off immediately. Chamberlain summed up the album alchemy when talking to Jay S. Jacobs, author of *Pretty Good Years*: 'It was much more of a band effort than ever before, much more a shifting of sounds and pulsing rhythms and massive beats.'

Producer Joe Chiccarelli, who has worked with Chamberlain for years, said, 'I love Matt. He's one of the best drummers of all time. He's just got such a beautiful touch, a beautiful tone, the greatest, steadiest pocket in the world. He's such a creative force. I mean, the kind of guy that you can give just a little bit of an idea to, and he takes it all the way, or just comes up with something that you're like, woah, I didn't hear that for the song but that's so unique. He's a very special musician, one of the best ever.'

'The idea was to capture the drums live, and then tweak them in Pro Tools,' Matt recalled in *Tori Amos: In the Studio*.

The chemistry that developed between Tori, Matt, bassist Jon Evans and guitarist Steve Caton was special: the kind that every artist hopes to obtain, and once that easy-going vibe was established, the actual studio recording merely took six months. Perhaps that ease underscored the decision to collaborate on subsequent recordings.

Typical of previous projects, change was a constant. Tori replaced the complicated but beautiful-sounding harpsichord that bled through *Boys for Pele* with a plethora of unique bells and whistles, courtesy of the Kurzweil. It was an exciting album to make, with a newly-established set of protocols. Tori enjoyed working directly with Chamberlain to create innovative rhythms. Chamberlain recalled that 'Playboy Mommy,' 'Pandora's Aquarium' and 'Black Dove' only required a few takes.

The ensemble toured throughout most of 1998, on the Plugged '98 Tour – Tori's first time using a full band on tour. In fact, she had written this new batch of songs with them in mind. How did this sea change affect her performance and piano arrangements? She told *BMG Music Service*, 'I think, that knowing I was planning to bring rhythm with me into these songs, I wanted a real band behind me, not a studio entity to jazz them up. I thought, if I'm going to do this, the piano has to be integrated, and yet, not lost in the mix.'

The innovations were duly noted by industry professionals. In the year after its release, Tori was nominated for two Grammy Awards: Best Alternative Music Performance and Best Female Rock Vocal Performance for the track 'Raspberry Swirl.'

As far as production resources, the album was recorded in her husband, Mark Hawley's home studio – Martian Engineering in Cornwall, England – with Tori returning as producer.

Unlike the keyboard-friendly *Boys for Pele*, *From the Choirgirl Hotel* generated energy with a nod towards electronics and hard rock. In keeping with the tradition set during *Boys for Pele*, Tori green-lighted two album tracks as remix versions: 'Raspberry Swirl' and 'Jackie's Strength.'

Tori suffered a miscarriage three months into her pregnancy during an extended tour. She and Mark had been lamenting the loss of the child, but rather than keeping her grief hidden from fans, she expressed emotions through the airing of new material. In doing so, she gave voice to others who had shared the experience but couldn't find the words to express their pain or didn't feel safe sharing their experience with others.

'Spark,' in particular, created awareness and dialogue among fans. She told *Q* magazine in May 1998: 'Y'know, once you've felt life in your body, you can't go back to having been a woman that's never carried life.' Against layers of ambience lies the song's fiercest line: 'She's convinced she could hold back a glacier/But she couldn't keep the baby alive.'

The album served an additional purpose: the 'choirgirl hotel' concept refers to the imaginary place where the album's songs cohabitate but still retain separate identities. Tori was wrapping a maternal arm around these song girls, sending them out to the public while keeping a watchful eye out: 'Go, go, go, go, now/Out of the nest…' she wrote in 'Mother.' Traces of *Little Earthquakes* were bleeding into the album – like *déjà vu*, in a good way.

The album achieved platinum status from the RIAA on 18 December 2000, more than two years after its initial release. In June, John Aizlewood of *Q* wrote affirmatively about Tori, 'At last, she's putting the songs first, and the band-led *From the Choirgirl Hotel* is, by any reasonable yardstick, a glorious coming of age.'

John Everson wrote on *blogspottingtrends.blogspot.com*: 'The album feels very much like a transitional work for Amos, a significant turning point.' Everson supported this comment by stressing that this was Tori's first time working in a home studio, as well as working with drummer Matt Chamberlain, who would heavily influence Tori's sound and comfort level on stage and in the studio.

Working with this excellent band allowed Tori the flexibility to experiment with non-traditional vocal styles and alternative musical genres. She was still committed to writing on the piano yet didn't need to feel wedded to the instrument. She could engage in call and response or sit back for a few measures and take in the big picture. She could derive energy, not just from the audience but from her colleagues.

'Spark' (Tori Amos)

Released as an A-side, 20 April 1998 (US) b/w 'Purple People (Christmas in Space),' 'Have Yourself a Merry Little Christmas,' 'Bachelorette,' 'Do It Again,' 'Cooling.'

Tori leaves little to the imagination but a lot to ponder. 'She's addicted to nicotine patches/She couldn't keep her baby alive.'

Bravely and with insight, Tori examines female trauma. Her vocals sound distant and muted, as though she's emoting from a chamber, although musically, there's no sense of compromise.

The video shows her as a kidnapping victim, as the perpetrator lurks ahead. Spoiler alert: If you're hoping for a happy ending, you won't find it here, but the visuals make strong social statements about modern-day violence.

'Cruel' (Tori Amos)

Remix released as an A-side single ('Cruel-Shady Feline Mix') with 'Raspberry Swirl,' July 1998 (UK), 24 November 1998 (US), 18 December 1998 (CAN) b/w 'Ambient Raspberry Swirl-Scarlet Spectrum Feels,' 'Mainline Cherry-Ambient Spark.'

There's little trace of Tori Amos, concert pianist. Instead, there's an explosion of blips and bleeps amid self-assured percussion. Then, the counterculture lyric: 'Dance with the Sufis/Celebrate the top ten', and 'I can be cruel/I don't know why.' Lyrics go from obscure to blatant; the gyrating instrumental is fascinating. Chamberlain's marimba shimmers.

'Black-Dove (January)' (Tori Amos)

The slightly under-the-radar dissonance is reason enough to stay the course, but Tori's lyrics and tone validate the experience. With the simple line, 'She was a January girl,' Tori sets into motion the plight of a mysterious protagonist, although some lines only give a nod to a sense of innocence: 'How a lion becomes a mouse.'

When she sings, 'By the woods' initially, the vocal quality is tenuous. But with repetition, the phrase gathers steam.

The 'On the other side of the galaxy' line instigates a rise in volume and a blinding array of textures: Caton is a triple-threat wunderkind, switching from electric guitar to guerilla mandolin strums. When anticipating an utterance, all players are airtight. Ultimately, Tori achieves a fever-pitch progression on her own terms.

'Raspberry Swirl' (Tori Amos)

Remix released as an A-side single ('Raspberry Swirl-Lip Gloss Version') with 'Cruel,' July 1998 (UK), November 1998 (US), 18 December 1998 (CAN), b/w 'Ambient Swirl-Scarlet Spectrum Feels,' 'Mainline Cherry-Ambient Spark.'

After a few bars of muffled voice, we're ensconced in Tori's imaginative, electronic universe. What follows is a cluster of vocal ambling and celebratory rhythms that fly like ping pong balls across a net and lead to a sweaty, heated jam.

Tori pays supreme homage to her enduring female friendships. 'Raspberry Swirl' is a sensual and virtual Shinkansen. Industry professional Tony Bonyata spoke highly of 'a heart-pounding beat and neck-bending sonic guitar tones straight out of Adrian Belew's song bag' on a concertlivewire.com review from 5 August 2014.

'Jackie's Strength' (Tori Amos)

Released as an A-side single, 15 September 1998 (US), 23 February 1999 (Remixes), b/w 'Never Seen Blue,' 'Beulah Land.'

This straightforward, gripping storyline is dual purposed: pairing a pivotal moment between Tori and her mother with personal reflections. Mary Amos idolized Jacqueline Kennedy Onassis. When she recalled John F. Kennedy's death and how the tragedy affected his stoic spouse, Tori retained the memory for years. That the assassination occurred during Tori's birth year further cemented that date into her subconscious. Tori explained on the *VH1 Storytellers* Special, 'I remember my mother telling me that the day Kennedy died – John F. Kennedy – that she put me down and she couldn't breathe. Mama lay me down on the front lawn and prayed for Jackie's strength. And all she thought of was Jackie and the strength that it would take Jackie to lead the nation.'

Tori wonders how Jackie endured her husband's assassination and questions the concept of legalized marriage and commitment, given society's high divorce rate: 'Feeling owned by 21 / Never knew my day would come,' she sings earnestly against shifting chords.

'Jackie's Strength' is one of the most transparent tracks on the album. Arranger Shenale's breathtaking fifteen-piece string arrangement assures that the song retains its majestic status. The related remix shot to number one on the US Dance Club chart.

'i i e e e' (Tori Amos)

Consider E. E. Cummings and Lewis Carroll on steroids reciting poetry set against a swarthy backbeat in an opium den. Tori's vocal improvisation is innovative, especially against Chamberlain's arresting percussion. There's no sign of hesitation or ennui in her performance – it's like, she's singing the song for the very first time.

The bittersweet content references a little girl Tori lost in a miscarriage; the exciting vocal execution makes the song sparkle. Caton displays outlandish chops in a mid-point solo.

'Liquid Diamonds' (Tori Amos)

Starting off in a medium tempo, this seven-minute, atmospheric track assures a vacation from reality with its searing effervescence. The band eases into the groove a few measures before Tori chimes in and then supports her from the sidelines during the zany melodic transitions, like when she mumbles in a monotone before letting the glass-breaking begin.

At first listen, it's convenient to categorize 'Liquid Diamonds' as a venture into smooth jazz, but it's more. The freedom here is carried out in ad-lib vocals and even the production. After all, there's that cool fade-in and fade-out: perhaps a sign of contemporary times; that technique hadn't been associated with Tori's work previously.

She rants, 'I guess I'm an underwater thing, I'm liquid running' in verse one; waxes rhapsodic about a 'sea secret' in verse two; but then shrieks hysterically about 'jeans' ... um, what's the rationale? Who cares? It's kooky, but unquestionably cool.

'She's Your Cocaine' (Tori Amos)

Caton's stupefying electric guitar sets the gold standard. Then, a dramatic shift in tempo distracts us from the punk alchemy. But when Tori grabs the mic, the miasma temporarily fades, for she's a flipping banshee of the highest order. This might not be the Tori you signed up for, but hear her out; she's worth the gamble. *Vive la difference*.

St. Eve did a brilliant cover for the 2001 *Songs of a Goddess – A Tribute to Tori Amos*. She intuitively recognized the virulence in Tori's original and respected the pace.

'Northern Lad' (Tori Amos)

In a grand departure from the previous tracks, Tori returns to traditional singer-songwriter mode. Her voice is pure and heartbreaking. The 'sonic architecture' – a term Tori frequently uses to describe her songwriting strategy – is impressive; she knows how to nuance and how to get back home after she feigns being unhinged. It's exciting to hear her take vocal liberties.

'Hotel' (Tori Amos)

For this curious, technologically progressive arrangement, Tori experiments freely with tempo while exploiting the boundaries of her range. A wild electronic component threads throughout. The escalation and edge-of-the-seat tension make it a fun but inhibiting ride, where all concerned get box-seating.

'Playboy Mommy' (Tori Amos)

The aftermath of Tori's miscarriage is revisited in 'Playboy Mommy.' She explained to *Q* how the ordeal and residual feelings of hurt and anger influenced the lyric:

> 'Playboy Mommy' dealt with my feelings of rejection – 'Wasn't I enough to be your mother, didn't you want me?' – 'Well, don't come then. Go choose some little right-wing Christian for your mother.'

As if the bluesy ensemble architecture wasn't captivating enough, Al Perkins' steel guitar adds buoyancy, and Willie Porter's slide adds grit.

During a live concert, Tori explained that after writing most of the song, she still had trouble figuring out the first line. Then, after drinking champagne at a nightclub in France, she fell flat on her face after climbing a winding staircase in her signature platform shoes. When Beenie asked if she was okay, Tori replied, 'Oh, Beene, I need more champagne. I feel awful, but… oh my god, I have the beginning to the song.'

This line put more than a little sparkle in Tori's step that night: 'In my platforms, I hit the floor, fell face down, didn't help my brain out.'

'Pandora's Aquarium' (Tori Amos)

'This little song came when I was living by the water, dancing by the water, eating by the water,' Tori explains to a live audience. 'She dives for shells with her nautical nuns,' is the opening line, which Tori sculpts from here on in.

The rubato piano allows space for her voice to escalate and descend. She does extraordinary vocal tricks here, and to appreciate her skills fully, I find I have to let this new Tori in, and not compare her to what I thought she was about on earlier albums or in concert.

Each section has its own unique beauty and method of movement. Tori's voice is light as merengue, but after she sings 'Ripples go and ripples go and ripple back to me,' the meter changes, and for a moment, we're suspended in time, but the band keeps the interest level high during the transition.

She creates mind-numbing suspense during the final phrase: 'The lord of the flies was diagnosed as….' Before blurting out the mystery word, she taunts us with a series of scalar aerobics. 'I'm not asking you to believe in me,' she coyly confides, yet her performance couldn't be more authentic.

'Purple People' (Tori Amos) (Japanese edition bonus track)
Tori was inspired by a friend's recollection of this simple introduction: 'Hi, I'm Betsy Brown, do you do judo? I do judo.'

While it's not unusual for Tori to turn a casual greeting into gibberish, it is unusual to achieve the final result. Despite the curious title, 'Purple People' is no lighthearted ditty: it's a demonstrative ballad with a gorgeous melody that would sound sexy in a *The Threepenny Opera* knockoff or a Broadway smash like *A Chorus Line*. Vintage.

Related Tracks:

B-sides:

'Purple People (Christmas in Space)' (Tori Amos)
The battling horns, frantic piano fills and distinguished drumming make this a satisfying rendition. But even without the flash, it's impossible to disengage from this gorgeously-written-and-performed melody, flush with idyllic images snared from Mother Nature's bounty: 'Thunder wishes it could be the snow….'

'Have Yourself a Merry Little Christmas' (Traditional)
Tori's expressive soprano makes this the perfect cover version; although the disturbing video cancels out the innocence of the commanding performance.

'Bachelorette' (Tori Amos)
This track also appears in *A Piano.* If some steamy film noir required an under-three-minute theme, this would absolutely do the job.

After a few bars of clanky percussion, Tori begins this beguine by hammering out a singular piano note alongside a weird electronic effect that sounds like rubber bands being stretched from bureau knob to bureau knob but duly amplified. No doubt, the strangled rubber band effect was the brainchild of Steve Caton, who would only stay aboard another year, but the contagious giggle at the end was all Tori.

'Do It Again' (Walter Becker, Donald Fagen)
Tori sings against hollow industrial beats. Hearing this track sans, the typical Steely Dan accouterments took some getting accustomed to, but ultimately, it gets under the skin.

'Cooling' (Tori Amos)
Also, on *A Piano* in 2006. Who can argue with the impact that these strong words have on romantic partners? 'You got too many brambles, but I always like a good storm.'

'Cooling' has, understandably, acquired many fans who agree that it's probably about the end of a relationship, with sensitive descriptors that back up the theme. The main motif reminds me of Marc Cohn's exuberant 'Walking

In Memphis': the accompaniment is easy on the ears but strong enough to uphold the ballad's expressive viewpoint.

'Never Seen Blue' (Tori Amos)
Against swelling arpeggios and tone clusters, Tori relies on her upper register and Joni Mitchell-style delivery. 'Where the razor's been' led to theories that self-harm is a sub-theme, while 'red' and 'blue' brought to mind fire and masculinity, leaving room for complex discussions.

'Beulah Land' (Tori Amos)
Also, in *A Piano*. A straight-ahead ballad, similar in tone to 'Desperado' and heightened by the second verse harmonies.

'Cruel' (Shady Feline Mix)
Tori's words range from muddled to precise, against a host of thrashing percussive iterations. This cantankerous track simply explodes with stops and starts.

'Raspberry Swirl' (Lip Gloss version) (Tori Amos)
Tori's vacuum-packed voice gets lost within the swells of space-age ambience.

'Raspberry Swirl' (Scarlet Spectrum Feels) (Tori Amos)
Frequently referred to as the 'Goth Mix,' and rightly so. The fierce, vertigo-inducing components make stoner music sound unbearably tame. Fantastically engaging in small doses. How many syllables can you make out of the title, Tori fans?

'Mainline Cherry' (Ambient Spark) (Tori Amos)
The incessant use of cymbals is merely one highlight, or perhaps, aberration? Tori's repetitive and often eerie vocal machinations are especially intrepid. It's fresh and addictive.

Album Art

Katerina Jebb's cover portrait showcases Tori's profile. Her fingers are outstretched, grasping at random strands of hair. Her expression is somber. Jebb's technique involves using Xerox photocopiers to photograph her models. Tori acknowledged that the final version was 'very ghostly, ideal for the project,' and that the image 'stayed true to the text.' (*torismaze.com*)

The hand-drawn map inside the jewel case shows locales, the likes of 'Pudding Dungeon,' 'Wannabe Rockies,' 'Mr. Grumpy's Maze' and the 'Nautical Nuns Casino.' As far as the Tori shots: in one, she wears a long, black dress. In another, a denim skirt, fancy top and shiny shoes. Those images are pedestrian compared to one, in which she's laying down on tree stumps, barely covered except for a dark sheet. The background is a beguiling Picasso blue.

To Venus and Back (1999)

Personnel:
Tori Amos: Bosendorfer piano, synthesizers, vocals
Steve Caton: guitar
Jon Evans: bass
Matt Chamberlain: drums, percussion
Andy Gray: additional drum programming on 'Suede,' 'Riot Poof' and 'Datura'
Produced by Tori Amos
Recorded in Cornwall, England
Label: East West (UK), Atlantic (US)
Release date: UK and US: 21 September 1999
Highest chart rank: UK: 22, US: 12
Running Time: Disc one: 47:49, Disc two: 75:33

To Venus and Back, the fifth studio album, was also Tori's first official live album. It was released as a double CD/cassette collection. The first disc – 'Venus: Orbiting' – contained eleven original studio cuts recorded with long-term colleagues: drummer Matt Chamberlain; bassist Jon Evans and guitarist Steve Caton.

The second disc, 'Venus Live, Still Orbiting,' consisted of thirteen tracks from Tori's 1998 world tour, which was titled Plugged '98' Marathon World Trek. This disc stands as a celebration of Tori's first live concert recording.

Five days after the album's release, Tori completed a tour with Alanis Morissette and set to work promoting the album's tracks. Although, back in mid-August of that year, she had already jump-started the promotion process by performing 'Bliss' on *The Late Show with David Letterman*. But on the same night the album got released, Tori hit the ground running by singing '1000 Oceans' on *The Tonight Show with Jay Leno*. Both songs were eventually listed in the top 25 of the *Billboard* Top Singles Sales charts, according to a press release.

The album was not only a surprise to fans but to Tori, as she had only intended to release a live disc, plus a disc of B-sides and rarities. But eighteen months after last setting foot in the studio, inspiration returned.

The album would not be released in vinyl, as that format was losing its legitimacy within the industry. Like *From the Choirgirl Hotel,* it was also penned specifically with small band arrangements in mind.

Mark Hawley and Marcel van Limbeek multitracked every performance – soundcheck or concert date – as Tori often created new songs on the spot.

To Venus and Back is a contemporary-sounding album, varnished with riveting dance club rhythms. Tori stays true to her piano, but with the band, liberally employs electronics. Old-school fans may consider this choice to be an unnecessary evil. I enjoyed some of the outlandish effects, but there were times when I pined away for a stripped-down ballad.

Natasha Stovall of *rollingstone.com,* in her review of *'To Venus and Back,'* called the album 'autobiographical as ever.' But the album's content went way beyond Tori's personal reflections. By this point in her career, she'd fully established herself as an artist who not only shared her most intimate thoughts with her fanbase but stood by her principles with an action plan. That sometimes meant writing about an alarming news event and educating people about the emotional cost, as she did evocatively in 'Juarez.'

The album title came about in an organic way when a friend referred to her as 'the eternal explorer' and said that she would go to Venus if she could. Since Venus also represents female energy, it was a perfect fit for a feminist-leaning artist.

To Venus and Back visits two fascinating sides of Tori. Listening to her hits in a live context connects us with her loyal fanbase and allows us access to her interactive ad-libs and compositional elaborations. She also lets her hair down, seemingly unrestrained by studio limitations and time crunches, energized by the love of her fans.

Similarly, to past projects, changes materialized. In this case, although Chamberlain and Evans would continue on for an ambitious decade, Tori and long-standing guitarist Caton parted ways.

Disc One – 'Venus: Orbiting'

'Bliss' (Tori Amos)

Released as an A-side single, 24 August 1999 (US), (CAN), b/w 'Jupiter' (Live); The 'maxi' includes 'Upside Down' (Live '99).

Chamberlain's crisp four-on-the-floor, Caton's Merseyside strumming and Evans' infectious bassline create a superb canvas. When Tori splashes on lyrics – 'Father, I killed my monkey' and 'A hot Kachina who wants into mine,' with a gouache of 'yeahs' – the sheen proves irresistible. Not all lines are rad, but all contribute to the blistering rock attitude.

'Juarez' (Tori Amos)

Tori's voice morphs from muted to expressive against a cantankerous electronic background. 'Juarez' stems from an article about the brutal murder and sexual assault of several hundred women in Juarez, Mexico. Tori explained to *songfacts.com*, 'So as the song started to develop, I really began taking the voice of the desert, singing in that perspective.'

The ugliness of this aggressive act comes through in both the aching vocals and cacophonous arrangement. The anguished line, 'No angel came,' probably reflects the fact that the perpetrators were never found and the survivors' families received no justice.

'Juarez' is an especially moving song, executed in an unapologetic, contemporary manner. Bob Dylan's 1965 recording, 'Just Like Tom Thumb's Blues,' also depicted the Mexican city in a bleak light, but the two recordings share no other common thread.

'Concertina' (Tori Amos)

Released as an A-side single, 8 February 2000 (US), b/w 'Famous Blue Raincoat' (Live), 'Twinkle,' (Live), video for 'Glory of the 80's'.

On this fourth and last single from the album, Tori likens the instrument to the discomfort and compression felt when being inside a 'squeezebox.' Ironically, her voice is so pretty, that that kind of tension doesn't surface; but no complaints here, as it's a delightful pop song. The electronic drums against the lithe piano add to the charm. Evans' input is cutting-edge. Tori flaunts her vocal range with ease and confidence. The electronic drums add oomph.

'Glory of the 80's' (Tori Amos)

Released as an A-side single, 11 October 1999 (AUS), 1 November 1999 (UK), 1 November 1999 (EU), b/w 'Famous Blue Raincoat' (Live), 'Twinkle' (Live); version 2 includes: 'Baker Baker' (Live), 'Winter' (Live).

A YouTube fan commented: 'I want to marry this song and have its tiny song babies.' I can understand! This is Tori at her most vibrant. Her voice is in tip-top shape, energy is high and the stream-of-consciousness phrases roll off her tongue with seemingly little effort.

It sounds like a swan song dedicated to her challenging *Y Kant Tori Read* days. After all, when she sings, 'In the glories of the '80s, I may not have to die,' and adds digs about the superficial times, we need no further explanation. 'Joan of Arcs to the right!'

'Lust' (Tori Amos)

In *Piece by Piece*, Tori elaborates: 'Similarly, the song 'Sweet the Sting' on *The Beekeeper*, makes my hips sway. This to me is a musical example of the marriage of the sacred and the profane.'

Driven by a quirky ping-pong rhythm and contrapuntal piano, Tori's soft voice renders sensuality, as the title suggests. The down-to-earth subtext is about trust and boundaries.

'Suede' (Tori Amos)

This swampy song – with a texture not as striking as her debut's 'Leather' – crosses over to Americana but then gets fairly emo at the bridge. It's sultry and ever-changing. Tori takes chances by cross-bleeding into alternative worlds, with entertaining word flow.

'Josephine' (Tori Amos)

Here's Tori's take on Napoleon Bonaparte's wife and how she endured their relationship amid stormy times, with 'Not tonight, Josephine' being the imperative line. As a curious and voracious reader, Tori has the ability to condense facts and distill the essential components of an event or relationship when she tackles a narrative. Thankfully, she humanizes her characters at the same time. The length allows time for introspection.

'Riot Poof' (Tori Amos)

Filled to the brim with dynamic dance music and layer upon layer of swirling vocals, Tori aces the imagery with groupings like, 'A bath, a glitter and a tiny shiver,' elevating generic dance genre lyricism to a loftier plane. For this LGBTQ tribute, she references David Bowie *glam.*

'Datura' (Tori Amos)

Clocking in at over eight minutes, 'Datura' is tasked with chronicling the flora in Tori's garden, with a focus on the most toxic and hallucinogenic specimen of all. Tori chants plant names over a steady beat – the hypnotic rhythmic effect comes in part from the use of two different drum kits. While the time signature goes berserk in the A section, all is calm and bright in the bridge.

'Spring Haze' (Tori Amos)

Instrumentally, Tori's admiration for Debussy and Stravinsky comes to the fore in her velvety, nuanced voicings. Conceptually, she intrigues, with a roster of inner-rhymes and truthful detail. 'Spring Haze' is about the fatal death of John F. Kennedy, Jr., who perished in a private plane crash. The first two lines prepare us: 'Certainly these clouds go somewhere/Billowing out to nowhere.' The last line, 'Why does it always end up like this?' leaves us in tears.

'1000 Oceans' (Tori Amos)

Released as an A-side CD single and Cassette, 9 September 1999 (US), 10 January 2000 (AUS), b/w 'Baker Baker' (Live); also, vinyl single and enhanced CD versions.
This beautiful ballad came to Tori in a dream. Although she claims that connecting the text with the soaring melody line was a challenge, she apparently puzzled it out. Her presentation is enigmatic. She perfectly captured the harsh reality of grief, with her late father-in-law in mind. 'I can't believe that I would keep, keep you from flying,' is a disquieting but moving image.

Note: 'Zero Point' was bumped, but later released on *A Piano: The Collection* in 2006.

Disc Two – 'Venus Live, Still Orbiting'

'Precious Things' (Tori Amos)

Heavy percussion and space-age effects set the tone. The crowd cheers in anticipation of Tori's piano lead-in, to which she adds a tapestry of new chords. Anyone familiar with the recording expects her to take off from here, and she does, with a delightful mélange of vocal madness, emphasized in expected places by her savvy cohorts.

'Cruel' (Tori Amos)
Amazing electronic effects form the prelude. In the beginning, the vocals initially come across as cavalier but get increasingly gutsy. The juxtaposition of wacky blips against gritty phrasing is seductive. Tori then tears into an atonal quasi-aria against the space-age fusion. When you wonder how much crazier the track can get, she settles the score with breathy harmonies.

'Cornflake Girl' (Tori Amos)
Tori introduces her 'wonderful brothers on stage,' Evans name-checks 'The Peter Gunn Theme,' and Tori breaks out into a hip, rubato version of a most successful hit. She seasons this live version with terrific blues licks, and there's no shortage of manic ingenuity in her scatting, as she's completely in the moment.

'Bells for Her' (Tori Amos)
Tori does Rachmaninoff on the lower notes, then purrs the sing song story over airy arpeggios. The rapt concentration on the bass notes gives this stunning ballad new life.

'Girl' (Tori Amos)
Chamberlain ignites the starting flame. Tori starts out slowly. When Cato joins in, he commits to the task with lightning force. Finally, the song enjoys a huge reception.

'Cooling' (Tori Amos)
'She's one of my best friends of all the songs,' Tori confesses, then laments that the song never became an album cut. As she performs, the concert hall stays pin-drop quiet. This cut features Tori's fluid range, but the piano's inner voicings are also compelling.

'Cooling' is flush with metaphor: 'Brambles turning to bushes,' and images of 'fire' and 'water' – is it about a perplexing love affair? Or a different type of loss? This ambiguity exists but doesn't interfere with the expressive beauty.

'Mr. Zebra' (Tori Amos)
Tori begins with wordplay: 'Rabbits, plinkety-plinkety-plink!' When feeding off the cheers of the audience, her joy is palpable.

'Cloud on My Tongue' (Tori Amos)
Mercifully, Tori plays this ballad solo. The move from chest to head voice is effective against the dirge-like chording. The band adds excitement to the majority of these songs, but a few standards require a little fuss; this particular version made fans rejoice.

'Sugar' (Tori Amos)

Tori's voice remains low and empathetic, lingering over a handful of chords. She amps it up when the other instruments fill in and proceeds to ad-lib with fervor.

'Little Earthquakes' (Tori Amos)

After a dark, distilled piano introduction, Tori inches into the powerful storyline. She stays cool and collected in the A section, and becomes more impassioned in the B section, repeating 'And I hate…' as the band supports her soulful singing.

'Space Dog' (Tori Amos)

The full band sound fleshes out this thrilling arrangement. They lay back on the B section but make up for it with exuberance. I can't get Chamberlain's cool rhythms out of my mind.

'The Waitress' (Tori Amos)

After an atmospheric intro., Tori sends shivers up the spine with her maneuvers on this complex melody. Performing live allows for lots of room to play and settle into the groove. This is an extended version, and the audience eats it up.

'Purple People' (Tori Amos)

The aria-like melody reverberates across the stage. Because this cinematic song evokes the image of a country café in the south of France, I long for Tori to break out into a romance language or at least a patois…. Well, maybe next time.

Album Art

Lauren Haynes photographed Tori for the *To Venus and Back* cover, in which the bright-eyed vocalist is focusing on something in the distance. It's not clear where she is, as we simply see muted streams of light and dark. There's nothing staged, unnatural or mysterious about this fresh image, so it's fitting for an album of contemporary songs. Unobtrusively, the album title is in lowercase and off to the right, as if it's only there to blend in with the image. The gatefold opens to reveal a full body shot. Here, Tori's more animated.

Strange Little Girls (September 2001)

Personnel:
Tori Amos: lead vocals, Wurlitzer, Bosendorfer, Rhodes, ARP
Matt Chamberlain: drums, military drum, Taos drums
Adrian Belew: guitar, drill guitar, acoustic and rattlesnake track
Justin Meldal-Johnsen: bass, 'bass painting'
John Philip Shenale: arrangements and performance track, strings and synths
Jon Evans: bass
Dr Edison Amos, Daniel Bocking, George W, Bush, George H. W. Bush: voices
M & M: additional guitars, string pads
Produced by: Tori Amos
Recorded at Martian Studio, Cornwall; The Nut Ranch, Los Angeles, February-July 2001
Label: Atlantic
Release date: UK and US: 18 September 2001
Highest chart rank: UK: 16, US: 4
Running time: 62:09

Strange Little Girls is Tori's sixth studio album. This concept album features twelve tracks that were written and originally performed by male recording artists and which Tori set about reinterpreting through the perspective of thirteen fictional females (one song is conveyed by twins).

She even looks the part; the jacket features flashy images of the dolled-up songwriter – one to match each subject's unique personality. While it's ambitious, did it work? I've got mixed feelings about this album. And spoiler alert: I do feel that some of her re-imagined renditions are over the top. Perhaps I'm too much of a fan of those originals.

Now, I know Tori has been selective with cover songs in the past: her version of 'Smells Like Teen Spirit' was phenomenal, and anytime she comes up with a Beatles, Stones, or Led Zeppelin classic, I'm in – but this was a stretch. I was often surprised by her choice of artist or song, especially when it came to Neil Young's 'Heart of Gold' and 10cc's 'I'm Not in Love.' Then again, a fan sometimes has to suspend disbelief. I reminded myself that Tori is often the first artist to throw her hat into the ring when it comes to generating new album ideas. Since the *Little Earthquakes* era, she has committed herself to research, album to album, whether that comes in the form of reading copious numbers of books, observing humanity with all its grandeur and ills, digging into family history, or reflecting back on heartaches and achievements.

Perhaps what's striking, is that Tori had come full circle and was in a position to examine her music from a completely different angle. She'd done her homework. She had drawn from mythology and folklore in the past with stellar results, but at a certain point, anthropological research becomes labor-intensive. Writing from an intuitive, experiential perspective is potentially enlightening. I was curious about this next step.

But as a long-time fan, I wasn't sure *I* was ready for this dramatic excursion. I was apprehensive about listening to Tori's rendition of Slayer's 'Raining Blood.' I assumed I'd be banging my head against anguished vocals for six-plus agonizing minutes. Then, I listened. It's far from my favorite track, but it's genuine and progressive enough to attract a new audience.

Shortly after the album release, Tori embarked on a national tour, beginning on 28 September 2001 in Miami and ending on 21 November in San Francisco. This tour marked her return to performing as a solo act: her first since 1994.

Strange Little Girls received the following reaction from *Slant Magazine*'s Sal Cinquemani: 'This is a cover album that covers about as much of Amos' split-psyche, as it does her diverse musical differences.' Cinquemani concludes, 'Transposing her postpartum crisis into someone else's world, seems perfectly out of place and right on time.' ('Tori Amos, Strange Little Girls' by Sal Cinquemani: 6 September 2001, *slantmagazine.com*)

Amos told *seattlepi.com* about the pre-studio strategizing: She prepared for the album by 'hanging out in men's heads, taking their seeds and planting them in women's voices.' (Gene Stout, 8 November 2001, *seattlepi.com*). Arranger John Philip Shenale noted: '*Strange Little Girls* was the intro to *Night of Hunters* in a way, because it shows her ability to switch and change everything into her own space. She's very immediate. For example, the songs on *Strange Little Girls*: I'd never thought of any of those, but she does. It's a perception that these creative people have, in buckets.'

'New Age' (Lou Reed)

On this original from the Velvet Underground's 1970 album, *Loaded*, the filmic introductory instrumentation inches along in steamy slow motion. Guitarist, Adrian Belew, and Beck/Nine Inch Nails bassist Justin Meldal-Johnsen starts out spare but dreamily expands into overdrive, all the while retaining the shimmer and optimism of the futuristic theme. It's an about-face when the two guests approach the bridge with admirable aggression.

Tori's new wave vocals are especially persuasive on the phrase, 'I'll come running to you.' Check out the Tori Amos influence in Florence Welch's (Florence and the Machine) performances near the end of the decade.

''97 Bonnie & Clyde' (Marshall Mathers, Jeff Bass, Mark Bass)

This Eminem cover from 1999's *The Slim Shady LP* is super creepy on any level. It's about a man who murders his wife, throws her into the trunk, and with his daughter alongside, heads towards the lake. Are we having fun yet?

In the victim's defense, Tori stated: 'She had to have a voice.' I sympathize with Tori's viewpoint that the victim – as opposed to the perpetrator – is not served in most violent songs. Tori definitely stretched the experimental envelope if that was her intent. I can certainly see the appeal if you are a horror fan, but I had trouble focusing, as the theme was so chilling.

Shenale recounted, 'We morphed that and turned it into her own sentiment musically. She is not one to conform. She will use her muses, her instinctual connections to a song, in order to extract, maybe, things that had been unseen before – much like a performer will perform Schubert in a new way.' Shenale underscored a salient aspect of Tori's writing process: 'Generally, she really reworks things.' She creatively re-imagined this; it scared the daylights out of me.'

'Strange Little Girl' (Jet Black, J. J.Burnel, Hugh Cornwell, Dave Greenfield, Hans Warmling)

On this Stranglers song from 1982, Tori's voice reflects a high degree of anxiety, which is echoed mid-song by the cacophony of electronics and hushed harmonies.

In response to journalist Greg Shapiro's query about choosing to cover a Stranglers song, Tori replied: 'I was just drawn to them because … what a catalog they've written.'

'Enjoy the Silence' (Martin Gore)

Dissonant harmonies and a droning effect in this Depeche Mode cover align perfectly with the lead vocals.

'I'm Not in Love' (Eric Stewart, Graham Gouldman)

A stoic, hollow drum rhythm and tinny electronic sounds wreak havoc on the nervous system. These background effects are weirdly fascinating at times but certainly a distant cry from the carefully constructed and lush 10cc original, on which the ironic lyrics exuded a sense of longing for romantic love. This spare, industrial background – uncharacteristically devoid of keyboards – left Tori shining the spotlight on her vocals.

On 25 January 2021, music writer, Eoghan Lyng, wrote a review for culturesonar.com, which included this observation: 'Tori Amos subverting the 10cc classic, translated Eric Stewart's revelatory 'I'm Not in Love' to exhibit the latent violence that exists behind a lover's dispute.'While I can't argue with that rationale, I do have qualms about the aesthetic. I grieve for the cover this could've been had Tori's gorgeous and expressive voice brought out the essence of the heartfelt lyrics against a more accessible background. On the other hand, as a tableau for guitarist Adrian Belew's breakaway embellishments, this version rocks.

'Rattlesnakes' (Lloyd Cole, Neil Clark)

In stark contrast to the Lloyd Cole and the Commotions ballad – which has rich orchestration, striking guitar, and vocals brimming with personality – Tori tones the song way down, rendering it melancholy. Her take is curious but all-consuming.

'Time' (Tom Waits)

Without mimicry, Tori reproduced the world-weary timbre of Waits' sandpaper voice; throwing her heart into the story simultaneously.

'Heart of Gold' (Neil Young)

This angry re-imagining of an earnest love song leaves me wondering what Tori was thinking about in the studio. She explained her reasoning to *windycitytimes.com* journalist Greg Shapiro: 'When I stripped it back, I saw that there was a sort of fury that the song itself had in it.'

I'm lost here. The original found Young searching for love with such open-mindedness. Fury? What fury? Still, Belew's fretless guitar synthesizer adds the edge that the lyrics just can't.

'I Don't Like Mondays' (Bob Geldof)

The high-pitched keys draw attention away from Tori's spot-on vocal on this Boomtown Rats cover about the 1979 Cleveland Elementary School shooting by a sixteen-year-old who claimed she committed the crime because 'I don't like Mondays.' Despite the spare arrangement, this anti-gun-violence plea more succinctly addresses the issue than on the following Beatles cover.

'Happiness Is a Warm Gun' (John Lennon, Paul McCartney)

Putting America's fanatical gun laws under fire through recorded speech is laudable, and Tori's vocals are, at times, spectacular. But this confusing collage demands much patience. Starting with the announcement of John Lennon's tragic death, it clocks in at over nine minutes.

Tori took too many liberties – the original took two-and-a-half minutes and includes dynamic stylistic contrasts. U2 took about four-and-a-half minutes, and Joe Anderson, just a bit over three, but both covers were satisfyingly melodic. With that element missing, Tori's venom is directed toward George W. Bush and George H. W. Bush. She even talked her dad, Dr. Edison Amos, into recording a voice-over, which she promised not to edit, but energies are scattered.

Still, there are some cool bits: Belew's tremolo provides a shimmering after-effect.

So, this was a gamble, but protocol was followed. Yoko Ono sincerely gave her blessing, and perhaps Lennon would've given this rendition a thumbs-up.

'Raining Blood' (Jeff Hanneman, Kerry King)

After hearing the Slayer original, Tori was immensely moved; she equated the theme with traumatic events occurring in Afghanistan. But her own version was a far cry from the often-covered 1986 *Reign in Blood* track.

Author D.X. Ferris, who wrote the 33 1/3 book about *Reign in Blood*, observed: 'Performed with just her voice and piano, 'Raining Blood' turns into a slow, gothic drone….'

Doing a stripped-down version was certainly a wise move, as opposed to simulating Slayer's bizarre electronics, as many copycats have done. Slayer's arrangement forges strength from bombastic guitar, deranged effects and loaded themes like purgatory and death; in other words, an open invite to a deafening catharsis.

To a point, Tori abides with atonal lunges and a lugubrious dirge that conveys street cred. She adds an extra minute-and-a-half for good measure. Certainly, she had guts to attempt this song. But despite her efforts, she falls short in terms of dynamic intensity and pacing; when Tori wanted to 'kill this waitress' ('The Waitress' 1994), we heard the aggravation loud and clear. Where's that rage now?

'Real Men' (Joe Jackson)

Tori injects the straight-talking lyric with soul. Sung from a woman's viewpoint, 'We wonder who the real men are?' becomes a controversial statement. As in the original, the instrumentation is uncluttered and focused. Adrian Belew and Jon Evans create a terrific chemical reaction. Tori's vocals are refreshingly effusive.

Related Tracks:

Original B-sides, 'After All' and 'Only Women Bleed' were called back after distribution in Europe. Thus, this is the first Tori Amos album that did not include an officially released single. There are no vinyl versions available in the U.S. or across the pond either.

'After All' (David Bowie)

With droning piano and pitch bends, Tori highlights the gravity of this lesser-known Bowie ballad by cherry-picking the most meaningful phrases.

'Only Women Bleed' (Alice Cooper, Dick Wagner)

It appeared on the 'Silent All These Years' single and the *Little Earthquakes Deluxe Remaster*. Lita Ford also interpreted this song. Tori's take includes a gospel-rich solo, but her emotional tone is somewhat uneven.

Album Art

So, you found yourself glued to Thomas Schenk's photos of bold, personable females? There's more: the CD booklet features photos of Tori dressed up as each of the intriguing dozen that the songs inspired. Text is by *The Sandman* author Neil Gaiman, and makeup is by Kevin Aucoin, to whom 'Taxi Ride' was dedicated.

Scarlet's Walk (October 2002)

Personnel:
Tori Amos: Bosendorfer piano, Rhodes, Wurlitzer, ARP, vocals
David Torn, Mac Aladdin, Robbie McIntosh: guitar
Jon Evans: bass
Matt Chamberlain: drums, percussion
Sinfonia of London: strings
John Philip Shenale: string arrangements
David Firman: conductor
Peter Willison: director of strings
Produced by Tori Amos
Recorded in Cornwall, England, Winter 2001-Spring 2002
Label: Epic, Sony Music
Release date: UK: 28 October 2002, US: 29 October 2002
Highest chart ranking: UK: 26, US: 7
Running time: 74:09

Post-11 September 2001, Tori took off a year to explore America, starting in California and heading eastwards. She'd grown up hearing about the Trail of Tears tragedy and how it affected her Cherokee ancestors. So, in light of that trauma, this journey was more than a casual road trip: it was a time of learning and grieving, as well as a way to confirm her peoples' truths.

On Tori's seventh studio album – her first after leaving the Atlantic label – the fictional Scarlet takes on the role of avatar traveler. As she forms friendships, falls in love, or gets left behind, she chronicles her reflections and bears witness to rugged mountain ranges, luminous badlands, and Midwestern prairies through the eyes of a curious descendant.

'This is heady stuff. But even when the imagery gets dense; Amos' generous spirit lets you in,' wrote Laura Sinagra at *spin.com*. Bassist Jon Evans also reacted positively: 'I think this is some of Tori's best songwriting.'

Here's how Greg Kot of the *Chicago Tribune* summed up Tori's eighteen-track album: 'Sometimes she drifts too far into the new age mystic ('Crazy'), but *Scarlet's Walk* mostly sounds like the work of someone who shuts out the mundane and tunes exclusively to her own idiosyncratic frequency – and that's something to celebrate in this era of prefab, factory-approved pop personalities.'

Scarlet's Walk definitely 'shuts out the mundane.' The project may have been a long time coming, but when it did come to fruition, it breathed new life into themes often ignored or discounted by American historians. Work had to be done before its conception: *Little Earthquakes* was dynamic, but despite its brilliance, served the role of the quintessential debut, in so far as shedding light on the songwriter's reflections and travails, truly setting an autobiographical tone. *Under the Pink* was critically acclaimed, but a follow-up album often requires an artist to stay close to the vest; Tori was still in lockdown. *Boys for Pele* was fearless and feminist-friendly but somewhat constrained by its overarching theme. *From the Choirgirl Hotel* was often misinterpreted, and many say that *Strange Little Girls* worked better as a concept than an actual aesthetic.

But at this point in her career, Tori was in especially good stead. Moving to the Epic label granted her the freedom to create without constraints and consolidate the skills she'd acquired since the making of her debut. What she does best here – similarly to her maternal grandfather – is earnest storytelling, without hyperbole.

Tori buried herself in research, which she'd been prone to do over the course of subsequent albums, and assembled a team from Haskell Indian Nations University in Lawrence, Kansas, to map out obligatory sites, such as Wounded Knee.

In some essential ways, *Scarlet's Walk* is the best and most accessible album since *Little Earthquakes.* Here, she is not mired in experimental mode, nor does she brood about the past; she writes in real-time. Her vocal instrument befriends us and consoles us, as it always has, bringing us closer, measure by measure, to her true composer's heart. Her linear narratives change us, challenge us, and at times, confound us. But after so many pretty good years in, it's imperative to honor those iterations because the feelings Tori transmits set her apart from her more commercially-minded peers. Plus, the impassioned vocals we expect are in full tilt.

Besides arranger John Philip Shenale and the Sinfonia of London, bassist Jon Evans and drummer Matt Chamberlain, *Scarlet's Walk* welcomes aboard seasoned guitarists Robbie McIntosh and David Torn. Mark Hawley also contributes guitar and resumes responsibility as engineer with long-term colleague Marcel van Limbeek.

In *Tori Amos: Piece by Piece*, bassist Jon Evans noted: 'The classical influence in Tori's music comes through in her harmonic choices and articulation. Her voicings are very classical.'

But further adjustments were made instrumentally. Tori explained in the press release that the musicians 'tried to use instruments that were more indigenous of the songs' places.'

While the fans noted the album's immediate value, the industry waited a month to validate its excellence, which is when *Scarlet's Walk* reached RIAA Gold status in the US.

So, the themes are engaging, the structure sound, the production excellent, and there is an impressive cross-section of genres represented on *Scarlet's Walk*. The only issue: the 74-minute length. Certain songs are simply too similar to each other to warrant this running time. That said, the saving grace may be the Tori team (Scarlet's Web) information component, on which each song was fleshed out in detail within the context of the album at large. This helped the fans comprehend the sequential aspects of the project, so when listening, they could do so without fumbling for facts.

'Amber Waves' (Tori Amos)
The opening track's title doubles as a reference to a poetic line in an iconic American anthem ('Amber waves of grain') and the name of a character actress in the 1997 film, *Boogie Nights.*

This slow-mover is awash in passionate harmonies. Scarlet befriends and shows empathy for Amber, who has been exploited in the adult film industry. The lyrics are compelling from the onset: 'He lit you up like amber waves in his movie show.'

Because she's the first companion Scarlet comes across on her introspective journey, Amber is a highly significant character, although the two merely pair up on an L.A. bus for a short spell. Tori envisioned Amber 'reclaiming parts of her purloined life.'

'A Sorta Fairytale' (Tori Amos)
Released as an A-side single, October 2002 (US), b/w 'Operation Peter Pan.'
Director, Sanji, made the corresponding, surreal music video in which the female character appears as a head connected to a leg, and actor Adrien Brody, appears as a head connected to an arm. After a perceived slight, the female counterpart disappears on a skateboard, landing on a beach. When lovers reunite, body parts resurface; they become whole.

This bittersweet story is uniquely told: 'And I rode alongside till you lost me there in the open road.' The lyric sums up Scarlet's disillusionment: her lover doesn't know who she really is. 'I'm so sad, like a good book, I can't put this day back,' she grimaces.

But even without the visuals, you can glean the meaning behind this well-produced pop song on which the double-tracked, ethereal backing vocals are saturated with reverb.

There's a special quality about the articulation: perhaps it's that Tori doesn't over-enunciate; her tone is conversational, so the narrative comes off as if being spoken by a curious bystander.

The guitar work is inconspicuous but addictive. In addition, there's that lift when the hand drum resurfaces, and the instruments magically fall into line at the chorus.

Three commercially-released versions resulted from this first single off *Scarlet's Walk*: an album version, the 101 Mix, and the original single version.

'Wednesday' (Tori Amos)
The tumbling A section contrasts vividly with the dreamy B, but both parts express the disarming 'lost in America' theme. This is one bouncy, old-timey tune. But alas, the fun rhythm doesn't change Scarlet's karma, at least not yet. Scarlet may believe she'll find love again, but in the here and now, romance remains a distant fantasy.

'Strange' (Tori Amos)
Strong harmonic changes upload a sense of urgency in this melancholy ballad about romantic deception. It's succinctly stated: 'You said, 'We'll build

a nest' / 'So I left my life' With impeccably constructed lyrics and through Scarlet's increasing ennui, we recall the pain of losing oneself in a long-term relationship and how it makes us vulnerable. Tori's voice aches with sincerity; the observations are uncomfortably plausible.

Moreover, 'Strange' is an important marker in terms of the album arc. Hungry for truth and tired of being let down romantically, Scarlet is ready for change. To that end, she prepares herself to explore the sacred lands of her ancestors. But to get there, she had to reflect and evolve: 'Guess I was in deeper than I thought I was.'

The heartfelt images and delivery recall the more significant moments of *Little Earthquakes*. When Tori questions the fragile state of a fictional character's relationship – not with non-sequiturs as she'd often done in the past, but in a mature, linear fashion – she creates emphatically enduring stories.

The song was released as a single. Re-recorded for the airwaves, an Americana effect was achieved with bent-note guitar and overdubbed vocals.

'Carbon' (Tori Amos)

Chamberlain's precise send-off (like his lively outro) and Tori's spare, sporadic chording anchor the liquid vocals of this character study. Scarlet faces quite a conundrum when 'Carbon' – a wounded being whom she attempts to save – creates a tailspin. The piano line swirls in and out of the constantly changing percussive waves, creating a storm-cloud of sadness.

Similar to 'A Sorta Fairy Tale,' the backing vocals are evanescent. As for the narrative, Tori uses lyrical repetition to supplant the somber content into our subconscious minds. And although the lyrical meaning is not easily discerned – i.e., 'Behind crystalline irises, loons can dive where the world bleeds white' – the poetic images cast Tori in a new light. Once upon a time, Tori exploited the concrete: 'There's a bowling ball in my stomach'; but here, she divines an other-worldly aesthetic.

'Crazy' (Tori Amos)

The guitar work lends this ballad an infectious Americana feel. Scarlet feels a pull toward the charismatic 'Crazy' yet fears rejection. Ultimately, she can't resist the promise of a wild ride. After a few laughs, it's back to the desert, alone.

'Wampum Prayer' (Tori Amos)

Scarlet picks up the voice of the Native American ancestors on the a cappella 'Wampum Prayer' after visiting the site of a massacre of the Apache people. Although it's under 50-seconds in length, the song leaves a sobering impression. Tori told *yessaid.com* about Scarlet's trajectory: 'She has a dream, and follows the voice and prayer of an old woman who survived, and whose song is woven into the land.'

This moving and simply-arranged song is stunning in its word pictures, especially as Scarlet reflects on a 'trail of blood and amens.'

'Don't Make Me Come to Vegas' (Tori Amos)

Released as an A-side single, 27 May 2003, 'Don't Make Me Come to Vegas ('Timo on Tori'), b/w 'Don't Make Me Come to Vegas (Timo on Tori Alternate Version),' 'Don't Make Me Come to Vegas (Timo on Tori Breaks Remix).'

Tori's voice is steamy and provocative as she comps out simple chords. Featuring a dark, hollow intro., the arrangement is awash with carefree Caribbean rhythms. An exciting transformation occurs when Tori switches into head voice, parsing out fills between phrases.

The lyrics are richly detailed and informative – 'My old flame was a jester and a joker and a dealer of men' – but we're given enough latitude to form our own thoughts.

There's massive plot movement too: Scarlet's niece begs her aunt to bail her out; she's marooned in the land of Blackjack and all-you-can-eat buffets, but Scarlet can't fathom making the journey, with so many ghosts at bay.

'Sweet Sangria' (Tori Amos)

Set in Austin, Texas, 'Sweet Sangria' is an eclectic mix of rhythms; sharp piano excursions cut in and out, adding definitive color.

'Your Cloud' (Tori Amos)

Chamberlain's exploratory percussion, Evans' slick maneuvers and the contrasting vocals in the B-section beef up this ballad, where the sound production is first-class.

'Pancake' (Tori Amos)

When Scarlet meets a 'messiah figure' who fails to uphold the values he preaches, she confronts him and stands her ground: 'You used to look my god right in the eye.' But she's left disillusioned. Again.

Besides being a scaffold for political accusations, 'Pancake' serves as a backdrop for Tori's offbeat vocal chafing.

'I Can't See New York' (Tori Amos)

This gripping ballad eerily foreshadowed the events of 11 September 2001, when planes crashed into New York's twin towers. 'From here, no lines are drawn,' the narrative begins. Tori's voice is emphatic as she ponders the 'white clouds falling down.'

At 7:14 in length, this is the album's most expansive and contemporary-sounding piece. Most startling is that Tori conceptualized this song prior to the events of 9/11.

'Mrs. Jesus' (Tori Amos)

Tori commands our attention with the feminist title and the intense subject matter: 'Lifelines and suicide crimes,' are not easy topics to discuss – but this likable tune balances out the drama with colloquial English that keeps conversations hopping: 'How you been? I've been cruising.'

Shenale's emancipating strings and the bright harmonies work well against the rollicking rhyme schemes. In fact, 'Mrs. Jesus' may be the proverbial road song; one that makes you feel at home, even when navigating a strange dirt road at dusk.

Of course, being richly orchestrated, 'Mrs. Jesus' immediately stands apart from standard Americana-influenced material. Yet, the song reflects that genre: there's an infectious twang in Tori's vocal. True to form, she weaves in spirituality: 'Heaven,' 'John,' 'Paul' and 'The gospel.'

'Taxi Ride' (Tori Amos)

Released as an A-side single, January 2003 (US), b/w 'Taxi Ride' (radio edit).

The bonding of generations is expressed with thumping guitar and positive lines such as, 'I'm glad you're on my side.' Harmonies are delicate. Tori's lead vocal reflects a youthful optimism. Her long-term makeup artist Kevyn Aucoin was alive when the song was being composed, and after his untimely death, Tori dedicated the song in his honor. 'He is a master sculptor and not just of the face,' she exclaimed in Aucoin's bestseller, *Making Faces.*

'Another Girl's Paradise' (Tori Amos)

Throughout this personality-driven ballad, Scarlet studies and contrasts female fears and passions with enlightened eyes. With its soft country rhythm and bold harmonies, it's a bit of a black sheep compared to other tracks, but in a good way.

'Scarlet's Walk' (Tori Amos)

Scarlet sees a 'big, brave nation, now forgotten.' The wisdom acquired and the pain she's yearning to resolve scream out in the narrative and throughout the presentation. From the intricate guitar solos and Chamberlain's four on the floor to the distinctive chanting, 'Scarlet's Walk' aerates the senses.

'Virginia' (Tori Amos)

This is another character study featuring superb harmonies and rootsy instrumentation. Tori's female subjects are people we all know and can relate to, but she brings out their humanity.

'Gold Dust' (Tori Amos)

This underrated torch song is one of Tori's most artfully arranged compositions. Torrents of synth fuse with piano in the intro. and recapitulate between the verses, but it's Tori's resilient voice that earns the crown. The spiraling melody stands up to the best of Gershwin and Jobim.

Time and place are uniquely cited: 'Sights and sounds pull me back, I was here…' and 'How did it go so fast?'

'Gold Dust' may be the closing track, but Tori gives it fair shrift. Thankfully, rather than creating a jarring exodus, the team simply allows this beautiful melody to fade away.

Related Tracks:

'Operation Peter Pan' (Tori Amos) B-side of 'A Sorta Fairytale'

Written in response to the phenomenon that occurred between 1960 and 1962, in which 14,000 children were put on Pan Am flights from Cuba to Miami; the kids were labeled the 'Peter Pans.' This is a serene and sensitively-worded ballad.

Album Art

Scarlet stands on a dirt road, clad in a short-sleeved floral print dress and blood-red heels with tight ankle straps. Blue skies peek through a veil of clouds. Scarlet's facial expression conveys both a sense of wonderment and determination.

All shots of Tori/Scarlet were taken by Wild West photographer Kurt Markus, during a productive five-day stint in Montana.

Scarlet's Hidden Treasures (EP)

Personnel:
See Scarlet's Treasures
Tori Amos: Bosendorfer piano, Fender Rhodes, Wurlitzer, vocals
Mac Aladdin: acoustic guitar
Matt Chamberlain: drums
Jon Evans: bass
Release date: 18 May 2004
Recorded: 2003-2004
Running time: 33:48
Labels: Epic, Sony, BMG

This EP came packaged with the *Welcome to Sunny Florida* Live DVD, which was released in 2004. The six songs were all non-album tracks, although those who purchased the Limited-Edition Box Set were granted access to the unreleased B-sides, 'Tombigbee,' 'Seaside' and 'Mountain' via the *Scarlet's Web* site. Note that 'Mountain' does not appear on the EP.

'Ruby Through the Looking Glass' (Tori Amos)

Mostly about a 'girl unstrung,' and highlighted by an undulating progression and prophetic lyrics: 'Ruby sees things in you, things in me.' Tori revealed in

Pieces: 'Ruby is in utero, hearing her mother trying to protect her in the womb, while her mother is clearly in a fight.'

'Seaside' (Tori Amos)

In response to a bombing, Tori sings, 'Shells fired out, flowers mowed down.' The chorus is rife with nonsense words like 'jangle and jingle jangle', which juxtapose the gravity.

'Bug a Martini' (Tori Amos)

This ballad relies on a catchy chorus: 'Send me to Moscow lounge and return.' Tori employs fast-paced call and response between her own vocals and the Rhodes. Chamberlain's drumming is infectious; Evans' stand-up bass sounds jazzy and joyous.

'Apollo's Frock' (Tori Amos)

This illuminating song, inspired by Tori's love of mythology, is full of emotional detail: 'Apollo's Frock was always as beautiful as your sister's that your light shined on.' 'Santa' corrals us through this stream of consciousness, and along the way, we get to hear a pretty flute solo: something we've rarely associated with a Tori Amos composition, but which sets it apart from the guitar-and-piano-heavy fare.

'Tombigbee' (Tori Amos)

Tori's voice acts as the quintessential percussive instrument. The Native American moniker refers to a tributary of the Mobile River that runs through Mississippi and Alabama. Live, Tori plays the Rhodes and the Wurlitzer.

'Indian Summer' (Tori Amos)

This beauty, nearly eight minutes long, projects a profound message of peace: 'Is there another way? Teach me another way.' Midstream vocals and the backing vocals' echo effect reel us in.

'Mountain' – Scarlet's Web download (2002)

Unfortunately, since this song was only available as a download, fans have been scrambling to find an alternative means of access. Underscored by Chamberlain's demonic drumming, Tori's vocals sound fabulously amplified and circuitous. The unexpected outro is a monster.

Exclusive Session (Live EP)

Personnel:
Tori Amos: Piano and vocals
Produced by: Tori Amos
Release date: 7 June 2005

Running time: 17:47

This live EP – the first Tori Amos release made available through iTunes – was first distributed in May 2005 in the UK, followed by Germany. On 7 June, it became available in U.S. stores.

'Sleeps With Butterflies'/ 'The Power of Orange Knickers'/ 'Seaside'/ 'Crazy' (Live)

A Tori Amos Collection: Tales of a Librarian (2003)

Personnel:
Produced by Tori Amos, Eric Rosse
Recorded in 1990 – Summer 2003
Label: Atlantic
Release date: UK and US: 17 November 2003
Highest chart rank: UK: 74, US: 40, BEL: 34
Running Time: 78:00

For this compilation album, Tori reviewed earlier mixes to determine which tracks required a boost and were most descriptive of her personal life. She added two new songs that had been recorded for *Little Earthquakes*: 'Angels' and 'Snow Cherries from France' and two remastered B-sides: 'Sweet Dreams' and 'Mary,' that were recorded for *Little Earthquakes* but left behind. The 20 tracks were technically updated by engineers Mark Hawley and Marcel van Limbeek.

While the new songs were a great addition, some fans felt that revamping classic arrangements was aesthetically unnecessary. Others welcomed the novel twists. The revision did unveil a number of nuances: for example, Shenale claimed that parts he had previously composed – but that didn't appear initially – mysteriously crept onto this album (to his delight).

Author Thomas Wolfe said, 'You can't go home again.' Fine, but you can varnish the rails and repurpose the plants. And besides, who doesn't crave a little luxury?

'Angels' (Tori Amos)

The song features soothing backing vocals and stylish melodic leaps, but when Tori sings, 'They're trapping angels by the Potomac,' easy-listening becomes reflective.

'Precious Things'/ 'Angels'/ 'Silent All These Years'/ 'Cornflake Girl'/ 'Mary'/ 'God'/ 'Winter'/ 'Spark'/ 'Way Down'/ 'Professional Widow' (Armand's Star Trunk Funkin' Mix) (Radio Edit)/ 'Mr. Zebra'/ 'Crucify'/ 'Me and a Gun'/ 'Bliss'/ 'Playboy Mommy'/ 'Baker Baker'/ 'Tear in Your Hand'/ 'Sweet Dreams'/ 'Jackie's Strength'/ 'Snow Cherries from France'

Note: A DVD of live material from North American soundchecks also got produced: The soundchecks for 'Pretty Good Year,' 'Honey' and 'Northern Lad' were documented and packaged as *Welcome to Sunny Florida*, which was released on 4 September 2003. All songs were written by Tori Amos.

Other Related Tracks

'Putting the Damage On' was remixed. Two instrumental versions of 'Mr. Zebra' and 'Putting the Damage On' were released.

The Beekeeper (February 2005)

Personnel:
Tori Amos: lead singer, acoustic piano (Bosendorfer), B-3 Hammond organ, Hammond organ
Damien Rice: guest vocals
Matt Chamberlain: drums
Jon Evans: bass
Mac Aladdin: electric and acoustic guitar
London Community Gospel Choir: background vocals
Produced by Tori Amos
Recorded and mixed by Mark Hawley and Marcel van Limbeck at Martian Engineering, Cornwall, England, June-November 2004
Label: Epic
Release date: UK and US: 20 February 2005
Highest chart rank: UK: 24, US: 5, Billboard Top Internet Albums US: 1
Running Time: 79:31

The Beekeeper, Tori's eighth studio album, marked her first time back in the studio in three years. 2005 seemed like a *pretty good year*, as Tori had also become a published author, having co-written with *New York Times* critic Ann Powers, a quasi-autobiography, *Piece by Piece, A Portrait of the Artist: Her Thoughts, Her Conversations* (Broadway Books). She was also happily married and the mother of five-year-old 'Tash.'

Whereas in the past, the subject of her miscarriages became a deep topic for balladry, she was now in a position to celebrate motherhood. Still, having never shied away from tough topics, she included grief, adultery, religious hypocrisy and breakups.

Album to album, Tori has scouted out groundbreaking arranging ideas. She wouldn't opt for the prepared-piano concept as she did for the 1994 *Under the Pink* track, 'Bells for Her,' nor would she return to the electronica of 1999's *To Venus and Back*. But she had a definite instrumental blueprint in mind. She explained in a press release, 'The Beekeeper is musically inspired by the fact that the piano has realized that she has an organ – with my right hand on her organ and my left hand on her piano keys, I have been changed by the relationship between these two beautiful creatures, the Bosendorfer piano and the B3 Hammond organ.'

After trudging through America exploring her ancestry on *Scarlet's Walk*, Tori concerns herself with current political events while allocating breathing space to special guests: singer Damien Rice and the London Community Gospel Choir. All concerned are in excellent voice on the almost 80-minute recording of nineteen songs plus a bonus track.

On his website, bassist Jon Evans recalled: 'Playing bass on this record was a trip! So many styles.' Critical reception was overwhelmingly positive; *The Beekeeper* reached the top 10 on the *Billboard* 200: this was Tori's fifth time achieving such an impressive ranking. But unfortunately, she was facing other career issues: Tori had switched from Atlantic Records to Epic, in part to work with then-label president Polly Anthony. But things didn't go as planned: Anthony resigned shortly after Tori arrived, leaving the newly-signed artist to rebuild alliances. To that end, Tori formed the Bridge Entertainment Group to help her colleagues survive a rough patch taking place within the industry.

Then, another major change took place: the following year, Epic/Sony Music Entertainment and BMG Entertainment merged. What would that mean for their artist roster?

Clearly, a major tsunami loomed. *The Beekeeper* would be Tori's second album in a row to not have extra B-sides: a phenomenon that generally guaranteed artists more revenue and greater exposure. B-sides had originally been useful on the vinyl format, but technology had left them behind. With new formats taking over, alternative promotional opportunities took precedence.

There were other changes: 'Not David Bowie' was recorded during *The Beekeeper* sessions, it would not be made available until *Piano: The Collection* was released in 2006.

In addition, the non-album track, 'Garlands,' was also knocked off the project and would appear solely as a video on the DVD of the limited-edition album.

Tori took these unexpected setbacks in stride and set to work exploring new album ideas. Struck by Simon Buxton's book, *The Shamanic Way of the Bee* (2004), she concluded that 'The beekeepers were the parallels to our Native American shamans.' She found herself fascinated by the bee species. On the last day of 2005, she explored their properties on her website: 'They work with a tradition that forces you to look at those places that may need to be stung. And in order for you or I to gain the sweetness ... wisdom does not come without the sting.'

'I've always been drawn to beekeeping, the culture of honey, the sensuality of how it is created; if I see beekeepers, I pull over,' Tori told *Q* in January 2004.

Her next construct was that *The Beekeeper* would lead listeners through 'six gardens of life'. Listed on the back of the CD gatefold, they are: 'desert garden, rock garden, elixirs and herbs, the orchards, roses and thorns and the greenhouse.' The journey here reflected the six days God took to create the world. The number reappears again, as it bears relation to the six-sided cells of the honeycomb, as well as the hexagon, the latter providing a link to the human species.'See, the bee colony is based on a female hierarchy. The honeybee gathers the honey and feeds the hive…' she relayed in *Tori Amos: In the Studio*. She would explore female archetypes in the album tracks, as well as how women are perceived within the patriarchy.

Beyond the celebration of bees, Tori pursued another agenda. After researching Gnostic mysticism from the *Apocryphon of John*, she found herself getting upset about the historical downplay of Mary Magdalene.

Tori had also suffered the loss of her brother, Michael, who died in a car crash. And given the era, she was especially concerned about the heavy influence of the far-right in American politics. In fact, there was no shortage of subjects to write about; Tori has always had her ear to the ground, but through the execution of ideas on *The Beekeeper*, her vocals sounded more seasoned and mature. These lyrics weren't inflammatory; some critics claimed she'd lost 'her edge,' but she still focused on the essentials: cleanly produced, well-structured ballads with beautifully layered harmonies and stories that make people think. She'd been accused of histrionics, but she'd make her point now with carefully chosen words.

She'd also become more musically selective. Jon Pareles of the *New York Times* observed: '*Ms.* Amos had decided she doesn't have to pack every impulse into every song. Sometimes, now, a simple melody and a steady groove are enough.' On 18 February 2005, a reporter from *The Daily Mirror* wrote: '*The Beekeeper* is an eccentric album, a one-of-a-kind blend of soul and gospel flavors, classical flourishes, schoolgirl poetry, flights of choirgirl fancy and toe-curling confessionals.'

Tori's approach was inclusive in that she accentuated the songs with professionals outside of her immediate circle. As such, the London Community Gospel Choir augmented four songs.

'Parasol' (Tori Amos)

Structured like a traditional English folk song, and flavored with baroque-style vocal harmonies and the blazing-hot Hammond B3 organ, 'Parasol' is an awe-inspiring, melody-rich opener.

'Sweet the Sting' (Tori Amos)

Released as the second promotional single, 2005.

'The story started evolving soon after the B3 Hammond organ – whom I have named 'Big Momma' – was delivered,' Tori explains. With the exciting London Community Gospel Choir at her disposal, she swoons and stutters her way through this slick, soulful ballad, teasing her newly acquired instrument with legions of bluesy licks.

'The Power of Orange Knickers' (Tori Amos)

This oddly-titled offering features mellow baritone Damien Rice. Throughout the song, Tori and Damien engage in political sparring, but when they match tones, their voices blend flawlessly. That said, Tori flaunts her own *powerful* feminist petticoat.

'Jamaica Inn' (Tori Amos)

This joyful ballad, with especially bright harmonies, puts a positive spin on Tori's domestic life in Cornwall. But in an album of this size, it sadly gets lost in the shuffle.

'Barons of Suburbia' (Tori Amos)
'Do we fight for peace as they take another piece of us?' Tori inquires. Against a constant shifting of mood and meter, she gets politically heated.

'Sleeps With Butterflies' (Tori Amos)
Released as the first single, 11 January 2005.
Produced exceptionally well, with vocals that are delicate and stirring, this is the lullaby you wanted your mom to play to you – if only she'd understood your persistent wails.

'General Joy' (Tori Amos)
'It seems you need a soldier girl,' Tori sings. The backing vocals: 'Now they have liberty gagged.' The song has a strong anti-war message, with 'General Joy' – who doesn't really seem to love his bride – as a metaphoric foil. But even without verifying the underlying message, you can enjoy the groove.

'Mother Revolution' (Tori Amos)
Tori plays excellent, lounge-style piano, and her vocals are pure and expressive. But 'Mother Revolution' is more than just musical: it's a powerful testimonial.

'I've thought about this a lot since I had my daughter, and what I find really disturbing about this global war is you don't see any of the world leaders sending their children to be butchered,' she told *Uncut* in February 2005, 'Lucky me! I guessed the kind of man that you would turn out to be,' cuts through the hypocrisy of the patriarchy. You can enjoy the sheer musicality of 'Mother Revolution' or posit the underlying theme; either way, it's a revelation.

'Ribbons Undone' (Tori Amos)
Inspired by Tori's young daughter, Natashya Hawley, the story centers around fears children face growing up and the reassurances parents can provide.

'There will be time to chase the sun with ribbons undone,' Tori croons. It is immaculately recorded and clearly a labor of love – Kelsey Doblyn's backing vocals add an elegant touch.

'Cars and Guitars' (Tori Amos)
Released as the second promotional single in 2005.
'If I choke boys, you start me up again....' Tori employs cool, rhythmic vocal tricks during the intro. and beyond, asserting her upper range for dramatic effect. At the 'keep on driving' bridge, roll down the window to break your sweat; it's an exuberant, high-octane ride.

'Witness' (Tori Amos)
With screeching organ, Tori belts out, 'Thought I had a witness.' As her

pitch descends: 'I had life before you left me burning.' After grabbing our attention, she lays back. The contrasts uplift, especially when the gifted choir chimes in.

'Original Sinsuality' (Tori Amos)

For this surreal vision of Genesis, Tori employs startling vocals and memorable piano. She takes chances vocally yet respects the *sonic architecture* enough to abide by the structural rules.

'Ireland' (Tori Amos)

This doo-wop road trip should've taken place in a surrey or a Volkswagen, rather than a Saab, but the 1950s-style arrangement is sheer fun. This lighter fare balances out the heavies.

'The Beekeeper' (Tori Amos)

Performed with sensitivity, the lyrics, 'I'm the one who taps you on the shoulder' and 'I cannot accept that she will be taken from me,' melt the heart.

Tori tackles death in a caring manner, whereby the angel is the hero. Ironically though, the background is not spearheaded by a celestial choir but is instead ushered in on a hotbed of electronics (until the rockin' acoustic outro); but the juxtaposition works.

'Martha's Foolish Ginger' (Tori Amos)

Sparkling piano chords follow steady drum beats. Tori's boat gets star treatment with nautical directive 'the starboard side.' The sense of romantic regret is crystal clear: 'Love taking over your life was not your plan.' Tori's head voice is somewhat sorrowful. This pretty ballad pales in comparison to showstoppers like 'Sweet the Sting' and 'Hootchie Woman.'

'Hootchie Woman' (Tori Amos)

Seemingly buoyed by Evans' incredible stand-up bass line, Tori gets down and dirty. 'He's cheating on me with a hootchie woman,' she cries. Wait, she's not as vulnerable as we think. After all, this badass concludes, 'I've got the bank account because I bring home the bacon.'

When cutting her double-crosser down to size, this glammed-up blues pays enviable dividends, but I'll also put my money on Matt Chamberlain's Afro-Cuban drumming.

'Goodbye Pisces' (Tori Amos)

'There you go again, breaking porcelain….' With excellent enunciation and a sense of cool reflection, Tori ruminates on a doomed relationship. Again, with so many songs, this one runs the risk of being overlooked, which would be a shame.

'Marys of the Sea' (Tori Amos)

'Now, you have hijacked the son,' Tori sings. Why was the truth about Mary Magdalene ignored? Amid blinding percussion, Tori contrasts 'two scarlet women', but she's graced the biblical subject logically. Here's a rare chance to hike up the decibels on an otherwise low-fi album. Tori's not standing on ceremony: with a bee in her bonnet about biblical hypocrisy even before the release of *Little Earthquakes*, why would she curtsy anytime soon? 'Hey, I am not in your way / Hey, no need to push me again.' Stand down.

'Toast' (Tori Amos)

Some insiders suggest that Tori wrote 'Toast' about her brother Michael, who died in a car crash. Although the song is rife with gorgeous imagery, this line chills the blood: 'On your right standing is Mr. Bojangles/With a toast, he's telling me it's time to let you go.'

'Toast' is the most expressive song on the album. Grief is invariably a difficult subject to tackle, but Tori handles tough themes like a trucker in a hailstorm, with eyes on the road ahead, a steady hand and a clear conscience.

Related tracks

Bonus track: 'Garlands' (Tori Amos)

An overlooked and gorgeous arrangement.

Album Art

For the cover, photographer Kevin Mackintosh captured Tori leaning forward, smirking, surrounded by towering flora. Seven glam shots inside the CD booklet show her in varying poses. Song titles are grouped into various *gardens* and each set of lyrics is printed in the shape of a honeycomb. The colloquial expression, 'You catch more flies with honey,' immediately comes to mind.

American Doll Posse (2007)

Personnel:
Isabel: vocals (1, 7, 11, 18, 20)
Clyde: vocals (3, 9, 16, 17); background vocals (5)
Pip: vocals (4, 8, 12, 19, 22); background vocals (15)
Santa: vocals (6, 10, 12, 14, 23); background vocals (3)
Tori Amos: vocals (2, 5, 13, 15, 21); background vocals (20); Bosendorfer piano (1-7, 9-10, 12-23); electric piano (3); Fender Rhodes (7, 13, 23); upright piano (17); Wurlitzer (20); clavichord (22); Mellotron (23)
Matt Chamberlain: drums and percussion (2-7, 9-10, 12-13, 15-18, 20-23)
Jon Evans: bass (2-7, 9-10, 12-13, 15-18, 20, 22-23)
Mac Aladdin: electric guitar (2-8, 10, 12-13, 15-18, 22-23); ukulele (7, 11); electric 6 and 12-string guitars (10, 13, 18, 20); mandolin (11, 19); acoustic guitar (11-12, 15-16, 20); Ebow guitar (22)
Edward Bale, Matthew Elston, Holly Butler, Rosmary Bank: String quartet (9, 14)
John Philip Shenale: string arrangement (9, 14); brass arrangement (14)
Nick Hitchens: tuba; euphonium (14)
Produced by Tori Amos
Recorded at Martian Engineering, Cornwall, UK, June 2006-February 2007
Label: Epic
Release date: UK: 30 April 2007, US: 1 May 2007
Highest chart rank: UK: 50, US: 5
Running time: 78:42

American Doll Posse is Tori's ninth studio album and third release on the Epic Label. The album was released on CD, Vinyl, and CD/DVD. Always the progressive innovator, Tori conceptualized five female characters as the major players, based on Greek mythology. Each boasted a contemporary hairstyle and/or flashy wardrobe, and all performed specific album tracks, which Tori designated based upon the characters' personality traits. But their nine-to-five didn't end there: each doll corresponded to a unique aspect of Tori's personality, and when combined, well, just add Tori for a searing study of feminine complexity.

But a multi-faceted lining lurked beneath the framework. In this case, the goal was that the dolls would chronicle contemporary American stories, but not just generic stories. Tori's vision incorporated opposition to war, music-industry misogyny, sexuality and feminism; topics to which she lit an incendiary flame.

And who better to bear witness to hot topics than a gaggle of goddesses? Isabel – otherwise known as Artemis – represented the goddess of the hunt and was the most politically vocal; Clyde, as Persephone, 'wears her emotional wounds on her sleeve, but remains idealistic'; Pip represented Athena, an intrepid warrior; Santa (or Aphrodite) was denoted as the most sensual of the dolls; and, of course, Tori.

Guitarist, Mac Aladdin; drummer/percussionist Matt Chamberlain; and bassist, Jon Evans, reappeared; rumors circulating that Aladdin was actually Tori's husband, Mark Hawley, were affirmed. Well, mystery spouse reveal or not, Aladdin's ability to play multiple instruments and manufacture roller coaster riffs greatly contributed to the impermeable rock sound.

Bassist Jon Evans asserted: 'There's more distorted bass on this record than any other that I've made.' That mind-numbing distortion drove home a ton of emotions.

Tori's keyboard proficiency has never been debated, but she set the bar high, effortlessly switching between Bosendorfer, clavichord, Wurlitzer, Mellotron and electric, thereby making even a pedestrian arpeggio a centerfold.

With recording sessions beginning in June 2006, the final mixes were completed by February 2007. Before that time, Tori had been grappling with a maternal conundrum: when writing music for *The Beekeeper*, she worried about the effect her lyrical content might have on her daughter Natashya and friends. That said, some critics claimed that Tori had 'lost her edge.' But during a subsequent conversation, Natashya acknowledged the difference between the *public* and *private* mommy; parental guilt need not apply. In fact, Tori's hope was that Natashya's generation would be benefactors of her feminist visions.

Tori elected to air this familial topic with the public. She elaborated on her timing and ideology to journalist Paul Tingen: *www.tingen.org/toriamos07.htm.* 'I'm now taking on subjects that I could not have been able to take on in my twenties. With *Little Earthquakes*, I took on more personal things. But if you are going to be an American woman in 2007, with a real view on what's going on, you need to be brave and you need to know that some people won't want to look at it.'

Tori got considerable flak for 'Yo George' by comparing George W. Bush to King George of England. She also jackknifed into political terrain with the deceptively titled 'Almost Rosey'. But politics aside, *American Doll Posse* revitalized Tori's career. Early fans rejoiced in her return to conventional structure and conversational lyrics. Those that hopped on the bandwagon later celebrated her gutsy vocals and wicked sense of humor.

On the American Doll Posse World Tour, Tori was joined by drummer Matt Chamberlain, bassist Jon Evans and guitarist Dan Phelps.

Note: All songs were written by Tori Amos, but the fictional performer is listed in parentheses.

'Yo George' (Isabel)

'I was very vocal with the song 'Yo George.' I paid a price for that. And yet, I stand by it every step of the way,' Tori told the *Sunday Times* on 14 June 2009. Her detractors focused on these lines: 'Where have we gone wrong, America? / Mr. Lincoln, we can't seem to find you anywhere/Is it just the madness of King George?'

Against pedestrian chording, Tori – as Isabel – airs dissatisfaction with George W. Bush and his hawkish policies. Despite the brevity (1:25), she rammed home her perspective.

'Big Wheel' (Tori)

Released as an A-side single, 10 April 2007, b/w 'Drive All Night.'
Tori snipes and snarls against Mac Aladdin's robust riffs, Jon Evans' therapeutic thumping and Matt Chamberlain's shuffles in this entertaining Americana ballad where southern hospitality flies out the window, as Tori commands the room. This high-energy song was the first single.

'Turn that whiskey into rain,' she exclaims in this all-out swamp rocker. A host of ear-splitting stops precede each digit on a countdown to three. Against that tumultuous guitar riff and irreverent drums, she fiercely declares independence: 'Baby, don't need your cash.'

Tori also directed the video, which is based on a slideshow of her shoot.

'Bouncing off Clouds' (Clyde with Santa on background voices)

Released as the first single, 2007 (Europe); Released as the second single (US).
Tori's belligerent bass notes dominate the 88s, as Evans and Chamberlain masterfully fill in the crevices. Aladdin's tones are vibrant. There's flirtatious interplay between vocals and the electric guitar. The lead vocal sounds welcoming; the lyrics are pop bliss.

'Teenage Hustling' (Pip)

'You think you can come around here?' When Pip gets territorial, all hell breaks loose. What comes next? Bizarre vocal inflection, thrumming bass, and curious instrumental transitions. 'Teenage Hustling' is a far cry from the safe and sound lullabies on *The Beekeeper*.

If Tori *had* lost her edge, she'd gotten it back, using Pip's irreverent authority and finger-pointing lyrics: 'But you've been skanking around with your talentless trash.' The payoff comes when she channels high priestess Ronnie Spector: 'You'd better know, you better know-oh-oh.'

'Digital Ghost' (Tori with Clyde on backing vocals)

This feels very Bad Company/Beatles-sounding with the jangly minor chord sequence; the melodic leaps are contagious. I feel the desperation in the lyric: how the narrator wants so badly to connect with the lover, but alas, this dreaded machine, this 'digital ghost' acts as the interloper. 'The you I knew is slipping away' sounds the ultimate death knell.

'You Can Bring Your Dog' (Isabel)

'You'll be too busy, boy, to sue her for damages.' The stripped-down vocal and electric guitar call-and-response is but one lovable aspect of this party-time rocker.

'Mr. Bad Man' (Isabel)

Wistful on the surface, with a truculent instrumental background, 'Mr. Bad Man' doesn't skimp on detail. For example: 'There's a gold star on a gendarme.' It's structured much like a wry fairy tale – 'So the wolves try to dry her eyes 'cause the bad man made her cry.' For the detail alone, the song deserves multiple listens.

'Fat Slut' (Pip)

Listen to this after the kids are in bed! One fan simply wrote 'Ew.' The good news? This vulgar monologue is another shorty. Where track order is concerned, 'Girl Disappearing' deserves a more poignant preamble.

'Girl Disappearing' (Clyde)

'There was no protection from this urban light….' 'Girl Disappearing' has a distinctive melody and identifiable imagery, all enhanced by Shenale's pizzicato-friendly arrangement. The only thing is, I wish those strings were even higher in the mix.

'Secret Spell' (Santa)

Aladdin's swaggering guitar superbly mirrors Santa's contralto tones. If you need a reminder of how astounding Tori's vocal range is, bookmark here.

'Devils and Gods' (Isabel)

This shorty is appropriately strummed and plaintively sung. But as there are a dozen more songs down the pipeline, this is a good time for that outside smoke.

'Body and Soul' (Pip and Santa)

In the funkiest voice imaginable, Tori belts out 'Come and kneel with me, body and soul.' She lays it on thick in response to a perception of repression. A foot-stomping K. T. Tunstall-type bass line offsets some surefire sugary harmonies. It's spare lyrically, which works just fine, because the instrumental arrangement and Tori's empowering vocal hook go for the jugular.

'Father's Son' (Tori)

Chamberlain's stride and the old-school Fender Rhodes lend a Ray Manzarek feel, bringing to mind The Doors' 1971 classic 'Riders on the Storm.' Even the backing vocals sport classic rock bones, but Tori's performance reflects contemporary times.

Earnestly taking on the role of 'father's son,' and with lyrical maturity, she questions whether spirituality and femininity can coexist.

'Programmable Soda' (Santa)

With the dancing horns and cheery melody, this ditty would've been perfect for The Beatles' *Sgt. Pepper's….* Carefree, constantly moving strings, add whimsy.

Flavorful descriptors belie the deeper meaning: sometimes we adjust too much to others, to our own detriment.

'Code Red' (Tori with Pip on backing vocals)

'Leave them troubled boys all behind,' is the central sentiment. Aladdin adds spit-and-polish with his mid-point and post-finale assaults.

'Roosterspur Bridge' (Clyde)

Every once in a while, Tori takes on *place* as a metaphor, as she did in 'China,' and here too she exposes another world. 'Roosterspur Bridge' represents the renaissance of Tori's lyricism. When she writes lines like, 'I think I understand the fear in the boy, the fire in the man,' it's evident that she has kept that third eye wide open.

'Beauty of Speed' (Clyde)

On this velvety track – where emotions unabashedly escalate – the instrumental and vocals blend to perfection. Thematically, the lyrics may serve as a metaphor for drugs or a relationship that has spun out of control. Clyde teeters on the edge; the latter theory makes sense.

'Almost Rosey' (Isabel)

Released as the third single: an internet-only release through MySpace, 1 November 2007.

Like Don McLean's iconic 'American Pie,' 'Almost Rosey' is a fast-paced montage of introspective imagery. Musically, Tori finds her footing with brassy vocal leaps. The piano part is also in constant motion; the transitions that link the chorus and bridge; unquestionably solid.

Isabel, the keen-eyed journalist, takes command. The lyrics point to an internal struggle; perhaps between men and women or between peacemakers and warriors.

In any event, we're forewarned about viewing the world through a rose-colored scrim. Moreover, 'The blondes don't jump out of cakes,' is a telling line. Tori's disdain for industry sexism may be the trigger. 'Chin up, a happy mask was never your best disguise,' was likely related to her disenchantment with the Iraq War and how the news was disseminated.

'Velvet Revolution' (Pip)

If Jacques Brel and Kahlil Gibran smoked a hookah in a souk, they'd co-write similar lyrics: 'Aye-ee look at the sky and feel the tears of the prophets crying.' Against an oompah rhythm and Aladdin's definitive mandolin, Tori sounds as though she's finessing a French patois. Then again, she may be referencing the 1989 Czech Revolution of the same name or razing that thing called war. But vocally, she's at her Marlene Dietrich/Lili Marlene best.

'Dark Side of the Sun' (Isabel with Tori on backing vocals)
This percussive, warring theme benefits from Aladdin's demonstrative guitar on the bridge and final chorus, plus Tori's unrestrained lead vocal and powerful harmonies.

'Posse Bonus' (Tori)
Tori's repetitious vocals are totally in synch with the 1960s-style rhythm section. Lyrically, 'Posse Bonus' is one of the album's lightest offerings; unless you think 'Porcupine, burrow your way to freedom' is a covert message.

'Smokey Joe' (Pip)
What a study in quirky contrasts! Pip's piercingly high notes quiver against Tori's brooding chest voice. It's sporadic and surreal. At first, I despised it – likening the sound to nails against a chalkboard. Then, I loved it.

'Dragon' (Santa)
An album closer should whet one's appetite for more, and 'Dragon' makes that claim. Tori's vocals are triumphant, and her piano-playing gives goosebumps.

Bonus Tracks:
'My Posse Can Do' (Tori Amos) (available as a DVD on the limited-edition version)
Tori's breathy utterances under the guise of 'Santa' rise above a truculent piano ostinato and playful percussion. The comical presentation belies the clear feminist theme, where she drums up a series of barbs: 'I don't know what you've been playin'' – she sings in the first verse. In the second, her words suggest agitation, although the tone remains whimsical. 'I've got me some better things to do.'

The chorus consists of nonsense words that Tori repeats over the steady tempo. At the bridge, where there's an abrupt harmonic change, she brings a competitive love interest into the fold: 'She can flip her hair / I can flip you off.' Her piano work is also more melodic here; it mirrors her vocals. The electric guitar sequences strongly suggest John Doe of the Blasters.

In a latter verse, she divorces herself from the confines of competitive, romantic relationships to tag: 'a Formula 1 racer,' 'the pope' and 'presidential posts.' She puts her subject on the spot, accusing him/her of suggesting that these themes 'aren't for girls.' By the story's end, she's defined herself as separate from her lover's male-centered universe while also forging a new path: 'maybe this girl got a taste to misbehave.'

'Drive All Night' (Tori Amos)
Pushing fictional characters 'Santa' to the front-of-the-line and 'Isabel' to the back, Tori grants us a radio-friendly, country-inflected road song. We're

immediately ushered in with a guitar-driven intro. Tori's voice remains warm and low during the first verse, but she quickly moves into her evocative head voice on the chorus. When, as narrator, she references the subject, it's with more than a grain of humility: 'He said, 'Girl, maybe I can't play your hero in your last picture show, but I can drive all night.' A stronger image comes up when she claims that he/she 'drives and divides my flesh from your thorn.'

Similar to much of Tori's material on this album, tension sizzles beneath the melody lines and straight-forward pentameter.

'Miracle' (Tori Amos) (B-side to American Doll Posse) (available as a digital download for a limited time)

With Tori as 'Clyde,' the vocals commence immediately and the band is in full-throttle, with Tori's addition of strong chords. The song is also marked by gorgeous harmonies and a mix of regret and optimism: As for the subject-at-hand, 'Miracles,' she writes: 'Could have used one today.' On the bridge, Tori's voice rises dramatically. But in the chorus, she and the band maintain a catchy, poppy sound that pulls the listener back through the compositional vortex. Matt Chamberlain's expert drumming and the electric guitar on the outro. (possibly by Steve Caton) also add an excellent kick. The chorus was extracted from a demo dating back to *From the Choirgirl Hotel* which included 'Violet's Eyes.'

Limited edition copies of the album were ruled as ineligible for the UK charts due to the inclusion of free art cards depicting each posse member. To preserve the existing artwork, Tori did not issue a reduced package version of the special edition, so ranking was affected.

Album Art

Swedish-born, Blaise Reutersward, modeled and photographed The Sex Pistols, The Stranglers, Ramones, and Blondie, before working for *Vogue*. It's no wonder he was able to capture the *Doll Posse* images so vividly. The front cover: Isabel – in a white tunic with flowing sleeves – is holding up a camera; Tori – dressed completely in black – is squeezing a chicken, and Pip – flaunting a shiny white dress with a long sash and thigh-length black leather boots – strikes a catwalk pose. The back cover: Santa, with one hand on the hip, holds a martini glass. Clyde squats on the ground, her long disheveled hair hiding nearly half her face.

The enclosed booklet features additional images of the doll posse, with each proclaiming individuality through wardrobe, makeup, hairstyle and demeanor.

Abnormally Attracted to Sin (May 2009)

Personnel:
Tori Amos: vocals, piano, Rhodes, organ, synths
Matt Chamberlain: drums and percussion
Jon Evans: bass
Mac Aladdin: electric and acoustic guitar, 12-string, mandolin
John Philip Shenale: string arrangements, synths, B3 Organ
Mark Hawley: mixer
Marcel van Limbeek: mixer
Christian Lamb: videography
Karen Collins: photography
Produced by Tori Amos
Recorded at Martian Studios, Cornwall, UK, during the spring and summer of 2008. Final mixing/mastering continued into early 2009.
Label: Universal Republic
Release date: UK: 18 May 2009, US: 19 May 2009
Highest chart rank: UK: 20, US: 9
Running time: 72:03

Tori signed a distribution deal with Universal Republic Records to record two albums. *Abnormally Attracted to Sin* was the first; the second was *Midwinter Graces.*

In the summer of 2008, Tori returned to Los Angeles and reconnected with Doug Morris: the Atlantic Records executive who went to bat for her in the *Little Earthquakes* era. New song ideas had been brewing since the American Doll Posse World Tour, and now, they overflowed, as Tori revisited places (first seen in her twenties) with fresh eyes. She recollected living behind Hollywood's Highland Methodist Church, where she soaked up the sounds of sermons, incorporating the ideas into *Little Earthquakes*.

So much had changed. Tori had moved unquestionably ahead in her career, married and had a child; there were incidents left to mourn, but many to celebrate. Perhaps, with those thoughts in mind, Tori chose to create a truly heartfelt album. With four concept albums bagged, perhaps it was time to look inward, as she had so successfully done on her debut. And she wouldn't be reinventing the instrumental wheel; she'd already established a prototype. She explained to *Buzzine*, 'I've been working with the new keyboards, and ultimately, developing one sound. So, in a way, this record reminded me of the experience that I had {working on} *From the Choirgirl Hotel*, where technology and keyboards and the Bosendorfer were working together in an advanced way.'

Because several songs were highly personal, comparisons have been drawn to *Little Earthquakes*. But Tori's debut was helmed by four producers, and *Abnormally Attracted to Sin* only had one: Tori. That said, the album was unnecessarily long. An outside producer may have had the objectivity to edit where needed.

Drowned in Sound stated: 'Occasionally vague, sometimes incohesive and a little self-indulgent it may be, but ultimately, *Abnormally Attracted to Sin* is an abnormally attractive piece of work and another fine example of the shining talent that is Tori Amos.' *Spin* magazine concluded that: 'Amos writes no less penetratingly than she did on her first album, about the way women navigate the intersection between sex and power.'

The album was formatted as a digital download, a CD and a deluxe limited CD/DVD. The limited-edition came with *visualettes* for each track, which were shot by Christian Lamb: renowned for filming Madonna's final tour. Lamb filmed Tori primarily during her American Doll Posse World Tour, where she dressed as one of the *dolls* in related clothing. Tori promoted the album with The Sinful Attraction Tour, which hit the US, Europe and Australia.

Abnormally Attracted to Sin reached number 9 on the *Billboard* Top 200: Tori's seventh album to achieve that position.

'Give' (Tori Amos)

The percussion recalls loose wooden shutters snapping open during a windstorm. The synth effects are downright frightening, and the lyrics couldn't be more explicit. Tori's voice is wickedly witch-like when she sings, 'So you heard I crossed over the line….'

'Welcome to England' (Tori Amos)

Released as an A-side single digital download, 18 May 2009, b/w 'Welcome to England' (Digital), 'Maybe California' (Album), 'Fire to Your Plain' (Album version).
Parts of the instrumental recall a Philip Glass drone. 'You better bring your own sun, sweet girl,' is a recurring theme, but that seems to only cover what's happening on the surface.

'It's a story about one person leaving their world to go to their lover's world. It's England, but it could be anywhere,' Tori told *MusicOMH*, 9 May 2009. Leaving friends and family behind, coupled with a fear of losing oneself in a relationship, feels very genuine. And there's a strength in this southern woman's voice that suggests she's a little too familiar with feeling like an outsider.

'You lose pieces of yourself behind. Then you wake up thinking, 'Wait a minute. I have to make sure I bring my own perspective and who I am,' Tori told *JamBase*, 25 August 2009.

'Strong Black Vine' (Tori Amos)

With and against heavy-handed 'Kashmir' synth, layered harmonies and abrupt tempo changes, Tori achieves an exciting balance. At its core is a rant against religion-based intolerance.

Shenale recalls: 'I used a Chamberlin, but a lot of it has to do with the pitch-bend and multi-layers in order to get the effect. It's not just one sample doing that. It's multiple samples with different pitch bends; different ending pitches so that it sounds like it's an ensemble doing it.'

'Flavor' (Tori Amos)

'You must pick a side. Will you choose fear?' Tori felt this song was underappreciated, so she revived it for *Gold Dust*. It's a dreamy, lush production with clean percussion. Tori's tone is both angelic and tempestuous. Fans are on the fence about which version is best.

'Not Dying Today' (Tori Amos)

'Neil is thrilled he can claim he's mammalian.' This fast mover is full of colorful imagery. Weird wordplay can act as a safe house when emotions go over the top.

'Maybe California' (Tori Amos)

Released as a promotional single (digital download), 19 May 2009.

Regarding the ballad's central character – a wife and mother who contemplates taking her life – Tori says, 'There's nothing that she can give to stop this terrible emotional cancer that has taken over her family, her life – everything around her.'

Tori addresses how depression and the loss of dreams affect a human in a big city. The lyrics exemplify the far-reaching effects of the insidious Churchillian 'black dog,' as it relates to women, whom she feels 'quietly shoulder the burden of keeping a family intact,' during a crisis.

The production is low-fi, comprised essentially of light percussion, keys, vocals, and tasteful strings so as not to interfere with the essential message.

'Curtain Call' (Tori Amos)

'Right on cue, don't act surprised when they ask you to take....' The title gives away what you came for; Tori's wry spin on fame and the pressures due to what 'the looking glass reflects....'

Tori's contralto is magnetic. The backing vocals alight like whispering wind chimes, and when the song title reappears, the pitch is considerably higher. This epilogue of consequences and commitments is courted by beautiful broken chords and sensitive percussion. It recalls the way Frank Sinatra interpreted the line, 'When I was seventeen...', from 'It Was a Very Good Year,' but is more revealing; it's about the way female performers are sometimes treated as castoffs.

'Fire to Your Plain' (Tori Amos)

This is a light, breezy pop extravaganza. The strategically-placed synth hits and Chamberlain's steadfast percussion add a striking degree of ambience. Tori's voice sounds buttery and seductive. The theme seems to be feminine competition and personal empowerment. '...just buckle up girls/I'm stealing the night.'

'Police Me' (Tori Amos)

In complete contrast to 'Fire to Your Plain,' 'Police Me' is dredged in electronic distortion and Chamberlain's flamboyant fills. It's not just the gyrating time signatures that make this song infectious: the assertive guitar riff that ushers in the second verse is a monster. Tori, too, experiments with spoken-word and smoky inflections.

'That Guy' (Tori Amos)

Tori told *Veronica* on 5 September 2009: 'That Guy' has an orchestral feel from the late-'60s.' Shenale's streamlining made it Broadway/movie-theme-appropriate. He beefed up the modulation with a live string octet. Shenale comments: 'Previously, it was kind of internal, and focusing inside the sound, focusing into a much more personal space, and then it opens up completely when the other instruments come in.'

As for Tori's interpretation – I hear shades of Peggy Lee, Lani Hall and Billie Holiday in her graceful and mellow behind-the-beat phrasing. With its romantic descriptors, this moving character sketch carries a classic American songbook appeal. Tori considered including this ballad in her musical, *The Light Princess.*

'Abnormally Attracted to Sin' (Tori Amos)

Chamberlain's crisp drumming leads this title song on its way. When his sticks crash down on the cymbals, you could swear that he dragged his kit into your living room. This complex arrangement features sweltering counter-rhythms and strains of a bold organ. I wish vocals were higher in the mix; the choral lyrics sound muffled, but I loved the instrumental fever.

'500 Miles' (Tori Amos)

Released as final single, 2009.

I can imagine Fairport Convention covering this song. It's friendly and folky, but not necessarily a kindred soul for the surrounding tracks. Still, I enjoyed Mac Aladdin's acoustic guitar work and the way Tori's piano-playing meshed with her voice. The story conveys a refreshing innocence.

'Mary Jane' (Tori Amos)

'Mary Jane' tempers the tongue-twists of Gilbert and Sullivan and the sweeping melodic lines of Jacques Brel. This is the born-too-late Tori that may have time-traveled from another era; whatever the case, she's invented another fun world.

Thematically, the son tells his mother that he wants to 'discover the realms of the unknown.' The bottom line? 'She even bakes.' 'Mary Jane' is an Odd Fellow on this electronica-laden album, but still, very amusing.

'Starling' (Tori Amos)

'Starling ... screams in black and white.' This contemporary production, comprised of electric and acoustic piano, electric and acoustic guitars, bass, percussion and loops, forms an exhilarating backdrop for Tori's clear vocals.

The repetitive progression and the bridge harmonies got me in the door; I was hoping they'd reappear. The short electric guitar solo was a fiery add-on.

The theme engenders isolation due to romantic jealousy. In a mindful, poetic way, 'Starling' addresses the pain of being shut out of a loved one's life.

'Fast Horse' (Tori Amos)

The sharp, infectious rhythms loop together in the quickly-moving A section. But when the tempo slows, 'Fast Horse' really glistens. Aladdin's 12-string and mandolin play a big part in the overriding texture. Tori's amplified voice hits the spot.

'Ophelia' (Tori Amos)

Tori's in her element when using mythology as a muse. Perhaps using 'Jackie's Strength' as a blueprint, she came up with a sensitive piano arrangement that allows a wide berth for the troubling subject matter. The line, 'Ophelia, you must break the chain,' is meant as a warning and consolation. The father still 'rules from the grave.' The piano accompaniment is stormy and passionate, and when moved up an octave, the tragic beauty swells.

'Lady in Blue' (Tori Amos)

As thrashing ambient sounds canter across off-kilter chordal changes, Tori reaches for the slow burn. Think Lennon/McCartney's 'I Want You (She's So Heavy)' meets Holiday's 'Don't Explain.'

The sped-up, extended vamp – where Tori blends ascending and descending lines – is exceptionally animated. Think reincarnated Rachmaninoff woodshedding with Clapton.

Bonus track:

'Oscar's Theme' (Tori Amos)

Despite Tori's bent toward contemporary electronics, she invariably scores with acoustic piano and up-front vocals. This poetic study packed with strolling arpeggios was the only B-side associated with *Abnormally Attracted to Sin*.

Album Art

From the get-go, Tori conceptualized the album as a largely visual project. For the back-cover photo, fashion photographer Karen Collins shot Tori lying on a bed: her long red hair resting on one hand. In the other hand, she grips a decorative mask. She's wearing a sparkly, tight-fitting gown and silver slippers. Her body is angled in such a relaxed way that she resembles a mermaid. She's looking into the distance, her face with a somewhat melancholy expression.

The front cover reveals only half of this shot. The other stylized shots of Tori in this hotel room are in the CD booklet; the common denominator is that each depicts an aspect of female sensuality as it relates to power.

Live at Montreux 1991/1992 (2008)

Personnel:
Tori Amos: vocals, piano (Steinway and Yamaha)
Jon Astley: mastering
Recorded in Montreux, Switzerland, 3 July 1991 and 7 July 1992
Label: Eagle Records (CD), Eagle Eye Media (DVD)
Release date: UK: 22 September 2008, US: 30 September 2008
Highest chart rank: UK: Did not chart, US: Did not chart
Running time: 90 minutes

Tori Amos Live in Montreux 1991/1992 was recorded live at the Montreux Jazz Festival in Switzerland on 3 July 1991 and 7 July 1992. Both the sixteen-song CD and a DVD were released. The Blu-ray version was distributed on 1 December 2008 in the UK and 9 December in the U.S.

According to the press release: 'Eagle was the first visual music company to embrace High Definition,' thus giving fans an additional incentive for purchasing Tori's concert hits.

For the first concert, Tori was the 27-year-old opening act for The Moody Blues. Their fans had probably never heard of this American singer-songwriter before, but she fared well, got a decent response, and appeared genuinely surprised when she was brought back for an encore. A lifelong Led Zeppelin fan, Tori chose 'Thank you.'

Six months after the release of *Little Earthquakes*, she returned to Montreux as a headliner, and although the setlist was very similar, Tori had blossomed. More in command of her audience, she felt free to ad-lib between numbers or change up one of her classics: even if the audience expected a studio clone.

The promotion wasn't limited to North America and Europe. The double-disc version was also widely circulated in the Latin American market. In addition, a single CD was released in the US and Canada only, which – while it included the 1991 show – was only comprised of six tracks from the second concert. Lest fans feel compromised, the missing three tracks did become available as digital downloads. Finally, with the resurgence of vinyl, copies were made available in the UK and Europe in 2014, followed by additional vinyl pressings for the European market five years later.

The songs are largely taken from *Little Earthquakes*, with the exception of 'Song for Eric' and 'Upside Down' on disc one: songs that Tori originally intended to include in her debut and for which there wasn't enough space. The closer is a cover of the aforementioned Led Zeppelin's 'Thank You.'

Disc two is also mostly comprised of songs from *Little Earthquakes*, with the exception of two covers: 'Whole Lotta Love'/ 'Thank You' by Led Zeppelin (and in the case of the former, the late bluesman Willie Dixon) and the Nirvana cult-classic, 'Smells Like Teen Spirit.'

These concerts occurred at opportune times: the first, several months prior to the release of *Little Earthquakes*, when Tori was just starting to create a buzz; and the second, several months after the fact, when Tori was on her way to acquiring superstar status.

That said, on the DVD, you see her evolve from a somewhat shy singer-songwriter into a supremely confident all-round entertainer who is bold enough to banter with the audience. She even reprimands front row chatterers, knowing the rest of the house will have her back.

In hindsight, these live recordings would be considered legendary career boosters; and over the following years, a bit of a rarity, as Tori's trajectory moving forward would seldom include live recorded works.

Disc One (1991)

'Silent All These Years' (Tori Amos)

Still beautiful after all these years, it's a delight to hear Tori's pure, raw vocals and tempered progressions, with no interference.

'Precious Things' (Tori Amos)

Live, Tori's playing is more staccato, and her vocals more erratic than I expected. Because she's playing solo, she has the opportunity to take her time and ease into the mood.

'China' (Tori Amos)

This live version is similar to the album cut, except Tori adds a few bars in the middle with the lyric, 'You love to hit me, boy!'

'Crucify' (Tori Amos)

Tori inserts a few instrumental bars before plunging into verse one. The internal rhythms are breathtaking. 'You're just an empty cage, girl, if you kill the bird!' Minus the flourishes, the fascinating words come right at you.

'Leather' (Tori Amos)

'This is really different for me, because I usually play in my living room,' Tori confesses. She tells a story that a 'record man' told her: that if she plays this song, she'll 'have no career.' Bring out the easy chair. She sounds like she's in *your* living room.

'Song for Eric' (Tori Amos)

See 'Silent All These Years' single

'Upside Down' (Tori Amos)

See 'Silent All These Years' single

'Happy Phantom' (Tori Amos)
Tori's dynamics and rubato touches are incredibly exciting. She adds a barrelhouse piano feel; her falsetto is fine silk.

'Winter' (Tori Amos)
Sans the debut's orchestral touches, Tori takes on the role of conductor and choir. Her booming bass chords and right-hand staccato attacks do the honors.

'Thank You' (Jimmy Page, Robert Plant)
With reverence, Tori turns this sobering anthem into a proto-punk lullaby.

Disc Two (1992)
'Little Earthquakes' (Tori Amos)
Tori's vocals soar against the halting chords. The B section is where she goes off the rails with a maddening rush of rhythms.

'Crucify' (Tori Amos), **'Silent All These Years'** (Tori Amos), **'Precious Things'** (Tori Amos), **'Happy Phantom'** (Tori Amos)

'Whole Lotta Love'/Thank You' (Jimmy Page, Robert Plant, John Bonham, John Paul Jones, Willie Dixon)
Tori tinkles on the ivories of a Steinway prior to her Bosendorfer endorsement, but her playing still captivates. Rather than attempting to mirror the vociferous rock version sans guitar, she relies on her voice for dynamic contrasts.

'Me and a Gun' (Tori Amos), **'Winter'** (Tori Amos), **'Smells Like Teen Spirit'** (Kurt Cobain, Dave Grohl, Krist Novoselic)

Midwinter Graces (2009)

Personnel:
Tori Amos: vocals, piano, harpsichord, Wurlitzer
John Philip Shenale: strings, synths, samplers, string and brass arrangements
Matt Chamberlain: drums, percussion
Jon Evans: bass
Mac Aladdin: guitars
Kelsey Dobyns: guest vocals ('Candle: Coventry Carol')
Natashya Hawley: answer vocal ('Holly, Ivy and Rose')
Bruce Burchmore: lute
Lon Price: orchestration
Flugelhorn: Tony Kadleck, Bob Millikan, Brian Pareshi
Trombone: Tom Malone, Keith O'Quinn, Dan Levine
Trumpet: Tony Kadleck, Bob Millikan, Brian Pareshi, James De la Garza
Baritone saxophone: Ronnie Cuber
Clarinet: Bob Malach, Lawrence Feldman
Tenor saxophone: Sam Bortka, Bob Malach
Bass clarinet: Sam Bortka
Bass trombone: Dave Taylor
Violin: Bob Peterson, Norm Hughes, Charles Everett, Benedikt Brydern, John Wittenberg, Halm Shtrum, Francine Nadeau Walsh, Calabria McChesney-Foti, Phillip Vaiman, Razdan Kuyumjian, Mark Cargill, Margaret Wooten, Armen Garabedian, Gil Romero, Shari Zippert
Viola: Jimbo Ross, Evan Wilson, Dan Neufeld, Denise Buffum, Harry Shirinian
Cello: Nancy Ross, Armen Ksajikian, Timothy Loo, Giovanna Moraga Clayton, Ernie Ehrhardt
Produced by Tori Amos
Recorded at Martian Engineering, Cornwall, UK
Label: Universal Republic Records
Release date: UK: 9 November 2009, US: 10 November 2009
Highest chart rank: UK Album Tracks: 97, US Billboard Top Holiday Albums: 9
Running time: 58 minutes

The Deluxe edition (as opposed to the standard CD) was available in the US and Canada and included three bonus tracks, a 20-page photo book and DVD.

Tori branded her eleventh studio album – and second project for the Universal Republic label – a 'solstice album,' although it strongly mimics the optimism of a typical holiday recording, and the release date precedes the mistletoe and wraparound lights that would appear a few weeks later. Although five of the dozen tracks are originals, the remaining tracks are comprised of re-imagined, traditional holiday songs.

There's that elephant in the room: some may bristle at the very idea of Tori producing any album that espouses holiday music – after all, isn't this the same songwriter who got demonized for penning ballads like 'Crucify,' 'Father

Lucifer,' and 'God'? But then again, what's that ancient history got to do with bright and cheery melodies, sentimental refrains and triumphant blasts of baroque horn alongside the demonstrative Bosendorfer? Tori explains the meaning behind her 20-year accomplishment: 'I would say that it embraces the rebirth of light, but light means knowledge, light means consciousness. Everybody can attain that and have that in their life.'

She began the arduous writing process during the 2009 Sinful Attraction Tour. The whirlwind recording process took place in the North American coastal cities of Chicago and Toronto, and in England on the occasional day off.

The project was influenced by the aforementioned mentor, Doug Morris, who told Tori in March: 'I'm 70, and I want you to do this.' Although many of the classics had been written 'when things were really puritanical,' according to Tori, Morris encouraged her to view the material through a feminist lens.

Bassist Jon Evans was a major contributor: 'I played mostly upright on this one, as well as my nylon-string acoustic guitar,' he explained on his website.

Many reviews were favorable. *Drowned in Sound* reveled in 'the welcomed return of the long-neglected harpsichord on several tracks.' I concur: Tori executes exquisite timbre. *The Independent* chimed in: 'For a festive album with a difference, it's time to vote for Tori Amos.' *Slant Magazine* served up a sly, back-handed compliment: 'It's an ironic, pleasantly competent oddity.'

The number of players rallied to the cause was astounding – the personnel read like a New York City phone book: fifteen violinists? Three flugelhorns? Guest vocalists, strings, a lute player! *Midwinter Graces* became a celebration of epic proportions. Although the album wasn't promoted as a holiday project, it certainly lit up the tree. There were heartening results, both musically and lyrically. When it comes to anything resembling a holiday album, artists are not ordinarily held to a high standard, but *Midwinter Graces* became the rare bird that exceeds expectations.

Flaunting winsome vocals, sophisticated instrumental arrangements and a generally positive vibe, the album won critics over. Overall, it seemed like Tori satisfied her composer's heart by creating originals but also pleased the traditionalists – she even managed to avoid controversy!

With regards to the originals, though, there seemed to be clones: 'Star of Wonder' suggests a sugar-frosted 'We Three Kings'; and 'What Child, Nowell' marked its territory eons before this release. Then again, the synthesis is a clever one: 'What Child Is This' and 'The First Noel' make for a mighty-fine hybrid. Harmonies are precise and even. Lead vocals are easy on the ear. By eliminating the word salad of the past, Tori did come home for the holidays.

After she became her own producer, the average album gestation time yielded about eighteen songs, causing many fans and critics to question her editorial skills; but *Midwinter Graces* makes a comeback with a modest dozen. In terms of quantity and degree of sincerity, *Midwinter Graces* was a solstice-friendly success.

'What Child, Nowell' (Tori Amos)

For all you linguists, Tori must've already done the obligatory spell-check and a search: 'Nowell' is the British Middle Ages spelling, derived from 'noel', which means Christmas in French.

The verse harpsichord is lovely, and the strings merge effortlessly with Tori's vocal on the refrain. So, if the sleigh bells give you a migraine, have a little mercy.

'Star of Wonder' (John Henry Hopkins, Jr.)

This cover features canons that are airy and festive. It's architecturally sound as well. The years Tori labored over hymnal structures were well-reflected.

'A Silent Night With You' (Tori Amos)

Released as a promotional single, 29 November 2009

I love what Tori did with this song: 'The radio plays my holiday faves,' is how it begins. Further on, she sings, 'It takes me back to when our love was new.'

The 'joy to the world' section builds, as percussive textures come forth, and when the bell sounds are utilized, they accentuate all the right words. All in all, it's a contemporary look at a beloved classic, and Tori does a bang-up job.

'Candle: Coventry Rose' (Tori Amos)

This arrangement is decidedly baroque – which is inherently lo-fi by design – with simple chordal changes and muted ornamentation. The brass section adds an effective counterpoint. Tori sounds like she's reaching the highest point of her range, and production-wise, she could use some sweetening. Her niece, Kelsey Dobyns, adds a welcoming taste of honey.

'Holly, Ivy, and Rose' (Tori Amos)

In the beginning, the cartoonish orchestral effects distract from the main theme. But the seasoned mid-eastern flavors save the day by sustaining excitement. Nine-year-old Natashya Hawley adds a welcoming zest.

'Harps of Gold' (Tori Amos)

'I'll show you how it's done, you'll smile through the pain,' Tori sings. It's a three-ring-circus of sonics but with artful results. The namechecking of Handel's 'Gloria' chorus is delightful, and the recycled word 'echo' – embedded in call-and-response mode – is another compelling touch. 'Girl, take my hand, nothing has changed' contemporizes and rounds out the lyrical humanity.

'Snow Angel' (Tori Amos)

'Snow Angel' contains all the elements of a classic: an infectious melody, relatable word pictures and warmth. At the midway point, the orchestra softly echoes Tori's piano motif, so there's great teamwork all around. I hate to be finicky, but the ending is abrupt: a nice fade would've been easier on seasoned eardrums.

'Jeanette Isabella' (Tori Amos)
The pretty instrumental progression – which begins in the intro and continues throughout – adds a weighted texture that contrasts well with Tori's soprano. 'Night after night, the lights they will guide you.' The lyrics float like first snowflakes from section to section.

'Pink and Glitter' (Tori Amos)
The intense bluesy feel comes as a welcome surprise. Tori's lower range gets quite the workout. She vamps on the phrase 'Shower the world with pink and glitter,' as heavy brass competes.

'Emmanuel' (Tori Amos)
Tori's vocals are the richest they've been on this album. Her rendition is soulful, but the militaristic drumming and synched-up orchestration sometimes overwhelm.

'Winter's Carol' (Tori Amos)
I'm hearing heartfelt and familiar phrasing – the kind that drew me to Tori's early work – but also a hip urban freshness. There's no gimmickry, just subtly-articulated call and response, with a do-it-yourself directive. The dynamics are equally pleasing.

'Our New Year' (Tori Amos)
'I don't know why you went away....' The tone contrasts greatly with the other typically optimistic themes. But a ray of hope, with a toast, occurs by the end: 'Could this be the one?'

Rumors still circulate that the song was written about Tori's brother, Michael, who died in a car crash. It's a curious choice for a closer, but a beautiful ballad nonetheless.

Note: All songs are traditional unless indicated otherwise. All cover songs are reworked, and all contain new lyrics courtesy of Tori Amos.

Deluxe Edition Bonus Tracks

'Comfort and Joy'
The bagel man said, 'What will you have?' This laid-back version of a holiday song screams *The Threepenny Opera.*

'Stille Nacht, Heilige Nacht (Silent Night, Holy Night)' (Josef Mohr, Franz Xaver Gruber, John Freeman Young)
The rollicking piano provides a great foundation for Tori's lilting phrases.

iTunes Bonus Track

'Good King Wenceslas'

This is a glistening version of the classic. It's nice to hear straight-ahead piano without all the fuss and muss. Tori's patient interpretation inspires.

Album Art

Miranda Penn Turin was the album photographer. Clearly, this project was a family affair; Tori conveys that succinctly: 'So the next generation is represented.' Her nephew, Casey Dobyns – a New York model – appears on the front as a suspended angel about to take flight. He's wearing a sleeveless, open-faced vest adorned with billowy white feathers and sports a set of pliable wings. His white jeans are a tight fit. His feet are bare; there's a look of total serenity on his youthful face. His figure rises against a clear sky with powdery clouds.

Other images in the enclosed booklet are of Tori: wearing thigh-high boots and a tailored, two-piece suit, all in eggshell white. Her arms are akimbo, holding up a lantern under a pale moon; a red, Queen-of-Hearts-type collar snug around her neck. Resting against a tree made of deep green leaves, she's a study in black and white: while the eye is first drawn to Tori – with arms snugly wrapped across her shoulders – her multi-shaded robe also commands attention; like her nephew, she is flying, but without the benefit of wings, and in a simple blue dress, with the free-flowing *train*, serving as a makeshift rudder.

From Russia With Love (Live Album)

Recorded: 3 September 2010
Released: 13 December 2010
Running time: 101:01
Material for this exclusive two-CD release was drawn from a live concert recorded at the Crocus City Hall in Moscow, Russia, and was solely available through the Tori Amos online store. The audience was spellbindingly quiet during each song; then, as if on cue, exploded in unison.

Night Of Hunters (2011)

Personnel:
Tori Amos: vocals, Bosendorfer piano
John Philip Shenale: arranger
String Quartet (Apollon Musagete)
Piotr Szumiel: cello
Piotr Szumiel: viola
Pawet Zalejski: violin
Bartosz Zachlod: violin
Woodwind:
Laura Lucas: flute
Andreas Ottensamer: clarinet
Nigel Shore: oboe, English horn
Peter Whelan: bassoon
Luke Whitehead: contrabassoon
Additional vocalists:
Kelsey Dobyns: The Fire Muse guest vocals on 'Night of Hunters'
Natashya Hawley: as Annabelle; guest vocals on 'Snowblind,' 'Cactus Practice,' 'Job's Coffin' and 'The Chase'
Produced by Tori Amos
Recorded by Mark Hawley, mixer
Marcel Van Limbeck: mixer
Jon Astley: Mastering
Dr Alexander Buhr: Executive producer
Label: Deutsche Grammophon
Release date: UK: 19 September 2011, North America: 20 September 2011
Victor de Mello: Photography
Highest chart rank: UK: 27, US: 24; Billboard Top Classical Albums: 1; Billboard Top Rock Albums: 7
Running time: 72:17

Tori earned the status of becoming the first female artist to place an album in the top 10 of the classical, alternative and rock charts simultaneously.

Tori's twelfth studio album came about through serendipity. After decades of conceptualizing and fine-tuning her own projects – including a few that were excruciatingly personal – Tori got an offer that a prodigy couldn't refuse when Dr. Alexander Buhr, of Deutsche Grammophon, got in touch. Dr. Buhr queried Tori about writing a 21st-century song cycle based on rock or pop but using classical music themes.

She would be on a restrictive diet of classical music for a spell, as Dr. Buhr grounded her in recordings of some of the greatest composers of the last 400 years. These A-listers included Pole Frederic Chopin; Frenchmen Claude Debussy, Charles Valentin Alkan and Eric Satie; Austrian Franz Schubert; German Johann Sebastian Bach, and Spanish pianist Enrique Granados.

If Tori agreed to revisit her classical roots, she would undergo a radical interpersonal change: she wouldn't be working with Evans and Chamberlain. On the other hand, she would still enjoy working with arranger John Philip Shenale, with whom she'd shared a twenty-year relationship.She would also switch gears to work with Andreas Ottensamer, principal clarinetist of the Berlin Philharmonic and acclaimed string quartet, The Apollon Musagete.

Tori would enjoy the opportunity to collaborate with family: her daughter Natashya Hawley, and niece Kelsey Dobyns, as vocalists, and husband, Mark Hawley, back onboard for mixing.

Conceptual decisions were set in place. Tori made a commitment to use solely acoustic instrumentation. Of course, she'd have strings and woodwinds to flavor the arrangements, but her voice and piano would be under the hottest lights.

Then, there was the challenge of creating a unique narrative by drawing inspiration from classical compositions and creating her own original pieces and sub-plots. Tori ultimately chose a theme based on 'the hunter and the hunted and how both exist within us' through the story of 'a woman who finds herself in the dying embers of a relationship.'

More specifically, 'Annabelle is the shapeshifting creature and the story is set in (the video was filmed in Kinsale, County Cork) Ireland. It is really going into the myth of Ireland itself, back in time with a lover,' Tori explained to Jerry Nunn of *Windy City Times*, on 16 November 2011. When Nunn inquired about the onstage version, Tori responded: 'The live show is with a string quartet who played on the record; there is a quartet of woodwinds, as well as an octet.'

Natashya's shapeshifting fox/goose Annabelle convinces the protagonist to travel 3,000 years into the past to a disturbing era when the woman and her lover fought 'side by side.' Moving forward, they sail, 'abandoning her world, the new world, in favor of his world, the old world.' The intricate plot ultimately involves a 'peyote ritual': when the protagonist ends her journey, she 'sees the world from a higher perspective.'

Will Hermes of *rollingstone.com,* said on 18 October 2001: 'There are pretty moments: the clarinet-piano duet 'Seven Sisters'; the tag-team vocals on 'The Chase'; the lush closer, 'Carry.' But often it feels like musical theater in need of a stage production.'

Michael Tedder of *avclub.com*, said on 20 October: 'Just describing the album makes it seem like Amos has completely disappeared down the rabbit hole, but *Hunters* is actually her most enjoyable album in years.'

A long-term fan, who disappeared and then jumped back on the bandwagon, felt that Tori had been 'unfairly maligned by musical snobs,' and that this album was the first in a long time in which he'd had a genuine interest.

On 19 September, Jonathan Keefe of *slantmagazine.com*, expressed disfavor with 'idiosyncratic syntax', but went on to say, 'The more direct songs on *Night of Hunters* are genuinely beautiful, and transcend the trappings of the album's rigid construct.'

Chicago-based music journalist, Andy Argyrakis, attended the Chicago Theatre on 10 December 2011, and in his www.concertlivewire.com review, wrote: 'For Tori Amos' latest album and tour, she's turned extra-ambitious to pen a modern-day song cycle inspired by ancient classical works.' Argyrakis was also struck by Tori's 'stunningly gorgeous vocals.'

It seemed unanimous that Tori had come full circle with the completion of this challenging project in which she consistently came up with distinctive melodies. If the ghosts of the classical forefathers ever resurfaced from the graves, I believe, they'd joyfully hum a few bars; Debussy might even request a co-write. *Night of Hunters* demystifies and recalibrates chamber music, into something that the popular-music-minded fan can readily access.

Says Shenale: '*Night of Hunters* is probably one of the deepest things we've done. I mean, the orchestra stuff is big, but it's deep because there were layers of emotion. I loved Tori's piano-playing, and I love the fact that she has great inner-voice work.' Shenale had his work cut out for him: during this time, he also prepared octet arrangements for the two American concerts and for *The Light Princess.*

'Shattering Sea' (Alkan)

Tori's singular notes and sweltering bass expand on Alkan's simple melody, but rather than stay the course; she imbues further turbulence. She sings, 'That is not my blood on the bedroom floor,' after which strings add a coarse layer of angst.

The next interlude is more subdued, as is Tori's singing. Now, it's sounding like a traditional ballad as she echoes her own lines. A swarm of violins lead into Tori's recant. The pizzicato effect is mesmerizing. Tensions build as quickly as they dissipate. A thrill.

'Snowblind' (Featuring Natashya Hawley)

Based on 'Anoranza' from Enrique Granados's *6 Pieces of Spanish Folksongs*, 'Snowblind' features powerful imagery and resounding vocals from the eleven-year-old Natashya Hawley, whose steady contralto belies her age. Tori's pounding arpeggios uphold the narrative.

The original version is intricate with its striking fills, but Tori flourishes her own rendition with controlled dynamics and a lithe, recurring motif.

'Battle of Trees' (Satie)

Revisiting prepared-piano, Tori takes off on Eric Satie's dissonant 'Gnossienne No. 1,' which the French composer wrote in his early twenties. Amid lush cello double-stops and violin pizzicato parts that serve as a spine – yet quickly resolve, Tori spins a web of searing imagery. She borrows liberally from Satie's original melody line – which was recently popularized in Netflix TV series *The Queen's Gambit*.

The truest instrumental moments come when the melancholy strings echo Tori's central piano line. Remarkably – despite a limited use of dynamics – Tori's voice expresses an urgency, with the dramatic lyrics teasing us into a trance. We could argue about which lyrics make the most impact, but for my hard-earned cash, I'd wager: 'Only to be felled by the blade of a vow.'

'Fearlessness' (Granados)

A cacophony leads us in. 'We sailed like the ancient ones.' On the line, 'Teams of horses on the brine,' harmonies erupt. When the lovers part ways, genuine sadness surfaces. The call and response, 'Did you hear me?' emphasizes their desperate plight.

While Granados featured thirds, arpeggios and ornamentation, this version's core consists of droning, reverberating woodwinds and the text's frantic movement.

Shenale recalls Tori's sadness when learning about Granados and his wife's sad end: the composer and his wife drowned at sea.

'Cactus Practice' (Chopin)

This duet between Natashya and Tori could've been set in the poppy fields of *The Wizard of Oz*: close enough, as the storyline involves peyote. The duo asks, 'Will you induct me into the drink of the cactus?' Obviously, that's not a rhetorical question. Tori captures the essence of Chopin's most thrilling nocturne, with descending bass and subtle voicings.

'Star Whisperer' (Schubert)

This time, the call and response come from the orchestra. Tori breaks the word 'sky' up into eons of syllables. In the next section, the celli and violins hold the reins; Tori responds with a full-on, explosive solo. A tender flute sweetens the tale – and it all begins again.

Schubert's composition (Piano Sonata in A Major, D 959) – marked by broken chords – clocked in at eight minutes; Tori's at 9:53. When Schubert wrote this, he knew he was going to die. Did Tori know about this? In any case, the vocals reflect a profound sadness.

'Job's Coffin' (Mendelssohn)

Inspired by 'Nautical Twilight,' this version features Natashya Hawley. With simple text, as opposed to the ethereal nature of the other tracks, her warm, forceful voice hits the spot. She's a youthful Nora Jones/Adele. I can't wait to see where life takes her.

There's major introspection here: 'Why do we women give ourselves away?' Tori's asked this before. Maybe we'll find the answer on the next album?

Mendelssohn favored pretty trills and escalating intervals. Tori followed suit with colorful piano and special attention to dynamics. Orchestrally, a *releve* of strings and rosy clarinet conflate with sunny harmonies. The melodic skips near the end are compelling, but the optimism distinctly comes alive with the lyric: 'She is boundless.'

'Your Ghost' (Schumann)

Shifting from major to minor tonality, light to dark, with a pallet of orchestral textures, 'Your Ghost' is structurally innovative. Schumann's 'Ghost Variations' were spare; Tori's take is far more complex. The composer wrote the piece days before being committed to a mental institution. In both versions, the tenderness is deeply felt. The vocals are plaintive, but purposeful. 'I understand, you've been wounded.'

'Edge of the Moon' (Bach)

As Tori sings counterpoint to the brass, there's a remarkable tear in her voice, tempered by a cross-section of constantly moving lines. Her piano solo against a plucking bass leads us down a path to peaceful harmonies.

'The Chase' (Mussorgsky)

'Out there are hunters, let's say predators.' The oboe enhances the exposition. 'Show her the riddle, it is serious.' The complicated plot thickens: 'Watch me change to a grain of corn.'

Natashya and Tori trade curious phrases; on occasion, they sing in unison. The piano's piggyback passages remain true to the title. Orchestral instruments scramble to find room between spaces.

Mussorgsky's original was a Russian classic, which featured constant interplay between instruments, and this *Night of Hunters* version proclaimed high regard for his vision.

'Night of Hunters' (Scarlatti, Gregorian chant)

The ornamentation is exhilarating. Kelsey Dobyns is the featured vocalist. Scarlatti's original illuminated two independent instrumental lines. Here, the vocal lines collide against mercurial orchestral blasts. Dobyns confidently takes turns with the other players.

'Seven Sisters' (Bach)

Discussing *Night of Hunters*, Tori told Noah Michelson, the Editorial Director of *HuffPost Personal*: 'I always hoped that it would be a ballet.'

Perhaps 'Seven Sisters' was the likeliest contender.' While Bach's original relied on a staccato bassline and undulating right hand, Tori's hypnotic piano writhes against Andreas Ottensamer's clarinet: his instrument flirts and chases her ivories in a suspenseful *pas de deux.* But 'Seven Sisters' also features an unblemished rush of woodwinds. On this sole instrumental offering – and in less than three minutes – these expert musicians sweep us into their fanciful world.

Shenale described Ottensamer as a 'one-take guy,' who, in this case, said, 'Let me try it one more time.' Shenale claims: 'He did it perfectly from top to bottom.'

'Carry' (A variation on 'La Fille aux Cheveux de Lin' by Debussy)
Released as a digital download, 18 August 2011.
In the French composer's original, there is tearful hesitation between phrases. Tori expands on that notion by putting the lyrics in the second person: 'Love, hold my hand….'

The promise, 'You will never be forgotten by me,' ignites universal acceptance. This elegant overture is about preserving our images of loved ones. The piano and strings – along with Tori's vocals – yield warm, healing waves. Furthermore, after all the compositional drama that precedes it, 'Carry' re-calibrates us.

Deluxe Edition Bonus DVD

'Documentary'/ 'Carry' (Music video)/ 'Nautical Twilight' (Music video)

Sin Palabras (Without Words)

The instrumental version was released 13 December 2011. Simon Smith of *higherplanemusic.com*, wrote: 'It's essentially the karaoke version of the album itself,' and 'What is there not to love?'

Album Art

Victor de Mello's cover shot shows Tori, arms outstretched, her long ginger locks gleaming. Standing in front of a roiling lake, surrounded by the Kelly-green Irish countryside, she's entranced by something outside our field of vision. The sky is grey; it has that look of oncoming rain, and the lake glitters with similar shades.

Gold Dust (2012)

Personnel:
Tori Amos: Vocals, Bosendorfer piano
Produced by: Tori Amos
John Philip Shenale: Orchestral arrangements
Jules Buckley: Conductor
The Metropole Orkest
Mark Hawley: Engineer, mixer
Henk Heijink: Artistic producer
Danielle Levitt: Cover photo, photography
Dennis Martin: Photography
Dirk Overeem: Assistant engineer
Sean Mosher-Smith: Photography
Marcel Van Limbeek: Engineer, mixer
Recorded at Martian Engineering, Cornwall, UK
Label: Grammophon, Mercury Classics
Release date: UK: 1 October 2012, US: 2 October 2012, Germany: 28 September 2012
Highest chart rank: UK: 36, US: 63; Billboard Top Classical Albums: 3; Billboard Top Alternative Albums: 16; Billboard Tastemakers: 23; Billboard Top Rock Albums: 25; Belgium (FL): 24, NL: 34
The album either did not chart in Canada.
Running time: 61:08

Surviving twenty years in the music business is a laudable achievement and what better way to celebrate than by getting back into the studio. Listening to the fourteen tracks of Tori's thirteenth studio album is an excellent way to take stock of her essential – and perhaps, most intimate – work since her debut. Having been re-immersed into the world of classical music only one year earlier with *Night of Hunters* – when she created a song cycle from scratch based on past works – Tori likely needed a respite.

Here, she places an illuminating spin on old favorites, harkening back to four must-haves from *Little Earthquakes* and beyond. Tori's exhilarating orchestral debut with The Metropole Orkest took place on 8 October 2010 at Heineken Music Hall in Amsterdam and fueled the decision to rearrange and record *Gold Dust*. The majority of the material chosen was lifted from that performance.

With conductor Jules Buckley and the Metropole Orkest, Tori had the unique opportunity to re-imagine her favorites with fresh orchestral arrangements and minimal overdubbing. As expected with an artist of such stature, she could've anticipated judgments: would the re-imagined cuts pass muster with contemporary fans and critics? For that matter, would dedicated fans allow for change?

For many, the original versions spoke to pivotal moments in their lives: moments that intersected, at times, specifically with a poignant piano progression or profound vocal phrase. I know how this goes, as many of those originals still affect me deeply. So, would such intimate moments get lost in the orchestral kerfuffle?

I was concerned that the most insidious orchestral touches might distract the listeners and cause them to lose interest in the actual backstories: but while a few measures here and there overwhelmed, this was just not the case.

Tori's familial connections feature prominently in these tracks. 'Jackie's Strength' is not only about Jackie Kennedy's bravery during her husband's assassination, but also Tori's mother's heart-stopping reaction to that event. 'Winter' traces paternal lineage, and 'Snow Cherries From France' smartly illustrates Tori's everlasting love for her husband, Mark Hawley.

As for critical acclaim, *American Songwriter* roared its approval of these updated renditions, lauding the album's freshness; while Jonathan Keefe of Brooklyn's *Slant Magazine* suggested that the album 'doesn't really work as a stand-alone project' and that it 'has the feel of a concert album, and is thus inessential to everyone but her die-hard fans.' On the other hand, Keefe concedes that 'Flavor' 'benefits from the new heightened sense of drama.'

On 9 October 2012, Annie Zaleski of avclub.com voiced a mixed reaction about the tracks, asserting that Tori 'doesn't just perform them, she empathizes with them,' and that the 'sonic upgrades to some of her best songs are sublime,' but that, 'with a few exceptions, these new versions rarely improve upon the originals.'

Instrumentally, arranger John Philip Shenale appeared to be the barometer Tori used when deciding upon which albums to draw. As such, *To Venus and Back* (1999) and *The Beekeeper* (2005) were kept aside as roadkill, as neither album enjoyed the benefit of Shenale's astute, orchestral alchemy.

Strange Little Girls (2001) was also a non-contender due to the contents being cover versions of all shapes and sizes and not necessarily conducive to whinnying violins or growling celli. And of course, *Y Kant Tori Read* – despite the legendary bootleg hoopla and eventual renaissance – would always have to fight for a seat at the studio table. God help us if the critics ever forgive Tori for posing on the cover with ratted hair and bustier! 'Flavor' and 'Gold Dust' were two of the more dolled-up numbers. Notable long-form tracks were cut down to a more fashionable and accessible size.

So, what made this album unique? 'On all the records before, I'd never recorded with a string or brass section. You unzip the skin and sing to an engineer. You sing alone,' Tori explained in October to Jenn Selby at glamourmagazine.co.uk. Tori was after a new rush that could only come from 'singing these songs with 56 other people in the other room all listening in, and the control room packed with people.'

'Flavor' (Tori Amos)

Released as an A-side single, 6 September 2012

On *thelineofbestfit.com*, Tori explains: ''Flavor' stepped forward for all kinds of reasons. I think that she was overlooked on *Abnormally* a bit. She took me by the hand and said, 'I have a message."

What the original *Abnormally Attracted to Sin* version loses in terms of an organic feel, it gains in sophistication and purpose. The rising and falling strings and the lead vocal double-tracking allow the lyrics to shine. The embellishments are especially noticeable in the song's second half, where the orchestral touches magically sweep against Tori's melodic lines.

This first *Gold Dust* single also enjoyed life as a remix by Austrian DJ Peter Rauhofer. Deutsche Grammophon released the 28-minute dance recording on 1 January 2012. It included 'Club Mix,' 'Big Room Mix,' 'Old Skool Dub Mix' and 'Club Mix/Radio Edit.'

'Yes, Anastasia' (Tori Amos)

The orchestral introduction is stunning, and Tori's voice retains the haunting nature of the original. Here, the original nine-minute song is halved, so building and resolving suspense earlier becomes a crucial factor: and the orchestral team nailed this. I love how – when Tori's voice rises – the orchestra accents create a hollow din.

'Jackie's Strength' (Tori Amos)

Wisely, Tori's elaborate voicings are ever-present. During the latter part of verse one, the orchestra creeps in discreetly, and thereafter, the instruments wisely punctuate – rather than compete with – Tori's vocal phrases.

During the second refrain, textures deepen, but by this point, we've already settled into the song, so the vivid strings feel natural and more of a structural asset. By the third refrain, I'd feel that something was amiss if the strings jumped ship.

'Cloud on My Tongue' (Tori Amos)

Thank you, orchestra, for leaving Tori's piano front and center. I was so worried! I enjoyed how the orchestra whispered back Tori's phrases; and when the lyrics got repetitious, I enjoyed the novel conversation that transpired. My one qualm was with the crescendo at the final 'circles again' chorus, which sort of left us hanging in thin air.

Tori told thelineofbestfit.com that she included the song 'because it is an overlooked piece of music that I have really grown with.'

'Precious Things' (Tori Amos)

The percussion on the first verse is magical. The orchestra holds back until the refrain. Tori's double-tracked screams sound messed with here, more canned and formulaic than expected.

After Tori sings 'In my peach party dress' and goes ballistic, the strings add a fullness that grew on me. Thankfully, the soul of this epic was retained and expanded upon with care.

'Gold Dust' (Tori Amos)
A tasteful rendering: the harmonies are exquisite and the transitions are dreamy. Tori had the opportunity to finish the last verse without competing forces.

'Star of Wonder' (Tori Amos)
The orchestra greatly enhances the mid-eastern influence at the core of this arrangement. The inventive percussion pushes the story forward, too.

'Winter' (Tori Amos)
I held my breath, murmured a wish and it was granted – Tori soloed for that gorgeous first verse, and when the orchestra entered, it was with much grace and deliberate bursts of beauty. I was also grateful that Tori left her phrasing pretty much as it was in the original. There's so much to take in here that there's little room for random embellishment. That said, when the orchestral solo did commence, it was uplifting and appreciated. Timing is still king.

'Flying Dutchman' (Tori Amos)

'Programmable Soda' (Tori Amos)
The strings, brass and flute create a cartoonish and comical canvas, but the most notable juxtaposition occurs between the voice and strings. It's an uplifting arrangement, but over all too soon. But this was certainly a good opportunity for expansion of a really fun track.

'Snow Cherries From France' (Tori Amos)
This is one of the album's most well-balanced arrangements. The strings don't just lurk; they creep. Tori's pungent bass line is immaculately repurposed.

'Marianne' (Tori Amos)
I wanted this sensitive theme to be treated with dignity, and I was not disappointed. Tori's central piano passages are handled with care; powerful strings enhanced thoughtful imagery.

'Silent All These Years' (Tori Amos)
Verse two was the right time to herald in the violins while leaving enough white space for Tori's nuanced noodling. The overall counterpoint is also effective. The newly-arranged vocal harmonies sweeten the mix; the slight dissonance midstream somehow doesn't feel forced.

'Girl Disappearing' (Tori Amos)
This is a beautiful closer, and works exceedingly well with lush strings. The brass can be distracting, but what's really bewitching, is how the orchestra underscores the harmonies.

Album Art

Danielle Levitt captured the contemporary Tori for this shoot. When the star peers out of the open window of a big yellow taxi, her expression is so welcoming that you want to ride shotgun. There's Tori in her black leather, against a tagged background; Tori seated, alone, at a coffee shop, surrounded by urban locals; and Tori gripping her bike's handlebars in front of a bustling marketplace. Then, alongside lively New York baseball fans, she poses in a stylish outfit with skintight boots. It's like having a personal tour of the city without braving the gridlock.

Unrepentant Geraldines (2014)

Personnel:
Tori Amos: vocals, Bosendorfer piano, Hammond organ, Wurlitzer electric piano, Mellotron, Fender Rhodes
Mac Aladdin: guitars
Mark Hawley: additional instrumentation, producer, mixer, programmer
Natashya Hawley: vocals on 'Promise'
Karen Binns: style and concept
Marcel van Limbeek: producer, mixer
Amarpaul Kalirai: photography
Desmond Murray: hair
Nora Nona: makeup
Matt Read: package design
Adam Spry: chief technician
Ann Walker: piano technician
Produced by: Tori Amos
Recorded at Martian Engineering, Cornwall, UK, July 2012-May 2013
Label: Mercury Classics
Release date: UK: 12 May 2014, US: 13 May 2014 (In the US, the format was vinyl and digital download; in the UK, the format was CD and DVD)
Highest chart rank: UK: 13, US: 7
Running time: 59:24

Tori spent more than five years renewing her creative energies before making *Unrepentant Geraldines*. She'd written an original musical – *The Light Princess* – performed with a big band and orchestra and re-arranged and re-recorded compositions. What was left?

Or maybe the answer is that 'less' – as architect Ludwig Mies Van der Rohe pointed out – really 'is more.' Previous albums like *Gold Dust* and *Night of Hunters* were production extravaganzas that challenged Tori in an affirmative way. But by the same token, they enabled her to put up the fourth wall, and because many fans were clamoring for the *old Tori*, *Unrepentant Geraldines* came along at exactly the right time. She had, undeniably, garnered admiration in the classical world. But the idea of hearing fresh Tori material, featuring vocals up-front and center, echoed by purposeful piano and first-person observations: well, just that thought, gave fans goosebumps.

Andy Argyrakis covered the Chicago Theatre concert of 5 August 2014, when Tori opened with 'Parasol.' Leaving with a favorable impression, he told concertlivewire.com: 'Any place Tori Amos turns up, becomes a scene of angelic enchantment.'

In hindsight, *American Doll Posse* granted Tori permission to be a holy terror of an extrovert, and it really was fun to examine the different aspects of her complex psyche, in concert and via the record.

Midwinter Graces was a festive, songwriting hybrid. But being released close to the holiday season, it came off as somewhat formulaic; fan appetites were craving genuine introspection. Tori hadn't written an entire album of originals since *Abnormally Attracted to Sin* in 2009. It was high time. But as always, she needed a muse. And this time, that muse would come to her through the discipline of visual art. Tori explained to *Rolling Stone:* 'Through the visual artist's application of tone, shape, pattern and pigment, I not only begin to see, but I can honestly say I began to hear.'

Being no stranger to intensive research, Tori was especially drawn to ancient works of art: such as Cezanne's 1870 painting, *The Black Marble Clock*. A drawing of a nineteenth-century wood carving for a songbook by Daniel Gabriel Rossetti inspired the song 'Maids of Elfen-Mere.' In a Spotify commentary in 2014, Tori claimed that after she spotted the image, 'I started hearing the maids singing to me, and I started wondering what their message would be, then, and in the 21st century.' Additional visuals would similarly beckon. Tori's instincts were spot-on. The album reached the *Billboard* top ten: the first time since the release of *Abnormally Attracted to Sin.*

But why the unorthodox album title? In essence, Tori's fourteenth studio album is an effervescent toast to feminism, as it's about acquiring agency and refusing to apologize for one's actions and beliefs. This concept album pretty much mimics Tori's trajectory. Paying her dues had not always been easy: it had meant negotiating with multiple record labels and skating on thin political ice over the course of her career, Tori has had to butt heads over creative freedom. How unrepentant is *that?* And perhaps this album would serve as a clarion call to other women facing difficult challenges.

While critics sparred over which aspect of *Unrepentant Geraldines* was the best, most agreed that the album was a winner. Dave Thompson of *The Guardian* said on 8 May: '*Unrepentant Geraldines* is more likely to thrill old fans rather than win new ones, but her voice has rarely sounded as powerful or pure.'

On 15 May, Caitlin White of *time.com* and with *Consequence of Sound* had this to say about Tori's work: 'Although her lyrics on this album deal heavily in legendary and fictional elements, it also feels like they're more connected to Amos' own life than anything she's written before.' White goes on to say, 'Amos manages to weave her own mythology into larger fantastical stories, and fight societal norms in the process, all with a fierceness that will please old fans and likely win over new ones.' Alex Macpherson of *thequietus.com,* said on 3 June: 'Amos seems more at ease with this than ever before.'

Skeptics agreed that if it had indeed been lost, Tori had regained her footing. True believers wagged their fingers as if to say, 'I told you so.'

Touring in tandem with the release of *Unrepentant Geraldines* (a tour which began in Ireland on 5 May 2014 and ended on 21 November 2014), Tori reiterated her support for LGBTQ rights worldwide by taking a stance against homophobia in Russia. At the Crocus City Hall, Moscow, she covered 'Not Gonna Get Us' by the openly lesbian duo, t.A.T.u.

'America' (Tori Amos)
'Once they wake from their rest,' refers to the rampant political divisions in the U.S. that Tori observed then and that still exist now. Early on, she cites 'the other America….' Tori doesn't rile fans up through her tender vocal quality or lilting phrasing but through pacing and insightful, dynamic lyricism. There are shades of *Scarlet's Walk* here – Tori's political views come off as intelligent and persuasive, but not abrasive. Musically, Mac Aladdin's acoustic guitar pulls the complex structure together without a hitch.

'Trouble's Lament' (Tori Amos)
Released as a promotional single, digital download, 28 March 2014.
This lead promotional single was sent out as a digital download, and what an excellent choice that was! Living in Cornwall simply can't eradicate the soul of a southern girl. When Tori sneers 'Trouble needs a home, girls,' and proclaims that the subject 'fell out with Satan,' she's a punchy PJ Harvey. On the edge is exactly where 'trouble' wants to stay. The spirits of Duane Eddy and Johnny Cash manhandled their way into the chunky strums and moaning bass lines; the percussion is swampy and contagious.

'Wild Way' (Tori Amos)
When a songwriter begins a romantic ballad with the phrase, 'I hate you,' even the most blasé ears will perk right up; but the explanation is just as powerful. This is an incredibly gorgeous song, in which Tori takes stock of her marriage: 'Don't forget you were the one who loved my wild way.' She explains: 'When I sang it, Mark was on the other side, on the controller, and when I walked in, he had tears in his eyes, and he said, 'That's a take. And I hate you too, wife, I hate you, too.'

Instrumentally, there's little to hate: Tori lays back on the piano, luxuriating in the art of simple chord outlining. Her vocals are pure, and her storytelling couldn't be more transparent. To me, this is Tori's finest Harry Nilsson moment.

'Wedding Day' (Tori Amos)
This baroque arrangement is sublimely romantic. 'I run back to your arms again,' Tori sings, against keen electric guitar. 'I swore angels were born,' she continues in that same vein. 'Now I take off the mask….'

'Weatherman' (Tori Amos)
This portrait study is intricate in all possible ways: lyrically, instrumentally and thematically. He knows 'every curve of every hill,' Tori marvels against infinite arpeggios. She's an integral part of the scene: 'I'll be dressing up in snow.' The repetitive choral refrain is striking. Tori's piano riffs flow as freely as the moving words.

'16 Shades of Blue' (Tori Amos)

'Are you telling me it's over?' The underlying theme is the aging process, but on the surface, there is a ton of musicality. This smoky ballad is flush with vocal harmonies, rock-solid bass and random ripples at the ivories. Tori used the artist Cezanne, as her primary inspiration, so it's an extremely visual piece of work.

'Maids of Elfen-Mere' (Tori Amos)

Using her voice as a pulley, Tori draws us into a nirvana, where the maids 'watch over the boy with chestnut hair.' The harmonic changes are jagged – the vocals, mellifluous.

'Promise' (Tori Amos)

'Promise not to judge,' 'Promise not to take,' but at the same time, 'be there.' This is probably what we're all seeking in an idyllic, familial relationship, but Tori maps it out efficiently. In the video, she duets with Natashya, and their blend is as appealing as their separate parts. I can't recall other songs in which a mother and daughter express future desires this way; it's special.

'What happens when a mom and daughter don't even get to the point of talking? They don't even get that far because the walls come up,' Tori told *CBS Sunday Morning* on 3 August 2014. Tori and Natashya did not merely analyze their inter-generational dilemma, they arrived at the solution through music.

Listen back to 'Playboy Mommy' from 1998's *From the Choirgirl Hotel* to get more perspective on Tori's personal history.

'Giant's Rolling Pin' (Tori Amos)

With digs at the 2013 NSA surveillance scandal – 'Everybody spies, so why the big surprise?' – and a 'Maxwell's Silver Hammer' zeal, Tori fuses a fun, quirky soundscape and sobering politics. The litany of sound effects is a hoot.

'Selkie' (Tori Amos)

Tori injects a tearful humanity into this age-old myth. The pacing is spot-on; she takes her sweet time with the vocals and the complex piano arrangement.

'Unrepentant Geraldines' (Tori Amos)

'I'm gonna free myself from your opinion.' The title song hits all the spots: it has a cool, poppy, confident rhythm, a virulent viewpoint, turbulent piano, and an infinite swirl of pretty vocals.

'Oysters' (Tori Amos)

Tori's melodic piano trails each vivacious vocal phrase. 'Oysters' serves as an extraordinary palette for her multi-octave range. It's a song about coming to terms with one's demons: a common theme in her discography. The beautifully sung, recurring phrase, 'I'm going to turn oysters in the sand,' could be a metaphor for facing challenges.

'Rose Dover' (Tori Amos)

This complex, fugue-like arrangement actually carries a simple message for today's youth: 'You don't have to throw it all away.' As sonic narrator, Tori is the proverbial *Catcher in the Rye*, saving the youth from becoming jaded adults. This is about believing in one's imagination, even when the cost is dear.

'Invisible Boy' (Tori Amos)

'You could go under cover, make your great escape.' Another anthem of encouragement for those who soldier on but never get a byline. The plaintive piano is of the Broadway musical variety. Tori's vocal is echoed, but other than that, it's unfettered.

Bonus Tracks

'Dixie' (Tori Amos) (Amazon bonus track)

In homage to her mother, Mary Ellen, Tori wrote this simple but moving ballad. The piano interludes are embracing. Tori uses imagery to evoke touching memories. For example, 'Without any fingers, the peach ones,' refers to a pair of gloves. She repeats the line, 'holding my hand,' perhaps as a metaphor for the unconditional love she received during her southern childhood. With utmost sincerity, she describes herself as 'the richest girl in Dixieland.'

'White Telephone to God' (Tori Amos) (iTunes bonus track)

In only 2:17, Tori disseminates a great deal of information. 'Do we have to get older?' she inquires. The immediate answer: 'We do.' The structure is that of a call and response, in which the response imbues warm harmonies. 'When the white telephone rings, it's him,' she exclaims. She ticks off a series of high-caloric but satisfying foods that might lead one to an early death. This is one of Tori's lighter songs about the grim reaper, but definitely a fun one.

'Forest of Glass' (Tori Amos) (Deluxe edition bonus track)

'Steal me away from where I stand although I'm kneeling down on the ground,' Tori pleads. Come the bridge, lovely harmonies replace her lead vocals. With the piano, she creates a fragile counterpoint. At the chorus, syllables are stretched out with abandon: 'If you love him, you will follow.' Finally, her romanticized version of love is fiercely challenged: Will she follow her lover when the stakes are high? Even to his 'forest of glass?' Live, Tori uses both acoustic piano and synthesizer to establish and continue the undulating background. In promotional interviews, Tori has said: 'Making art cannot be a job. It has to go beyond that to be great.' On this song, where she freely experiments with imagery and vocal structure, her efforts show.

Deluxe edition DVD contents

'Album Trailer'/ 'Interview with Tori'/ 'Studio tour'/ 'Album photo shoot'.

Album Art

Canadian art director and fashion photographer Amarpaul Kalirai's name boasts associations with Hermes, Burberry and Topman. When he masterminded the cover image, he made sure that every element of the composition was established in harmony.

To that end, Tori is dressed in plain clothes, most notably a long-sleeved, blue denim shirt. She poses against a giant-sized replica of the cover, a white canvass decorated with splotches of eye-catching paint and oversized letters. Tori's petite frame hides the complete set of words, but what peeks through looks like: 'laugh' and 'sleep.' A glance at Kalirai's website reveals that he has a profound respect for his models. In all of his images, their personalities shine through. This shot is similarly constructed. Tori is posed but focused. Her stance is confident and she looks straight into the camera. She looks calm and in the moment.

The back cover contains more scrawled letters, but without Tori's presence. A few distinctive words pop out, though: 'bomb' and '16 shades of blue.' With Tori's artistic vision at the helm, Kalirai's vision serves as the perfect companion.

The Light Princess (Original Cast Recording) (2015)

Label: Universal/Mercury Classics

I'll briefly touch on this project, as it was a one-off. In 2013, Tori collaborated with Samuel Adamson on a musical entitled *The Light Princess*. Unlike *Night of Hunters*, Tori had not been asked to create the storyline from scratch, as the book was based on George McDonald's Scottish folk tale. Tori wrote the entire score, but she and Adamson collaborated on the lyrics. The plot breakdown is complex, but the basic idea is that the protagonist – Althea – is at odds with the gravitational force; she can't keep both feet on the ground – that is, until she falls in love with Prince Digby.

The musical premiered at the Royal National Theatre in London in 2013, but the cast recording of this London production was not released until October 2015. Time was tight; after all, Tori was committed to the *Unrepentant Geraldine's* Tour, and the making of that album in 2014. Work had to be completed on various stops along the way. As such, Tori relied on Mark Hawley and Marcel van Limbeek to oversee the production. They had already recorded the orchestra in April; no small feat with such a huge cast. The recording project was a colossal undertaking, resulting in 30 original tracks, plus three bonus tracks; two sung by Tori.

Simon Edge of the *Daily Express* said of Tori's contribution: 'stirring and sweet music by Amos,' and 'Tori Amos' musical is a wonderful, unforgettable feast for the senses.' *The Telegraph*, however, commented: 'Amos' music is lacking in standout numbers.'

Album Art

The album cover shows the barefoot, fictional protagonist, Althea, with her tulle skirt flying as she attempts to ground herself by standing on one leg. Red shoulder-length tresses cover her eyes, and her trim arms – stretched out on either side – offer another means of staying *weighted*.

Native Invader (2017)

Personnel:
Tori Amos: vocals, Bosendorfer, Hammond, keyboards, programming
Mac Aladdin: guitars
Mark Hawley: programming and additional instrumentation
John Philip Shenale: synth programming and additional keyboards on 'Mary's Eyes' and 'Reindeer King'
Tori and Tash: vocals on 'Up the Creek'
Ann Walker: Piano Technician
Paulina Otylie Surys: hand-colored photographs
The Glams:
Style and Concept: Karen Binns
Hair: Desmond Murray
Makeup: Michelle Rainier
Package Design: Matt Read at Combustion
Produced by: Tori Amos
Recorded and mixed at Martian Engineering Studios, Cornwall, UK
Engineers: Mark Hawley and Marcel van Limbeek
Assistant Engineer: Adam Spry
Mastered by Jon Astley at Martian Engineering, Cornwall, UK, 2016-2017
Assistant Dog: Pete
Label: Decca
Release date: UK and US: 8 September 2017
Highest chart rank: UK: 16, US: 39; Billboard Alternative Albums: 3, US Top Rock Albums: 6
Running time: 61:48

Native Invader, Tori's fifteenth studio album, signified a transition to the Decca Records label. It was during a *Billboard* interview that Tori first announced plans to do a promotional tour for a new album of unique original songs. She left out the specifics, perhaps to create a sense of mystery, but the album was much-anticipated.

During that spring, she used Instagram to post visual hints depicting a studio and a 'sacred fire.' On 23 April, her website provided the details. An important concept entailed finding 'different ways of facing unforeseen challenges, and in some cases, dangerous conflicts.' Tori's major thesis, concerned humans and their relationship to nature. She outlined the laudable goal: 'Sonically and visually, I wanted to look at how nature creates with her opposing forces, becoming the ultimate regenerator through her cycles of death and rebirth.'

However, Tori switched conceptual gears in the summer of 2016 after taking a road trip to the mountains of Tennessee and North Carolina: the latter, of course, her childhood home, where she'd been privileged to live among serene woodlands and was privy to familial stories. She went there to reconnect with her maternal family; but that winter, her mother, Mary Ellen, unexpectedly suffered a stroke, which set Tori into a tailspin of grief. That incident coincided with the U.S. election of Donald Trump. At that point, Tori's creative agenda was destined for change. 'It wasn't going to be a record of pain, blood and bone when I began,' Tori lamented on the album's press release. But she did hope that the project would facilitate healing.

As typical of her work ethic, she studied the experts prior to putting pen to paper. She told Sara Morosi of *The Wall Street Journal* on 14 August 2017 ('Tori Amos's Favorite Things'): 'The books – Robert Graves' *The Greek Myths* and Joseph Campbell's *The Mythic Dimension* – were pivotal research for the new record.' She also took to heart the teachings of Carl Sagan.

Working with Dr. Alexander Buhr for *Night of Hunters* and on her original musical *The Light Princess* between the years of 2011 and 2013 enhanced Tori's understanding and appreciation of the classical form, which is, perhaps, another reason why her most recent album features such elaborate and finely structured arrangements.

Critics nitpicked about individual tracks, but reviews were primarily positive. Neil Z. Yeung of *AllMusic*, observed: '*Native Invader* stands tall with its own vital voice and energy, alluding to beloved touchstones from throughout Amos' oeuvre while remaining fully of its time.' On 7 September, Emma Madden, of *drownedinsound.com*, wrote: 'What makes *Native Invader* a work of genius – a kind of great American novel, perhaps – is that it seamlessly blends the personal, political, natural and cosmic, into the same story.' On 8 September 2020, Nicola Rayner, of *udiscovermusic.com*, wrote: 'Tori Amos meant business on her 15th album, *Native Invader*: a work of great beauty, that's built from love, fury and personal and political despair.'

It's easy to draw comparisons with 2002's *Scarlet's Walk* due to the political machinations, a tendency to focus on multiple, sobering themes, and the singer-songwriter's deep regard and affection for rustic, physical landscapes.

Then again, *American Doll Posse* certainly didn't minimize Tori's wrath at George W. Bush – Tori explicitly expressed her political angst in both the latter and the current project at hand.

Overall, *Native Invader* solicits a musical nod to *Little Earthquakes*, particularly when Tori shucks away the gizmos, and returns to the fundamentals that fueled her stardom.

Of course, having had frequent exposure to right-wing lobbyists as a teen playing the Washington, D.C. piano bar circuit, Tori had developed an acute radar for political hyperbole. As we've seen, she's incorporated her political views on some albums more than others, but some of the strongest opinions feature here.

On the Native Invader Tour – where Tori played solo – she took in Europe and North America, beginning on 6 September 2017 in Cork, Ireland, and ending on 3 December in Los Angeles, California. The American tour alone accounted for 30 concert dates, but for all of the 49 shows, she relied on trusty friends: the Bosendorfer, plus a Nord keyboard and organ.

Says Shenale: '*Native Invader* is a fusion of both electronic and acoustic-sounding instruments. We didn't have the ability to use live players, and it wasn't really necessary.'

Native Invader was voted one of the Top 10 Best Albums of 2017 in the *Rolling Stone* poll.

'Reindeer King' (Tori Amos)

Released as the final single, 25 August 2017.

This is a seven-minute-plus opus for melting polar icecaps, where the thundering instrumentation imitates the mournful sound of icecaps calving. The related video intersperses shots of wolves and stark snowdrifts as lyrics roll across the screen. The thought-provoking imagery acutely echoes the printed lyrics: 'Crystal core, your mind has been divided from your soul.' After the lingering lead-in, more imagery tumbles from Tori's lips.

In this song of heartbreak and high stakes, the narrator longs to 'skate all the way just to hold your hand.' But the most magnetic line – 'Gotta get you back to you' – reveals even more about unbearable grief: 'Reindeer King' was written after Tori's mother, Mary, survived a stroke, and could only communicate with her eye movements, after which time, Tori sought out a shaman.

Although we can't directly experience Tori's pain, we can approximate her grief, through her phrasing. She carefully enunciates each word, and when she breaks a single syllable up into six segments, it seems she is hanging on to every utterance, for dear life.

Instrumentally, there's a predictable heaviness in the low-pitched piano tones and the celestial cello. The electronic effects are mesmerizing, especially the addictive ostinato.

As in 'Bells for Her,' these unique effects move the story forward with grace. Shanele used 'a lot of natural sounds, modified. I tracked her bass on the piano, with a Moog sound.'

'Wings' (Tori Amos)

'You've been suffering, hiding your pain,' the lyric begins. After setting the contextual stage, Tori's voice rises in pitch, and the backing vocals kick in for support. The programming, which, in texture, is tinny against her pure pipes, anticipates every thought.

'Broken Arrow' (Tori Amos)

Although it begins with a surprise wah-wah and a bluesy guitar vamp, don't expect a jam session to follow. 'Broken Arrow' is definitively a political song. 'Have we lost her?' Tori inquires. 'Are we emancipators or oppressors of lady liberty?'

'Broken Arrow' targets America's foremost institutions – 'our Senate' and 'the House' – and demands righteous responses. But along the way, Tori chimes in with visions of North America's physical beauty: i.e., the 'Great Lakes' and 'the Badlands.' Heading toward the outro, the percussion feels frenetic and insistent, thereby recapitulating the songwriter's grievances.

'Cloud Riders' (Tori Amos)

Released as an A-side single, 28 July 2017.

In complete contrast, 'Cloud Riders' has an easy-listening vibe that belies the central message: 'a dead calm before the storm.' This song is, sadly, about suicide and possibly connecting with the victim once more. Tori's vocals grow sharper and sharper at each turn. Fortunately, the whispering hum of the Hammond organ and light strumming allow them to shine, but it's also delightful to hear the acoustic guitar and organ interact during the extended outro.

At the chorus, the tone lightens: Aladdin's guitar reverberates with arpeggios, and there's an early 1960s girl-group feel to the rhythm and content. Lines like 'under the blue stars' smack of primal innocence. There are fascinating images here: 'A chariot pulled by cats purring/Will be returning from the other side.' Essentially, Tori fuses clever poetry and heartfelt emotion.

'Up the Creek' (Tori Amos)

Released as the second single, 11 August 2017.

Tori peppers this song with a phrase spoken by her beloved maternal grandfather: 'Good Lord willing and the creek don't rise.' It was her wish that Natashya should connect spiritually with the great-grandfather she'd never met.

This is one of the album's best arrangements. It's as if Jah Wobble, Ringo Starr and Joe Bonamassa had an impromptu session and asked Tori to front. Elements of classic rock and Delta blues form the instrumental bones.

The resounding phrase is 'desert sister.' Natashya's mature contralto sharpens the harmonic turns. The easy-going feel is infectious. But at 2:21, Tori's piano – which had been restrained amid the cacophony – explodes. That vivacious energy drums up memories of *Choirgirl*.

'Breakaway' (Tori Amos)

If Tori's *modus operandi* was to clone an operatic aria, she came awfully close. There's absolutely nothing to trim in this rich and very present track. Fans that disregarded her experimental and male cover-song phase will embrace the return.

'Siding with the soldiers who say, we cannot win the day,' is, first of all, a muscular opening line. Structurally, she starts out as the omniscient narrator, then switching to the second person for a more personal touch: 'You feel betrayed. I feel played.'

The gorgeous piano introduction recalls a Chopin ballade. At specific cadence points, Tori uses bright, suspended chords. This anthemic song also whittles its way through three tempo changes – 4/4, 7/8, 9/8 and back to 4/4 – and a myriad of keys. A succession of pretty grace notes tops it all off like twinkling candles on a birthday cake.

Vocally, Tori's tone is clear and stately, but the last few bars are reserved for the real diva: her liquid 88s. In a return to form, her piano-playing radiates warmth and reason.

'Wildwood' (Tori Amos)

The Greek goddess, Demeter, longs to reunite with her abducted daughter, Persephone. Inspired by Greek mythology and nature, Tori romanticizes rustic woodlands, 'Alders and the Oaks' and 'the pilgrim's path.' Clinically, drum loops season the sonic landscape.

'Chocolate Song' (Tori Amos)

The early bars of electronic music are as eerie as the wail of a hungry seabird. A sudden rhythmic shift and layered backing vocals in the 'I don't hate you' section create a balance.

'Bang' (Tori Amos)

Tori uses astronomy as a metaphor for the debate on illegal immigration. A big fan of Carl Sagan-isms, Tori infuses such lexicon – 'molecular machine' and 'star stuff' – into the lyrics, ending by ticking off essential elements: magnesium, chromium, cobalt, etc.

'We all are molecular machines, goals and dreams,' she concludes. Without being preachy, this is a positive song that explores our human potential and our obligation to achieve and excel given our unique human DNA. It's a celebration of our complex surface composition, but more importantly, a cry for inclusivity.

It's unique, stylistically. We've heard Tori scream, scat, draw out vowel sounds until we believe her vocal cords will snap, whisper and purr. Here, she presents a light rap.

'Climb' (Tori Amos)

On this ballad, Tori's voice is a penetrating salve. The lyrics are direct: 'Climb over the church wall' and 'You can feed the koi in the pond.'

Similar in harmonic structure to 'Past the Mission,' the story starts with open-voiced piano chords. As the story progresses, lyrics grow more personal: 'Wrap yourself in linen, holding Jesus close' and Tori's vocal machinations get more pronounced and complex. Thematically, she doesn't stray from the dominant fray: 'Only when you hold, can you forgive.' 'Climb' is a validation of feminine authority.

'Bats' (Tori Amos)

After a dreamy introduction, Tori tackles the lead vocal, accompanied by echo-driven backing vocals: which, although we know they're well-planned, seemingly appear at random intervals.

Her recurring themes are trance-like and hypnotic. It's as though she's channeled Steve Reich or Philip Glass. In any event, this minimalist approach gives 'Bats' a singular edge.

'Benjamin' (Tori Amos)

Singing over antiquated blips and bleeps, Tori enlightens or reminds us (depending on our age) – about the case of Juliana vs. the U.S., when a teen filed a lawsuit against the U.S. for 'failing to protect the environment.' Tori minces no words when describing related discrepancies – 'Sucking hydrocarbon from the ground' – thumbing her nose at the funding of fossil fuels.

The performance harkens back to *Little Earthquakes*; she uses her mid-range with confidence and transitions her vocal lines effortlessly from chest to head voice. 'Tell me when, I'm in your army then,' she cries. The programming near the end adds a sense of impending doom.

'Mary's Eyes' (Tori Amos)

This ballad was written straight from Tori's sorrow-filled heart and influenced by her mother, Mary Ellen, who suffered a stroke that disabled her speech. Tori, awash in admiration, sings of 'Hymns locked in her memory/I'm a believer.' It's about her mother, but it's also a homage to feminine self-containment.

'Mary is trapped. I don't know what she knows, is she with us in the present? Does she have long-term memory? We just don't know what is behind her eyes,' Tori explained in an interview. She asks guardian angel, 'Sister Despair': 'Can you bring her back to life?' The layered chording plays a significant role, as it's insistent and pervasive but simple enough to be a drop cloth over which Tori can overlay images that express extreme grief. Shenale counters the quivering motif with soaring lines of varying timbre.

Deluxe Edition Bonus Track

'Russia' (Tori Amos)

First, a female speaker repeats Russian words that sound like 'odnyorka' and 'pyatyorka.' Then Tori plays a march-like introduction comprised of tense, reverberating chords. The theme? Tori pretty much declares her own sonic war on the perceived alignment of Putin and Trump during the 2016 American election. As such, she offers her own set of directives: 'For those on the right / You need to build a bridge / For those on the left / You must build a bridge / For those in Washington / There is only one question'

The piano melodically echoes her angst, but after the probing line, 'Is Stalin on your shoulder?' – the piano bites back with Rachmaninoff-like responses. 'Time to wake, activate our native invaders.' The song ends with the female speaker broadcasting in Russian once more. It's uncanny how Tori manages to pack so much information into a 2:45 song.

Album Art

Polish-born Londoner, Paulina Otylie Surys, created beautiful hand-colored photographs exclusively for *Native Invader*. On the cover, Tori dons full native regalia. Other shots either show her posing in an austere setting or in stark natural surroundings. Surys studied both classical painting and photography at the Academy of Fine Arts. Using both mediums, she hand-paints her photographs with 'toners, chemicals and inks.'

Compilation Albums

Tales of a Librarian (2003)

Recorded: 1990-Summer 2003
Label: Atlantic
Release date: 17 November 2003
Highest chart rank: UK: 74, US: 40
This album was awarded Gold status in Australia and Silver status in the UK.
Running time: 78:00

Track listing

All tracks are written by Tori Amos
'Precious Things' (*Little Earthquakes*)
'Angels'
'Silent All These Years' (*Little Earthquakes*)
'Cornflake Girl' (*Under the Pink*)
'Mary' (B-side, *Little Earthquakes*)
'God' (*Under the Pink*)
'Winter' (*Little Earthquakes*)
'Spark' (*From the Choirgirl Hotel*)
'Way Down' (Extended) (*Boys for Pele*)
'Professional Widow' (Armand's Star Trunk Funkin' Mix) (Radio Edit) (single from *Boys for Pele*)
'Mr. Zebra' (*Boys for Pele*)
'Crucify' (*Little Earthquakes*)
'Me and a Gun' (*Little Earthquakes*)
'Bliss' (*To Venus and Back*)
'Playboy Mommy' (*From the Choirgirl Hotel*)
'Baker Baker' (*Under the Pink*)
'Tear in Your Hand' (*Little Earthquakes*)
'Sweet Dreams' (B-side, *Little Earthquakes*)
'Jackie's Strength' (*From the Choirgirl Hotel*)
'Snow Cherries from France' (*From the Choirgirl Hotel*)

A Piano: The Collection (2006)

There were 86 tracks on the A Piano: 2006 Box Set which represented the first 15 years of Tori's solo career.
Recorded: 1990-March 2006
Label: Rhino
Release date: US: 26 September 2006 – Did not chart.

Track listing

Disc A
'Leather' (*Little Earthquakes*)
'Precious Things' (*Little Earthquakes*)

'Silent All These Years' (*Little Earthquakes*)
'Upside Down' ('Silent All These Years' (U.K.) / 'Winter' (U.S.)
'Crucify' (*Little Earthquakes*)
'Happy Phantom' (*Little Earthquakes*)
'Me and a Gun' (*Little Earthquakes*)
'Flying Dutchman' ('China')
'Girl' (*Little Earthquakes*)
'Winter' (*Little Earthquakes*)
'Take to the Sky' ('Winter')
'Tear in Your Hand' (*Little Earthquakes*)
'China' (*Little Earthquakes*)
'Sweet Dreams' ('Winter')
'Mother' (*Little Earthquakes*)
'Little Earthquakes' (*Little Earthquakes*)

Disc B
'Cornflake Girl' (*Under the Pink*)
'Honey' ('Pretty Good Year' (U.K.) / 'Cornflake Girl' (U.S.)

'Take Me With You' (Tori Amos) (Previously Unreleased)
The piano work here is tightly woven around the spiraling melody. It's a superb assemblage of parallel fourths and fifths and It brings to mind the haunting 'Carbon' on *Scarlet's Walk*. Tori recorded it initially in 1990, and didn't add the lyrics until 2006; at that point she felt the project was complete. It's a song of extreme vulnerability: 'Even the rain can cut me up.' At the bridge when Tori settles into head voice, the tone is especially dark.

'Baker Baker' (*Under the Pink*)
'The Waitress' (*Under the Pink*)
'Pretty Good Year' (*Under the Pink*)
'God' (*Under the Pink*)
'Cloud on My Tongue' (*Under the Pink*)
'Past the Mission' (*Under the Pink*)
'Bells for Her' (*Under the Pink*)
'Yes, Anastasia' (*Under the Pink*)
'Blood Roses' (*Boys for Pele*)
'Mr. Zebra' (*Boys for Pele*)
'Caught a Lite Sneeze' (*Boys for Pele*)
'Professional Widow' ('Hey Jupiter')
'Beauty Queen/Horses' (*Boys for Pele*)
'Father Lucifer' (*Boys for Pele*)
'Marianne' (*Boys for Pele*)

Disc C

'Walk to Dublin' (Tori Amos) (Previously unreleased)

Tori focuses on the lowest keys on the piano, alongside jazzy beats and random hints of harpsichord. Her voice sounds desperate. Without a doubt, this is one of her zanier arrangements, complete with rambling, spoken word at the outro.

'Hey Jupiter' ('Hey Jupiter')
'Professional Widow' ('Professional Widow')
'Putting the Damage On' (*Boys for Pele*)
'Bliss' (*To Venus and Back*)
'Suede' (*To Venus and Back*)
'Glory of the 80s' (*To Venus and Back*)
'1000 Oceans' (*To Venus and Back*)
'Concertina' (*To Venus and Back*)
'Lust' (*To Venus and Back*)
'Datura' (*To Venus and Back*)
'Sugar' (*To Venus and Back*)
'The Waitress' (*To Venus and Back*)
'Snow Cherries from France' (*Tales of a Librarian*)
'Doughnut Song' (*Boys for Pele*)

Disc D

'A Sorta Fairytale' (*Scarlet's Walk*)

'Not David Bowie' (Tori Amos) (Sucker Reprise) (Previously unreleased)

It's not surprising, given the theme, that the song features an erratic beat and an overall wall of sound. Tori's voice at times even replicates Bowie's jittery instrument. Thematically, the lyrics imply that the narrator feels blamed because her friend/lover hasn't achieved success – 'Now you're filled with bitterness…' An ode to 'Fame'?

'Amber Waves' (*Scarlet's Walk*)
'Iieee' (*From the Choirgirl Hotel*)
'Playboy Mommy' (*From the Choirgirl Hotel*)
'The Beekeeper' (*The Beekeeper*)
'Jackie's Strength' (*From the Choirgirl Hotel*)

'Zero Point' (Tori Amos) (Previously unreleased):

After several bars of velvety acapella, where Tori simply utters: 'I found out at zero ground, I found out at zero point,' a steady series of blinding beats commence over which she resumes robotically ruminating. After a brief bridge, the indistinct vocals intensify and blur into a barrage of unsettling ambience.

These blips and bleeps vie for the singer's attention. Over the course of this 8:56 performance, Tori explores the repetitive melody through her chest voice; she uses her head voice, as well, but sparingly. The pentameter plays a more integral role than the lyric.

'Zero Point' is an enthralling piece of work. The eerie, percussive soundscape owes much to drummer Matt Chamberlain and programmer Andy Gray. For *To Venus and Back*, Tori had to make a tough choice. Both 'Datura' and 'Zero Point' ran about eight minutes long and she could only record one, so 'Zero Point' took the bullet. The theme was inspired by Zecharia Sitchin's *Earth Chronicle* series. In interviews, Tori points out more specifically, though, the collapse of the Roman Empire and the relation of that phenomenon to the actual concept of 'zero point.'

'Sweet the Sting' (*The Beekeeper*)

'Ode to My Clothes' (Tori Amos) (Previously unreleased)
Due to a mix-up, choice items from Tori's closet are given away to strangers. The song was written in response. Played with simple, block chords, Tori gives a straight-forward vocal performance. The odd ditty is told in only 2:06.

'Spark' (*From the Choirgirl Hotel*)
'Intro. Jam and Marys of the Sea' (Previously unreleased)
'Cruel' (*From the Choirgirl Hotel*)

'Dolphin Song' (Tori Amos) (Previously unreleased)
Tori's vocals are clear and resonant throughout. The chords move along at top speed at the verse, but slow at the chorus. It's a pretty song of faith and optimism: 'I know the lengths you would go…'

'Gold Dust' (*Scarlet's Walk*)

Disc E
'The Pool' ('Winter')
'Never Seen Blue' ('Jackie's Strength')
'Daisy Dead Petals' ('Pretty Good Year')
'Beulah Land' ('Jackie's Strength')
'Sugar' ('China')
'Cooling' ('Spark')
'Bachelorette' (Spark')
'Black Swan' ('Pretty Good Year') (U.K.)
'Mary' (*Tales of a Librarian*)

'Peeping Tommi' (Tori Amos) (Previously unreleased)
This arrangement is very reminiscent of Tori's piano work on *Little*

Earthquakes. The true emotion comes across at the B section, when she sings, 'Don't run away from me now.' Instrumentally, she creates a quiet drone behind her extended phrases.

'Toodles Mr. Jim' ('Caught a Lite Sneeze')
'Fire-Eater's Wife / Beauty Queen' (Previously unreleased)
'Playboy Mommy' (Previously unreleased)
'A Sorta Fairytale' (Previously unreleased)
'This Old Man' ('Caught a Lite Sneeze')
'Purple People' (*To Venus and Back*)
'Here. In My Head' ('Crucify')
'Hungarian Wedding Song' ('Caught a Lite Sneeze')

'Merman' (Tori Amos) (*From the Choirgirl Hotel*)
B-Side version. Exclusive digital release from 1999.
This soothing lullaby features melodic piano, Tori's signature melismas and a smattering of behind-the-beat backing vocals. 'Who could ever harm you?' she posits. 'Sleep now.'

'Sister Janet' ('Cornflake Girl')
'Home on the Range' ('Pretty Good Year')
'Frog on My Toe' ('Talula')

'Sugar' (Live) (Tori Amos)
Maybe a casual flip of the coin would help determine whether the live version on *To Venus and Back* or *Live from Sunny Florida*, is the champ. Maybe there's no contest: both versions retain the intended amount of sweetness.

Tori has performed many iterations of this beloved ballad, which was inspired by the memory of a childhood suitor. Hoping to win her affections, the lad asked how many sugars she likes in her tea. While the earnest suitor may have lost his dream girl, he certainly has fun stories to share. 'Sugar' was a surefire hit during the 1998 tour. Produced by Tori Amos.

'Honey' (Live) (Tori Amos)
The repetitive, instrumental drone effect pumps the conversational narrative with zest. 'It got kicked off at the last minute because I'm such a ding-a-ling,' Tori laments onstage about the track's omission from *Under the Pink*. Produced by Tori Amos.

'Professional Widow' (Merry Widow Version-Live) (Tori Amos)
Tori's organ emits a slow burn but gets exponentially more sinister, as she pants and screams the storyline in this condensed version. Produced by Tori Amos.

'Over the Rainbow' (Live) (Harold Arlen, E. Y. 'Yip' Harburg)
This American classic – which speaks to the universal theme of longing for something far better than what life ordinarily dictates – features hypnotic pacing. Tori emboldens each phrase with both a childlike innocence and a hard-wrought worldliness. While her breathy delivery made some fans bristle – they yearned to have her break out in full voice – it's the breathy delivery that makes this cover highly charged, distinguishing it from the Broadway belter. Produced by Tori Amos.

25 Really Deep Tracks

So, here we are at the end. 'Excuse me, but can I be you for a while….' I'll admit, I was a little reluctant to share this list, as we all know that Tori develops personal relationships with her 'song girls.' They ultimately become best friends, soulmates and confidantes; who am I to disrupt the natural order?

Some of Tori's songs have been wholeheartedly revised on stage or in the studio; others were pocketed until the muses reappeared. So, as I devised this list, I felt pretty conflicted: How would the left-out songs feel? So, I might have some misgivings come morning, but we had to arrive at some common ground, and these 25 really deep tracks are a pretty good blueprint for all-things Tori. You'll hear rich and whimsical piano, sensitive imagery, outrageous, heartbreaking vocals, and top-notch songwriting. The tracks come from these albums: *Abnormally Attracted to Sin, American Doll Posse, Boys for Pele, From the Choirgirl Hotel, Gold Dust, Little Earthquakes, Little Earthquakes Deluxe Edition, The Beekeeper, To Venus and Back* and *Under the Pink.*

These selections are in alphabetical *order;* not in preferential order, because taking on that untenable task would totally put me over the edge…

'Bells for Her'
'Big Wheel'
'Blood Roses'
'Caught a Lite Sneeze'
'Cornflake Girl'
'Crucify'
'Father Lucifer'
'Gold Dust'
'Happy Phantom'
'Hey Jupiter'
'Hoochie Woman'
'In the Springtime of His Voodoo'
'Liquid Diamonds'
'Mary Jane'
'Me and a Gun'
'Mother'
'Past the Mission'
'Precious Things'
'Silent All These Years'
'Take to the Sky'
'Winter'
'She's Your Cocaine'
'Spring Haze'
'The Waitress'
'Velvet Revolution'

Sweet the Spin: Ten-Plus Tori Amos tunes covered by other acts

Tori Amos has covered the work of Nirvana, Led Zeppelin, The Rolling Stones, Jimi Hendrix, Joni Mitchell and so many more. And once she chooses to do so, she commits to making her cover versions unique.

Below is an abbreviated list of acts (stemming from various genres) whom, I'm sure, hoped to achieve a similar objective. Some have disbanded, others are world-famous and a few are up-and-coming, but the major point is that Tori's work has been inspirational globally and that her versatility has fused endless creativity.

Some acts reiterated seminal riffs, but replaced Tori's piano with blazing electronics; while others echoed or imbued her piano style. Some remained true to the original lyric, regardless of gender, while others took liberties by leaving out or changing a word here or there. The common denominator is the collective passion behind these artistic choices, which makes each cover a stand-alone.

I was surprised to see that some of Tori's most personal songs have been covered by men. I asked myself, is that because Tori attracts such an inclusive fan base? Is this a trend? Does an artist's gender influence the listener's experience?

Noah Michelson – Editorial Director of *HuffPost Personal*, and the host of *D Is For Desire*: a love and sex podcast – has interviewed Tori frequently over the course of his career. Besides having a deep knowledge of her discography, he has an acute awareness of gender issues. Here is Michelson's take:

> Every time a singer chooses to sing a song, I think it reveals something about them. If someone who identifies as male, decides to sing 'Precious Things,' that is a specific choice, and it could mean a variety of things. The singer could simply admire the song – he finds it moving, he finds it dynamic, he relates to it on some or many levels. He may not even be thinking about the inherently gendered aspects of the song or that the song is very much about tensions between men and women. Then, of course, the singer may have chosen the song *because* of those tensions, and is interested in examining them or complicating them or upending them by giving a male voice to a song that is very much from and about a woman's specific experience of being a woman (and there will be some people who are not happy with or uneasy with that choice, and feel that because the song is specifically about that experience, someone who identifies as male, shouldn't attempt to cover it).
>
> I think hearing someone who identifies as male, sing 'In my peach party dress', can be disarming, as men typically do not wear dresses (at least in the West), and that choice can alert the listener to consider what the singer intended by that. Is he simply staying true to the lyrics of the song, or is he trying to convey something by making that choice? I think it'll be different for every singer, and we often do not and never will know the intention behind a creative choice like

that (just as we often don't know Tori's intention for choosing particular lyrics, as she prefers to let her listeners find their own way into the music.)

Regardless, I think the choice to keep the lyrics the same, and someone who identifies as male singing about female experiences, can be useful (though, as noted before, problematic,) because it can force the listener to (re) explore what the song is about; what it means (both in the general sense of narrative, but also in the specific sense of how the listener emotionally understands and/or relates to it), and how it exists in both the cultural landscape of when it was written and in today's cultural landscape.

I never think we should say 'This is exactly what is going on here!' or 'It means this', because there are so many factors and elements that are working together to create the song, create meaning, and create understanding. Even if we don't agree with or like a choice that an artist made, we can still learn from it. But I always think it's worthwhile to find new ways into artistic expressions and to continually challenge ourselves to try and understand why an artist made something or why an artist decided to cover a song and what that choice reveals about the artist, ourselves, and the world around us.

'A Sorta Fairytale'

When Taylor Swift performed this song live in August 2011 at Verizon Center, Washington, DC., she had no trouble nabbing those high notes because of her flexible range, but it was hard to hear over the screaming crowd.

'Blood Roses'

Although Daniel Versus the World didn't have a harpsichord on hand on 27 October 2014, he still played a soulful and condensed 3:48 version at The Fiddler's Elbow in London.

'China'

The now-defunct indie pop quarter, The Pains of Being Pure at Heart, performed this ballad on 26 July 2018 at the Oslo Culture Centre in Shanghai. Silky harmonies – courtesy of guitarist Kip Berman and Peggy Wang – swell above an arsenal of contrasting string effects.

'Cornflake Girl'

In 1996, Jawbox snuck 'Cornflake Girl' onto their self-titled final studio album as a hidden track. Reflecting back, J. Robbins told *AV Club*: '...deconstructing the actual song musically, it's pretty awesome, and it felt really great to play when we worked out all the parts.' And true to the former front man's word, this awesome iteration featured several distinctive parts.

'Cornflake Girl' was always a powerhouse sonically and lyrically, but Jawbox did this cover justice by exaggerating Tori's finest ideas. Robbins' baritone is in-your-face phenomenal, especially as he harmonizes with Bill Barbon's lucid, melodic tones. With drummer Zach Barocas, as co-conspirator, the feisty electric guitarist creates rubato changes of gladiatorial proportion. (Sources: *setlist.fm*, Ryan, K., 'J. Robbins walks us through Jawbox's 1996 swan song,' music.avclub.com, 22 September 2015.)

British artist, Imogen Heap, danced and sang against her own high-pitched vocal loops and a pre-recorded piano motif, on her Ellipse World Tour, with percussion tearing it up at the always-anticipated 'rabbit' coda.

In September 2018, Florence and the Machine produced a gasp-worthy rendition, making full use of vocalist Florence Welch's haunting vibrato. The ultimate high? She injected a blues lick against the thrumming bass line.

'Cooling'

Singer/pianist Charlotte Martin, did a relaxed but moving interpretation of this underrated think-piece, at Philadelphia's World Café on 7 March 2020.

'Father Lucifer'

On Michael Wollny's end-of-2020 compilation: 'Mondenkind,' the German pianist created a warm, expansive and jazz-centric instrumental version of the jubilant Tori Amos classic.

'Hey Jupiter'

Cemile Bora has a fragile quality to her voice, which is perfect for retelling this tale.

'Precious Things'

Californian alt-rock trio, Smile Empty Soul, re-staged the vocals with Sean Danielsen's gritty voice and subbed out Tori's keyboard kicker for sharply executed guitar tonalities.

Melbourne's Blueline Medic opted to start off with Shaun Lohoar's torrential blast of drums, followed by emphatic electric guitar by Adrian Lombardi, hypnotic bass by Dave Snow, and electrifying vocals by Donnie Dureau, for an exuberant goth-metal manifest. A YouTuber thanked the all-male quartet for not changing a single lyric.

Ithaca's Alex Reed – of electronica band, Seeming – created an exciting polar-opposite effect by flexing his rough-hewn baritone and juxtaposing it against his own auto-tune response.

Acoustic guitarist and vocalist Luca Freddi kept the song on an even keel vocally but used intricate classical runs as dramatic fills.

'Pretty Good Year'

In March 2016, post-punk Publicist OK, came out with a 4:11 version featuring the resplendent baritone of Zachary Lipez, whose performance added an extra layer of veracity to this time-tested ballad.

'Silent All These Years'

On this memorable rendition, the piano part is shaded similarly to that of the *Little Earthquakes* version, but the bittersweet, brooding vocals of George Lewis aka Twin Shadow, elicit a decidedly different timbre.

L'Aura's version with breathless vocals against folk guitar – at Teatro Valle, Chiaravalle, Italy, in the winter of 2016 – was the only American-penned ballad other than 'God Only Knows', on the Italian entertainer's extensive setlist.

'Winter'

Angel Olsen covered 'Winter' from her home during the height of the Covid-19 pandemic in April 2020. 'Took several tries to get this one down, who knew?' she exclaimed to Christopher Roberts at undertheradarmag.com on 7 April 2020. Angel's pure, resonant voice, made up for the pedestrian piano performance.

Amanda Palmer, on her Evelyn Evelyn tour, stayed remarkably true to the original version when performing at Space in Portland, Oregon on 24 November 2007. Similarly, to Amos, Amanda accentuated the tear-stained melody by using keyboard-spanning harmonies.

Interview With Joseph Chiccarelli

American producer and engineer Joseph Chiccarelli is based at Sunset Sound Studios in Hollywood, California. The multiple Grammy winner is acclaimed for creating superior chemistry with his high-profile clients, which have included: The Strokes, Elton John, Herb Alpert, Etta James, Morrissey, Beck and Alanis Morissette, among others.

The following interview, which took place between Chiccarelli and the author on 14 October 2020, was in response to queries about working with Tori Amos on *Y Kant Tori Read*.

Y Kant Tori Read was recorded in Los Angeles at a number of different studios: Capitol, Ground Control Studios; there were a couple of other studios in which we did some overdubs – Hollywood Sound Recorders: we did some stuff there. The project came about through a mutual friend. He introduced me to Tori and she and I hit it off immediately.

I remember her coming over to my house for the first time. She was special. She was living in an apartment behind a church in Hollywood. I remember meeting her there.

David Kirshenbaum was the executive producer on the project; I had worked with him in the past. I'd learned that he was involved from the manager at the time, Larry Kruteck. I knew this was professional and that I would be in good hands.

I needed a lot of keyboard programming, and Tori had some songs that needed finishing up on a writing level, so I introduced her to a keyboard player that I had worked with often, Kim Bullard. He and Tori got together and worked on touching up a few of her songs, and I got Kim involved in the album as a kind of co-producer.

The project really was, despite the myths out there on the street, not a band. It was just Tori. She'd played a few gigs in L.A. under the name Y Kant Tori Read. She'd met Matt Sorum – who was the drummer for Guns 'N Roses – as well as Steve Caton and Brad Cobb. They had done a couple of gigs together as a band, and at the time, you know, this was the late '80s, and everything was bands.

So, I think the record company and her manager thought going through the name of Tori Amos as a piano-playing female artist was not in step with the times. They thought it might be better suited as a band name. So, when *Y Kant Tori Read* came about, it wasn't a rock band per se, playing together, rehearsing altogether, being in the studio together.

Steve and Brad – two guys in the band – did play together on some of the songs, though. Matt, I believe, played on a couple of things, but it really wasn't a band per se, so that's how I got involved.

Steve Ferris and Vinnie Colaiuta, a few other musicians, and Tim Landers were people that I was working with a lot of the time as L.A. session players, so they were very sensitive musicians, people that I trusted. I thought they would get what Tori was all about, so I brought them in on some of the sessions as well.

Tori, I think, had a connection with Merry Clayton. I don't remember how Merry got involved, but she came in and did backgrounds and was absolutely wonderful. And needless to say, between Carole King and her solo albums, Rolling Stones and all those bands of hers, we were glad to have her aboard.

In general, the process of recording her was very, very simple technically; nothing really extraordinary. I remember we tried a number of different microphones at the time, and I had heard a demo of a Swedish microphone called a Milab VIP 50. I think somebody had loaned it to me to try out. It had a really beautiful tone. I tried it on Tori and loved it on her, and I think we used that for a large portion of the record. We also used a Telefunken 251 microphone on some of the songs.

We tried the vocal on 'Fire on the Side' on a number of different occasions. When we got to Ground Control Studios, it was just a matter of trying it on Tuesday, and if we didn't get it on Tuesday, maybe try it again on Friday, but just getting a couple of different looks at it for her to kind of get in the mood of singing it. That particular song was tough, but others were simpler and easier and didn't involve her diving deeper, so deep into the story.

We definitely had label involvement. Jason Flom was A&R. We also had Larry Kruteck, the manager, and David Kershenbaum was the executive producer, so I had a chain of command that was looking over me. I'd have to play tracks for and get peoples' approval and that kind of thing, so there was a fair amount of opinions involved.

Tori was definitely confident and passionate and, as she would like to say, 'a pirate' at the time, and definitely, we were going for something that was big and dramatic. If you think about the time, there were records like Peter Gabriel's So and Robbie Robertson's first solo album – these were records that were very big and landscape-y and had multiple layers, and so I think people were influenced by that; but at the same time, some of the songs were more intimate and storytelling, so they could get a simpler treatment, like 'Etienne,' and 'Fire on the Side' as mentioned.

As far as hearing Tori's work before our sessions? In all cases, there might have been a few songs that had demos or even a live recording of the band, but most of the time, it was Tori playing me a song at the piano, just going over to her place or having her come by the studio. I was working on a couple of different projects at the time, so she'd stop by, visit me, and say, 'Hey, I just wrote a new song.' But I don't believe there were fully fleshed-out demos on any of the songs.

There were a few songs – 'Cool on Your Island' and 'Pirates' – that she went and wrote with Kim Bullard, so they would have put together demos for songs that really were the backbone of the final master, so I would have used a lot of Kim's programming, you know, his drum loops or his synthesizers or whatever he did on those demos in his home studio.

The relationship between Tori and I was just fantastic. We were like brother and sister, just kidded and joked all the time. The sessions were really fun and playful and really positive overall. I know Tori loved the record when we were done.

To be honest, the only heartbreaking moment of the whole project was, she did this album cover that's somewhat infamous now if you will. We were at the studio mixing when she got the proofs in for the cover. I saw it and I was just aghast. I didn't know what to say because I just didn't feel that it represented the music, and I thought it made her look like some heavy metal singer. I just didn't think it was the appropriate thing for the music, but she was really in love with it. It was her 'pirate look' as she put it. And I remember saying to her, 'Hey, let's take a walk.' The studio was a residential studio up in Laurel Canyon. The musicians were gone. Ed (Thacker) was mixing. I said, 'Let's just leave Ed alone, let him work, and let's just take a walk.' So, we took a walk and I told her about the cover. I remember her being in tears because she really loved this cover. I said, 'I don't think it represents the music. I don't think it's you.'

I remember Tori saying, 'But it's my pirate look.' Tori's attitude about the cover had been happy. I told her, 'I get that, but I think a lot of other people will look at it and instantly cast you as this rock-chick singer, and I don't think it's the way you should be represented. If you're really that married to the cover, I'd do something that pokes fun at it, so it looks like a joke.'

I mentioned to her, there's a Monty Python album cover from the 1970s where, basically, it was one of those stock, very classical-looking music covers, where they usually have a pastoral scene and they have a typeface that looks very regal, if you will, and it's Brahms or Bach or whatever the record might be. But Monty Python took that very stock classical album cover, and they scribbled in black pen over it, 'Monty Python,' you know. It looked silly or almost blasphemous, if you will.

I said, 'Why don't you have somebody draw over this or scratch out your face or scratch out the cover, and put something on top of it or over it – think of it as a Monty Python cover, so people know you're not serious about this cover.'

Tori said, 'Oh, that's a good idea,' and her boyfriend at the time, Eric Rosse, I think, his mother was an artist – I might be wrong about that – but he got somebody to do those little figures that are on the cover, and that's as far as they went with it. That wasn't the kind of plan I was suggesting; maybe it helps lighten up the cover or makes it more playful, but it wasn't exactly the point I was trying to make.

That really was our only point of disagreement in the course of making the record, which was the album cover, and normally, as a producer, you really don't have input into the album cover. You'll suggest something to the artist, it will come up in conversation, you might offer an opinion, but I'm very reluctant to ever tell somebody, 'I think that's a bad cover.' This was extraordinary that I had to say this to her, and she was really miserably upset by it.

In some odd way, people have historically said it sounded nothing like the Tori Amos that followed, but I think if you put that in the middle of her career, it would sound just like a Tori Amos record. I think that the cover really swayed people, and the *Billboard* review was pretty harsh, and it just never had a chance. It was really sad.

For me as a producer, it was really heartbreaking because the one thing that you really look for is – when you finish an album and the artist comes to you, and this doesn't happen all the time – the artist comes to you and says, 'I love my record. I'm just crazy about this record. We achieved exactly what I wanted to achieve. I'm so proud of this,' and with the case of Tori, I remember getting the phone call from her, saying, 'Thank you so much, I just love this record, it's me, it's what I wanted to do. I'm proud of it; I'm crazy about it. It's what I wanted to do from the onset.'

Then, to have the album not be successful was really, really heartbreaking, because usually – and it's not always the case – but usually when you have the sense of something great here, there's a great artist here, there's a career to be launched; other people get it. I'm not saying I was foreseeing the future or anything, but usually, if you like it, other people like it. I was really heartbroken that it was so panned by the critics.

Since that time, Tori's played tracks live. That's really great. I'm so glad she didn't pass them over. I think there was a period of time in which she thought she had to disavow the record, you know?

Did I have a sense of Tori's future career? No, not at all. You can't ever really tell that. It happens so differently with every artist. Sometimes the first album comes out and explodes, and nothing happens thereafter. Sometimes it takes more albums. I'm not one to predict that. I would have predicted that Tori was a strong artist and had a point of view and had something to say that was really unique. I think that she really appealed to a lot of young women in the same way that perhaps Lady Gaga has in more modern times. I think she found a lot of girls who just felt like they couldn't find their place in the world; didn't have anybody that expressed their feelings, and I think she engaged a really, really large group of fans, female and male.

It was at a time where the female singer-songwriter was really starting to come back. We'd gone through the 1960s with the folk singers if you will, but it was all rock bands at the time.

But then, all of a sudden, you had Tracy Chapman, Tori, Suzanne Vega, Edie Brickell, that were starting to break at the time, so she was on the crest of that. Perhaps if *Y Kant Tori Read* came out a year or so later, maybe she would have been a little further along in the wave, and lines would have been a little bit more open, and the album might have been a little bit more accepted. I wanted to say that she was really at the beginning of the movement if there was such a thing.

Bibliography and other resources

Books:

Amos, T., *Resistance: A songwriter's story of hope, change and courage* (Sword and Stone, 2020)
Amos, T., Powers, A., *Piece by Piece: A portrait of the Artist – her thoughts, her conversations* (Broadway Books, 2005)
Amos, T., *Tori Amos: Anthology* (Amsco, 1998)
Brown, J., *Tori Amos: In the Studio* (ECW Press, 2011)
Ferris, D.X., *Reign in Blood (33 and 1/3 series)* (Bloomsbury, 2019)
Gentry, A., *Boys for Pele (33 and 1/3 series)* (Bloomsbury, 2019)
Jacobs, J. S., *Pretty Good Years: A Biography of Tori Amos* (Hal-Leonard, 2006)
Owens, D., *Where the Crawdads Sing* (Random House, 2018)
Rogers, Kalen., *Tori Amos – All These Years, The Authorized Biography* (Omnibus Press, 1996)
George-Warren, H., Romanowski, P., *The Rolling Stone Encyclopedia of Rock and Roll, Revised and updated for the 21st Century* (Rolling Stone Press, 2001)

Websites:

billboard.com
chicagoconcertreviews.com (Andy Argyrakis)
concertlivewire.com
thedent.com (March 25 1996 – May 5 2006) now archived
NME.com
www.pennyblackmusic.com
riaa.com
http://www.setlist.fm/
songfacts.com
toriamos.com (official website)
http://www.toriamosdiscography.info/
toriset.org
torismaze.com
undented.com
yessaid.com
Wikipedia.com

Articles:

Anderson, S., *Tori Amos to Get 'Unrepentant' on New Album* (rollingstone.com, 19 February 2014)
Cinquemani, S., *Review: Tori Amos, Strange Little Girls* (slantmagazine.com, 6 September 2001)
Conner, M. C., *Tori Amos's First Album, 'Y Kant Tori Read' Has Been Remastered* (m.huffpost.com, 4 September 2017)
Deevoy, A., *PJ Harvey, Bjork, and Tori Amos: Hips. Lips. Tits. Power* (*Q*, May 1994)

Everson, J., *Tight Socks and Feminist Freedom* (*Illinois Entertainer*, August 1994)
Lentini, L., *Tori Amos: Loud and Clear* (spin.com, 2 November 2020)
Nunn, J., *Tori Amos: Classical Music and her Gay Friends* (*Windy City Times*, 16 November 2016)
Pareles, J., *Critic's Choice: New CD's* (*The New York Times*, 21 February 2005)
Shapiro, G., *From Strange Little Girls to Real Men: Interview with Tori Amos* (windycitytimes.com, 17 October 2001)
Tedder, M., *Boys for Pele Turns 20* (stereogum.com, 2016)
Tingen, P., *Tori Amos Talks About American Doll Posse* (undented.com, 14 March 2007)
Wood, M., *Tori Amos, 'Abnormally Attracted to Sin'* (spin.com, 29 April 2009)
Zollo, P., *Tori Amos Finds Herself, Report and Interview* (*Musician*, May 1992)

Podcast:

Drive All Night: The Songs of Tori Amos (*stitcher.com*)

Left and below: Program covers for the *To Venus and Back* tour (1999) and Strange Days tour (2001). (*toriamosdiscography.info*)

Right and below: Program covers for the *Sinful Attraction* tour (2009) and *Unrepentant Geraldines* tour (2014). (*toriamosdiscography.info*)

On Track series

Tori Amos – Lisa Torem 978-1-78952-142-9
Asia – Peter Braidis 978-1-78952-099-6
Barclay James Harvest – Keith and Monica Domone 978-1-78952-067-5
The Beatles – Andrew Wild 978-1-78952-009-5
The Beatles Solo 1969-1980 – Andrew Wild 978-1-78952-030-9
Blue Oyster Cult – Jacob Holm-Lupo 978-1-78952-007-1
Marc Bolan and T.Rex – Peter Gallagher 978-1-78952-124-5
Kate Bush – Bill Thomas 978-1-78952-097-2
Camel – Hamish Kuzminski 978-1-78952-040-8
Caravan – Andy Boot 978-1-78952-127-6
Eric Clapton Solo – Andrew Wild 978-1-78952-141-2
The Clash – Nick Assirati 978-1-78952-077-4
Crosby, Stills and Nash – Andrew Wild 978-1-78952-039-2
The Damned – Morgan Brown 978-1-78952-136-8
Deep Purple and Rainbow 1968-79 – Steve Pilkington 978-1-78952-002-6
Dire Straits – Andrew Wild 978-1-78952-044-6
The Doors – Tony Thompson 978-1-78952-137-5
Dream Theater – Jordan Blum 978-1-78952-050-7
Elvis Costello and The Attractions – Georg Purvis 978-1-78952-129-0
Emerson Lake and Palmer – Mike Goode 978-1-78952-000-2
Fairport Convention – Kevan Furbank 978-1-78952-051-4
Peter Gabriel – Graeme Scarfe 978-1-78952-138-2
Genesis – Stuart MacFarlane 978-1-78952-005-7
Gentle Giant – Gary Steel 978-1-78952-058-3
Gong – Kevan Furbank 978-1-78952-082-8
Hawkwind – Duncan Harris 978-1-78952-052-1
Roy Harper – Opher Goodwin 978-1-78952-130-6
Iron Maiden – Steve Pilkington 978-1-78952-061-3
Jethro Tull – Jordan Blum 978-1-78952-016-3
Elton John in the 1970s – Peter Kearns 978-1-78952-034-7
Gong – Kevan Furbank 978-1-78952-082-8
The Incredible String Band – Tim Moon 978-1-78952-107-8
Iron Maiden – Steve Pilkington 978-1-78952-061-3
Judas Priest – John Tucker 978-1-78952-018-7
Kansas – Kevin Cummings 978-1-78952-057-6
Level 42 – Matt Philips 978-1-78952-102-3
Aimee Mann – Jez Rowden 978-1-78952-036-1
Joni Mitchell – Peter Kearns 978-1-78952-081-1
The Moody Blues – Geoffrey Feakes 978-1-78952-042-2
Mike Oldfield – Ryan Yard 978-1-78952-060-6
Tom Petty – Richard James 978-1-78952-128-3
Queen – Andrew Wild 978-1-78952-003-3
Renaissance – David Detmer 978-1-78952-062-0
The Rolling Stones 1963-80 – Steve Pilkington 978-1-78952-017-0
Steely Dan – Jez Rowden 978-1-78952-043-9
Steve Hackett – Geoffrey Feakes 978-1-78952-098-9
Thin Lizzy – Graeme Stroud 978-1-78952-064-4
Toto – Jacob Holm-Lupo 978-1-78952-019-4

U2 – Eoghan Lyng 978-1-78952-078-1
UFO – Richard James 978-1-78952-073-6
The Who – Geoffrey Feakes 978-1-78952-076-7
Roy Wood and the Move – James R Turner 978-1-78952-008-8
Van Der Graaf Generator – Dan Coffey 978-1-78952-031-6
Yes – Stephen Lambe 978-1-78952-001-9
Frank Zappa 1966 to 1979 – Eric Benac 978-1-78952-033-0
10CC – Peter Kearns 978-1-78952-054-5

Decades Series

Alice Cooper in the 1970s – Chris Sutton 978-1-78952-104-7
Curved Air in the 1970s – Laura Shenton 978-1-78952-069-9
Fleetwood Mac in the 1970s – Andrew Wild 978-1-78952-105-4
Focus in the 1970s – Stephen Lambe 978-1-78952-079-8
Marillion in the 1980s – Nathaniel Webb 978-1-78952-065-1
Pink Floyd In The 1970s – Georg Purvis 978-1-78952-072-9
The Sweet in the 1970s – Darren Johnson 978-1-78952-139-9
Uriah Heep in the 1970s – Steve Pilkington 978-1-78952-103-0

On Screen series

Carry On… – Stephen Lambe 978-1-78952-004-0
David Cronenberg – Patrick Chapman 978-1-78952-071-2
Doctor Who: The David Tennant Years – Jamie Hailstone 978-1-78952-066-8
Monty Python – Steve Pilkington 978-1-78952-047-7
Seinfeld Seasons 1 to 5 – Stephen Lambe 978-1-78952-012-5

Other Books

Babysitting A Band On The Rocks – G.D. Praetorius 978-1-78952-106-1
Derek Taylor: For Your Radioactive Children – Andrew Darlington 978-1-78952-038-5
Iggy and The Stooges On Stage 1967-1974 – Per Nilsen 978-1-78952-101-6
Jon Anderson and the Warriors – the road to Yes – David Watkinson 978-1-78952-059-0
Nu Metal: A Definitive Guide – Matt Karpe 978-1-78952-063-7
Tommy Bolin: In and Out of Deep Purple – Laura Shenton 978-1-78952-070-5
Maximum Darkness – Deke Leonard 978-1-78952-048-4
Maybe I Should've Stayed In Bed – Deke Leonard 978-1-78952-053-8
The Twang Dynasty – Deke Leonard 978-1-78952-049-1

and many more to come!

Would you like to write for Sonicbond Publishing?

We are mainly a music publisher, but we also occasionally publish in other genres including film and television. At Sonicbond Publishing we are always on the look-out for authors, particularly for our two main series, On Track and Decades.

Mixing fact with in depth analysis, the On Track series examines the entire recorded work of a particular musical artist or group. All genres are considered from easy listening and jazz to 60s soul to 90s pop, via rock and metal.

The Decades series singles out a particular decade in an artist or group's history and focuses on that decade in more detail than may be allowed in the On Track series.

While professional writing experience would, of course, be an advantage, the most important qualification is to have real enthusiasm and knowledge of your subject. First-time authors are welcomed, but the ability to write well in English is essential.

Sonicbond Publishing has distribution throughout Europe and North America, and all our books are also published in E-book form. Authors will be paid a royalty based on sales of their book. Further details about our books are available from www.sonicbondpublishing.com. To contact us, complete the contact form there or email info@sonicbondpublishing.co.uk